P9-DUJ-296

THE COMING OF AGE OF AMERICAN ART MUSIC

Recent Titles in Contributions to the Study of Music and Dance

Busoni and the Piano: The Works, the Writings, and the Recordings
Larry Sitsky

Music as Propaganda: Art to Persuade, Art to Control
Arnold Perris

A Most Wondrous Babble: American Art Composers, Their Music, and the American Scene, 1950–1985
Nicholas E. Tawa

Voices of Combat: A Century of Liberty and War Songs, 1765–1865
Kent A. Bowman

Edison, Musicians, and the Phonograph: A Century in Retrospect
John Harvith and Susan Edwards Harvith, editors

The Dawning of American Keyboard Music
J. Bunker Clark

Mozart in Person: His Character and Health
Peter J. Davies

Music for the Dance: Reflections on a Collaborative Art
Katherine Teck

From Sibelius to Sallinen: Finnish Nationalism and the Music of Finland
Lisa de Gorog with the collaboration of Ralph de Gorog

From Chords to Simultaneities: Chordal Indeterminacy and the Failure of Serialism
Nachum Schoffman

20th-Century Microtonal Notation
Gardner Read

Movement to Music: Musicians in the Dance Studio
Katherine Teck

The Coming of Age of American Art Music

New England's Classical Romanticists

Nicholas E. Tawa

CONTRIBUTIONS TO THE STUDY OF MUSIC AND DANCE, NUMBER 22

GREENWOOD PRESS
NEW YORK • WESTPORT, CONNECTICUT • LONDON

Library of Congress Cataloging-in-Publication Data

Tawa, Nicholas E.
The coming of age of American art music : New England's classical Romanticists / Nicholas E. Tawa.
p. cm. — (Contributions to the study of music and dance, ISSN 0193–9041 ; no. 22)
Includes bibliographical references and index.
ISBN 0–313–27707–4 (alk. paper)
1. Music—New England—19th century—History and criticism.
2. Music—New England—20th century—History and criticism.
3. Composers—New England. I. Title. II. Series.
ML200.4.T4 1991
781.6'8'097409034—dc20 90–22814

British Library Cataloguing in Publication Data is available.

Copyright © 1991 by Nicholas E. Tawa

All rights reserved. No portion of this book may be reproduced, by any process or technique, without the express written consent of the publisher.

Library of Congress Catalog Card Number: 90–22814
ISBN: 0–313–27707–4
ISSN: 0193–9041

First published in 1991

Greenwood Press, 88 Post Road West, Westport, CT 06881
An imprint of Greenwood Publishing Group, Inc.

Printed in the United States of America

∞

The paper used in this book complies with the Permanent Paper Standard issued by the National Information Standards Organization (Z39.48–1984).

10 9 8 7 6 5 4 3 2 1

CONTENTS

PREFACE

Who were John Knowles Paine, George Chadwick, Edward MacDowell, Horatio Parker, Arthur Foote, and Amy Beach? They were the most important art composers, save for Charles Ives, before the twentieth-century generation of composers represented by Copland, Sessions, and Thomson. They won national and international reputations owing to the high quality of their masterly compositions—songs, keyboard pieces, instrumental chamber works, cantatas, oratorios, masses, overtures, concertos, symphonies, symphonic poems, and operas. What does today's ordinary American know about them? What does the typical music student know? Nothing.

The convoluted pathway I pursued in order to gain some knowledge of these composers and their compositions can serve as an example of the usual difficulties that in the past have confronted anyone seriously interested in the concert and opera music written by Americans. I certainly knew nothing at all about this significant period in America's cultural history, when I was a boy and growing up in the West Roxbury section of Boston. Riding the streetcar home along Washington Street, I would hear the conductor call out the names of streets, "Mendelssohn, Haydn, Brahms, Liszt, Schubert," not having the faintest idea who these people were. Nor did I know who Beethoven was while I attended the Beethoven School. Nor did any teacher enlighten me. I also went with my parents on summer picnics beside the banks of the Charles River, in the Auburndale section of Newton, close to the house where Horatio Parker was born and brought up. If Beethoven was a mystery, Parker was a nonentity.

By high school I had discovered a hunger for concert music and knew the compositions of the Central European composers after whom the streets were named. This was owing largely to the free concerts given by what we knew as the local "WPA orchestra" and the urging of one teacher, Lucille Harrington. Nobody had yet even mentioned Parker to me. Much later, when I lived in Newton for a while, I asked the librarians about Parker and also about the Wa-Wan Press that Arthur Farwell had operated in Newton Center, from 1901 to 1908. They professed ignorance of both and showed no interest in learning anything further about either. Was there a conspiracy of silence?

In late adolescence, I commenced the serious study of music and travelled out to Waltham to study theory under an elderly Walter Starbuck. For the first time I heard of Chadwick and Foote, whom Starbuck had known personally and whose music he admired. He told me of Chadwick's bitterness and Foote's resignation over being shunted to one side by the younger generation of American musicians. Curious about these two unknowns, I sought to hear a composition or two of theirs but to no avail. At last, Koussevitzky and the Boston Symphony introduced me to Foote's Suite for Strings in E, which I thoroughly enjoyed. The experience was an isolated one; no other composition by any of these composers came my way.

I must also confess that after entering Harvard College in 1941, I constantly visited the music building, Paine Hall, having no idea who Paine was. Nor did the Harvard music faculty enlighten me. John Knowles Paine was apparently to remain a minor piece of Harvard's almost forgotten history. However, I did discover the scores of all six composers in the library, pored over them, picked out their notes at the piano, and vaguely came to admire them. For two years, beginning in September 1945, I worked as an assistant to Hugo Norden, music editor at the Arthur P. Schmidt Publishing House and music faculty member at Boston University. (I was getting my M.A. at Boston University at the time.) It was exciting to enter, day after day, the doors of the firm that had played such an essential role in the advancement of American art music and discuss with Dr. Norden the many compositions of these composers that Schmidt had published.

It was not until years later, and thanks largely to the recordings made by Karl Kreuger and the Society for the Preservation of the American Musical Heritage, that I at last heard the music of all six composers. In addition, there was the Strickland, Vienna Symphony and Chorus recording, on Desto, of Parker's moving oratorio *Hora Novissima*. Much of what I heard, I loved.

To read anything friendly to and supportive of these composers I had to go back to publications around the turn of the century. After the vast changes in taste that took place in the 1920s, not so much among the general music public as among composers, music critics, and music historians, publications either refused to take notice of these composers or dismissed them as mediocrities or worse. When, around twenty-five years ago, I complained to Gilbert Chase that the attack on these composers in his book *America's Music* was unjustified, he suggested I write a rebuttal and make a case for these composers and their music, which I now present.

This study is not intended to be the usual desiccated "the lives and music of . . ." that gives factual minutiae and detailed musical analyses of styles and fails to grapple with the questions: Who really were these composers? What did their music mean to their contemporaries? Can the music still be a source of enjoyment and pleasure for later generations of music lovers? What follows is a portrait of the American cultural world during the latter part of the nineteenth century, the place of art composers within their society, and the nature of the music created in response to the mandates of the time. If New England and Boston loom large in these pages, it is because they have to, not because I am yielding to provincial interests. I intend to show that what holds true for Boston's musical society is also true for New York City, Philadelphia, Chicago, and elsewhere.

Typical of an inquiry into cultural affinities involving music, tables and comparisons absorbed in technicalities may repeatedly substitute for the real state of affairs instead of divulging it. The reader may feel that he or she understands everything, not realizing that what is understood is the technicality dealt with, not the essential human or artistic quality behind it. The sociologist Charles Horton Cooley tells us that the elucidation of intricate states by uncomplicated ones of identical category can present us with useful correlations. So long as tables and technical comparisons are understood for what they are, ways of managing content, he suggests using them. However, as Cooley warns, the actual matters dealt with "are living wholes which can only be apprehended by a trained sympathy in contact with them." When conclusions are reached, "no presentation of them is adequate that does not restore the facts to their human reality."[1]

An important part of my research has comprised listening closely and repeatedly to the music and asking myself: What does the music itself tell me? Assuredly, I have enjoyed many compositions without recourse to who wrote them, to their au courantness, and to debate over their originality versus their imitativeness. What is more, these compositions have often moved me deeply with their expressiveness. Only after concentrated listening are scores examined. More often than not, a study of the scores confirms what my ears have heard—that knowledge, skill, logic, and economy have produced music of balanced structure, telling rhetoric, warmly sculpted melody, and effective contrast.

I urge music lovers not just to read about these six composers but to listen to their music with open minds. A few record companies have recently provided us with new recordings of a large number of their compositions. Writings about events and ideas are ultimately inadequate explanations of artistic works. In the final analysis, the music must explicate itself.

NOTE

1. Charles Horton Cooley, *Life and the Student* (New York: Knopf, 1927), 156.

THE COMING OF AGE OF AMERICAN ART MUSIC

1

COMPOSER, MUSIC, AND COMMUNITY

William Henry Fry wrote in the *New York Tribune*, on 9 January 1863, about the state of music in America. Born in Philadelphia, Fry was known as a composer, journalist, and lecturer on music both in New York and Philadelphia. He said art composers—"by composers we do not mean the writers of 'sheet music' any more than we would call poets the fillers-up of the corners of a village newspaper"—were rare, even in the largest cities.[1] Then, after the end of the American Civil War, well-trained composers did begin to appear in several American cities. Soon John Knowles Paine (1839–1906), George Chadwick (1854–1931), Arthur Foote (1853–1937), Horatio Parker (1863–1919), Edward MacDowell (1860–1908), and Amy Beach (1867–1944) would establish themselves as the first American composers to earn national and international reputations. When Louis C. Elson published his *History of American Music* in 1904, he named all of them, save Beach, who was still making her way upward, as the most significant American composers of his time, saying they had written works of high worth, received the most frequent performances of American art composers, produced major works in every musical genre, and won esteem in Europe.[2]

All came from New England, except for MacDowell, who was born in New York. His father's family had emigrated from northern Ireland around 1812. His mother's family, originally from England, had settled in Connecticut before the American Revolution. Herein lay his New England connection. His mother, in particular, watched over his upbringing, formal schooling, and musical training. Later, he married a New Englander, Marian Nevins.

These composers received their musical education in Germany or in Boston, which had given itself over to German music and German ideas on music. The composers' training was thorough; their knowledge of their craft, considerable. Amy Beach received little formal instruction in composition, but she did make an exhaustive study of the finest European masterworks and theoretical writings on music, translating some of them into English.

Paine, Chadwick, Foote, and Beach spent most of their creative lives in and around Boston. Parker maintained his Boston connections even after he went to live in New York and New Haven. MacDowell lived in Boston from 1888 to 1896. In the *American Grove*, Margery Lowens characterizes MacDowell's Boston years as his most productive period, when he composed with the utmost energy.[3] After leaving Boston to teach at Columbia University, MacDowell repeatedly visited the city, where his works received more attention than they did elsewhere. Moreover, he spent a great deal of his leisure time in Peterborough, New Hampshire.

These composers knew each other and took a keen interest in one another's music and thoughts about music. Foote mentions the happy meetings at the St. Botolph Club, during the 1890s, where the composers held lengthy after-dinner talks about their creations. Everyone was frank, even outspoken, in criticizing the others' creative efforts. Chadwick confirms Foote's statement, saying the composers knew each other well and met after concerts at one or another's home or at a club. They met "in convivial intercourse, whetting each other's wits with thrust and parry—rejoicing in each other's successes, and working for them, too, but ever ready with the cooling compress of gentle humor or sarcasm if perchance a head showed an undue tendency to enlarge." When, in 1893, Parker accepted the position of organist and choirmaster at Boston's Trinity Church, the "companionship of his old friends," says Chadwick, "the active musical life of Boston, his growing reputation, all stimulated him to further effort."[4] Neither Foote, Chadwick, nor Parker mention Amy Beach as participating in this companionship, possibly because she was relatively young, a woman, and married. However, she was a friend of all of them. Whatever the differences in their musical styles, they shared a common outlook on the relation of the creative artist and musical composition to American society. In short, ample reasons exist for seeing them as forming a group that had much in common.

Benjamin Lambord, a New York organist and choral director and a pupil of MacDowell, wrote in 1915 that he equated the American school of composers with New England and the "Boston group" of composers (designated in this study as the New England group). According to Lambord, they introduced "the first traditions of European musical culture" into American life and labored to get the American community "to look seriously upon the native composer and his achievement."[5] He warned readers not to look for a common style among their works. He added that, because of the achievements of these composers, Boston had to be taken as the birthplace of the first serious American art music, attributable also to the Boston Symphony Orchestra, the finest permanent orchestra of the time; the superb musical instruction available at Harvard University and other local schools; and the city's active intellectual and cultural life.[6]

In the late 1980s, Steven Ledbetter, a well-regarded musicologist, described these musicians as forming the first "*real* school" of American composers—talented, professionally trained, energetic, and idealistic. He characterized Boston as unique among American cities because of the excellence of its composers, schools, performance opportunities, and a social milieu that encouraged fellowship among composers, making them truly a school of American music.[7] Other fine specialists in American music, like Irving Lowens, H. Earle Johnson, William Kearns, and Victor Yellin, have made similar statements.

When Edward MacDowell returned to America after sojourning in Germany, he decided to locate in Boston because he knew that he and his music were already well known to local musical circles, a vigorous cultural life was in evidence, native composers were honored there more than elsewhere, and a musician could make a living in Boston and still find time to work creatively.[8]

A need for live composers existed, said Horatio Parker. He insisted a civilized nation needed an art of its own. "Every nation's [musical] life really centers in and radiates from its composers, unless it is content to import everything bodily."[9] The composers with whom this study is concerned were indeed the native artists who, in the words of Van Wyck Brooks, were able to "bring forth a [musical] culture, creating the living chain that we call tradition."[10]

This is not meant to cast aspersions on other composers of the time. Yet no other American artist received the universal recognition as a composer of major stature and talent that these six were accorded. The others were singles only, with little significant influence: Louis Moreau Gottschalk, William Henry Fry, George Frederick Bristow, Dudley Buck, Silas Pratt, and William Gilchrist, to name six. Of the six, the New Orleans–born Gottschalk had the greatest international renown, but this centered on his piano virtuosity and piano pieces, many of them of the salon type. Only recently are we rediscovering his audacious "Americanist" piano works, with their uninhibited rhythmic vitality and bold exploitation of the popular and folk music of North and South America.

THE POST–CIVIL WAR PERIOD AND BOSTON

What was the post–Civil War environment that seeded and influenced the art music that Americans would write? First was the swift industrialization of the United States and the growth in its population from around thirty-one and a half million in 1860 to ninety-two million in 1910. Over these years, some twenty-three million immigrants arrived in the United States. No longer predominantly from the British Isles and northern Europe, more and more of them now came from eastern Europe and the Mediterranean countries. A vast majority of them had left rural areas and had little education and less money. Uprooted Americans from farms or small villages and uprooted immigrants flocked to the cities to become anonymous wage earners, hungrily seeking musical entertainment to allay the tediousness of their everyday lives. In 1850 one out of eight Americans was a city dweller; in 1900, one out of three. Large urban centers made possible the variety of cultural resources essential for art music but also produced a sense of transition and social instability in Americans of an older Yankee stock with some education and pretensions to high culture.[11] Among these last were our six composers.

A new, brash urban popular culture burgeoned that struck these composers as fringing on coarseness.[12] If not countered, they felt, it threatened to obliterate the values of their older America. They saw an increase in yellow journalism, trashy novels, addiction to sports, and shoddy musical entertainments that went against the cultivated Yankee grain. Not that they repudiated all popular diversions—they could enjoy drinking in moderation, some involvement with sports, a few vaudeville and popular songs. However, for their own life's occupation, they elected to pursue another course—a fostering of idealism through what they created, a search for the finest and noblest in past music as models for their efforts, a pride in craftsmanship, a demanding from themselves of the best they could give. To them this embodied the authentic American spirit that they prized.[13]

Although thoughtful people throughout the United States shared in the composers' concerns and valuation of ennobling pursuits, they were by no means in the majority. More of them seemed to live in Boston than elsewhere. The attitude of other Americans toward high culture, when they thought of it at all, was one of suspicion. They approved of it as a leisure occupation for women but thought it had no other useful purpose. To them, art songs, string quartets, symphonies, and operas were not part of the real world; concert attendance was no preparation for life. They disdained intellectuals and artists of all sorts.[14] At the same time, these same Americans viewed (as did European travellers) Washington as the political, New York City as the financial, and Boston as the cultural capital of the United States. Postwar Boston "exhibited a superior cultural activity" sponsored by "old Americans," writes Howard Mumford Jones. He cites the *Atlantic Monthly*, the Browning Society, Harvard University, the Museum of Fine Arts, the Boston Public Library, and the Boston Symphony as proof of this superiority.[15] A musician would add to this list the New England Conservatory, several performing groups other than the Boston Symphony, and the publishing firm of Arthur P. Schmidt, dedicated to issuing native art music.

The *Musical Herald*, in its July 1885 issue, had virtues like the above in mind when it described Boston as the undoubted "musical centre" of America, where the quantity and quality of its music making were probably equal to those of "any European musical city." A large number of music lovers continually attended "lectures upon musical history and analysis, which pour enough musical information upon the inhabitants to make each one a critic." No wonder musicians clustered here.[16] By contrast, New York City, for all its size and wealth, was less attractive to these composers. Writing about the city in the eighties, Jerome Hopkins was despondent about the lack of good music. Performers, he said, avoided contemporary works. The profit line dominated the thinking of concert managers. The public felt contempt for unknown composers, skepticism over the existence of any native talent, and mentally handicapped when required to form an opinion on a new work. Churches rarely put on worthwhile sacred music. The whims of the fashionable, whose money and approval went to musical humbugs, had ascendancy. Referring to the two decades after the eighties, William Dean Howells said that the city's attitude toward the arts was embodied in the Metropolitan Opera, where the New Yorker's pride of wealth, vanity of fashion, and taste in music were revealed. Daniel Gregory Mason claimed such criticisms were still pertinent through the 1920s.[17]

To give a second example, Chicagoans reluctantly supported new musical undertakings, shunned artistic performances, and preferred brass-band concerts. String quartets were anathema. Amy Fay wrote to Henry Longfellow from Chicago, in 1880, that people were unmusical and altogether "out of the literary world." (In an earlier letter that Longfellow had sent her, he described Boston as "quite music mad.") The great orchestral conductor Theodore Thomas, trying to induce Chicagoans to accept fine music, used Boston as a whip. He said that in the nineties everybody avoided hearing symphonies. "When it seemed as if there were no immediate relief, the example of the Boston Orchestra came to our rescue and helped me to maintain the standard of our programmes. When fault was found with their severity, I would say, 'Do you wish our programmes to be inferior in standard to those of the Boston Orchestra?' 'No,' was the answer. 'Well, we give every year a number of programmes without a symphony. The Boston Orchestra does not.' That helped!"[18] Interestingly, when Cincinnati decided to claim eminence in music for itself, it styled itself "the Boston of the West."[19]

Gottschalk, an astute observer of the American scene, concertized throughout the country during the sixties. Although he chided Boston's conservative critic John Sullivan Dwight and lamented Boston's tendency toward the narrowly academic, he also enjoyed visiting the city. He called it "par excellence the aristocratic city" that had "made enormous progress in the sciences and arts." He praised its inhabitants for spending generously on music, finding them "intelligent, literary, polished, and musical"; for musicians like himself Boston was indeed "the Athens of America." He felt flattered when eminences like Longfellow took the trouble to call on him and lauded the "generous hospitality" of people like Annie and James T. Fields, at whose home he met the painter William Morris Hunt and the author Oliver Wendell Holmes. He concluded: "Boston possesses what New York has not yet obtained: two concert halls . . . in no way inferior to any of the largest concert halls in the world."[20]

THE NATURE OF THE MUSICAL PUBLIC

In an important aesthetic sense, these six composers acted as representatives of their social group. They had a mandate to express its principles at the highest artistic level. Yet, this social group did not comprise all of Boston's society. In 1889 Arlo Bates wrote that the Boston society of that decade was complex and enigmatical, "full of anomalies," and with "no fixed standards whether of wealth, birth, or culture, but at times apparently leaning a little toward each of these three factors of American social standing." Sylvester Baxter wrote ten years later that no one circle was representative of Boston: "Literary Boston, artistic Boston, scientific Boston, musical Boston, fashionable Boston—each constitutes a little social world in itself, each merges with the others more or less, and each has something typical of the whole."[21]

Certainly, not all wealthy or respectable people in Boston had a genuine love for art music or a regard for the six composers with whom we are concerned. An examination of the activities of "high society," revealed in biographies, autobiographies, letters, diaries, and novels based on its doings, will find little concerning native composers. Appearing with frequency are the names of European musicians, whether visitors or permanent residents in the city. Indeed, the fashionable and exclusive sets behaved like those of other cities, including New York, about which George Templeton Strong wrote: "In all matters of art, this community is Boeotian. It cares nothing for Mozart's and Weber's music, but is deeply interested in any 'kid-glove' performance, on the programme of which stand the names of Mrs. Astor, Mrs. William Schermerhorn, and the like, as a 'Ladies Committee' and to which people are admitted only by favor."[22]

Several writers inveighed against the Boston cliques that pretended an interest in music, talked nauseatingly about it, yet found musical evenings a form of slavery. They attended symphony concerts to be seen and to ogle each other.[23] Native composers could not expect support or appreciation from these people.

Insensitive behavior was sometimes witnessed at concerts. At an 1895 Apollo Club concert, Warren Davenport saw a man read a newspaper throughout the entire performance, "except when occasionally he, for a moment or two, rested his chin on his thumb and gazed vacantly on the disturbance below. As his seat was near the stage, he was in plain view of all the performers, and the largest part of the audience also. . . . It was a gross insult to the singers and the listeners alike. And this is Boston, and at a function of the swell singing society of that cultivated community."[24]

Several prominent Bostonians seem to have had no ear for music. Intellectually, they could esteem the six composers. However, they made no claim to understanding their or anybody else's music. Ralph Waldo Emerson once wrote to Dwight that he enjoyed reading Dwight's lectures on music but "with the drawback that I read them as a mute reads of eloquence." During a London visit, he mentioned Chopin in letters to his wife: "Last night I dined with Chopin at the house of Miss Stirling, &

heard him play; could the denying heaven have also given me ears for the occasion!" A week later: "Today I am to go to Chopin's Matinée Musicale, for which [Lord Lovelace] sent me a ticket yesterday, could he only lend me ears!"[25]

Similarly, William James was friendly with Paine. John Fiske wrote to his mother in December 1877: "We have been to a delightful grouse and potato salad supper party at Bro. Paine's. In the evening when the music was going on full tilt, William James called with his dog, and said dog howled and bellowed at the music and had to be banished to a distant room, amidst peals of laughter." But James did not comprehend Paine's music. Daniel Gregory Mason speaks of James's insensitivity to music. Once he coaxed James into describing his reactions to "the F major Ballade of Chopin, the one with the rather jerky rhythm. James wrote that this suggested to him a man going through life genially, placidly, amiably—'with one leg slightly longer than the other'."[26]

Several writers cite the five-day National Peace Jubilee, held in Boston in 1869, as the catalyst that induced many men and women previously uninterested in or unaware of art music to commence attending instrumental and vocal concerts. Patrick Gilmore organized the celebration, brought in the violinist Ole Bull as concertmaster, and assembled forty prominent performing artists, plus a huge orchestra of a thousand and a chorus of around ten thousand members. Seating was provided for an audience of around fifty thousand. Arthur Foote called it a musical "great awakening" of benefit to him and the other composers of the New England group. Gilmore, Foote recalled, purveyed an enormous amount of ballyhoo: "All the same, the music (mainly oratorio choruses) exerted its spell, and though we may smile at the occasion today, these concerts had a mighty influence, especially in New England." The musician Henry Dunham states that thousands came from outlying villages and towns in order to attend performances centered on oratorios like *Elijah*, *St. Paul*, and the *Messiah*. A selection of music from the Jubilee, issued in a special edition, "found its way into nearly every family in New England and . . . exerted a powerful influence for improvement in the musical taste of the community."[27]

The majority of the attendees, who later formed the greater part of the Boston audience for art music, barely knew any art music. Prior to the Jubilee, many of them had disesteemed music. To admit an affection for it, a wish to study an instrument or singing, or a desire to attend a concert might be regarded as moral weakness, states Dwight. Indeed, "the idea that music is an art of intellectual and spiritual consequence, that it should be respected and placed upon an equal footing with the recognized 'humanities' of a liberal education, would have been dismissed as one of the wildest and most dangerous of dreams."[28]

Although Boston's art-music audience grew to a size that commentators in other cities took note of, it was never huge. Local observers found no great hunger for music. When the native composers appeared, they had to act as missionaries trying to convert an indifferent public "to a due regard for the art as something worthy of a real man's life work," wrote David Stanley Smith, a friend of Parker. Yet, "these New England composers [Paine, Chadwick, Parker, MacDowell, and Whiting are named] did not resort to propaganda or the writing of articles to draw recognition for music or for themselves, but won their point by hard labor in the study. They produced much music but little talk."[29] Nevertheless, whatever its limitations, the local public for art music did grow and did encourage native composers to set their hands to original composition.

Contemporary observers recognized that composers had to satisfy an immense range of tastes and speak in ways that allowed ready understanding. Most of the music public in the United States, including Boston, had "neither the time nor disposition to cultivate insight into artistic subtleties and refinements or to develop their taste and powers of concentrated attention."[30] Fortunately, a nucleus of true believers did exist in America, mainly in Boston. This nucleus felt sympathetic toward Emerson's declaration in the poem "Culture":

> Can rules or tutors educate
> The semigod whom we await?
> He must be musical,
> Tremulous, impressional,
> Alive to gentle influence
> Of landscape and of sky,
> And tender to the spirit-touch
> Of man's or maiden's eye:
> But to his native centre fast,
> Shall into Future fuse the Past,
> And the world's flowing fates in his own mould recast.[31]

These true believers comprised a gentlefolk with urbane manners, polished speech, and elevated cultural pursuits. Contemporary writers constantly distinguished between them and an antidemocratic socioeconomic elite dedicated to fashion and self-aggrandizement and enamored of power and privilege. In contrast, genuine gentlefolk supported democracy, avoided ostentation, and chose responsible and worthwhile occupations, including cultural ones. Not all had wealth; some incomes were modest. Gentility was not a state achieved through birth; anybody could achieve it. It embraced doctors, lawyers, educated clergy, bankers, merchants, college professors, writers, publishers, editors, artists, and musicians. Upon such people fell the responsibility to uphold a serious cultural life. What is most important, the composers here designated as the New England group belonged in this category. To know the meaning of gentility as opposed to genteel can go some way toward discerning what these New Englanders held in common and how their communal outlook shaped the direction of the music written by native musicians. Without question, if the composer desired the character of gentleman or gentlewoman and acceptance as a creative artist, he or she had to comply with the social and moral standards dictated by the code of gentility.[32]

It was the fashion during the first half of the twentieth century to consider these men and women to be genteel and narrow-minded. The adherents of this point of view have been non–New Englanders enamored of musical styles other than those treasured by the cultivated individuals and the composers that here concern us. Their tastes have run to the vernacular or to works evidencing an originality that usually is an outgrowth of some avant-garde movement, as often as not having its origin in Europe. To not resemble what these critics demand music should resemble is prima facie evidence of unworthiness. Only at the end of the twentieth century do we begin to realize that the accusations made by these critics have nothing to do with aesthetic quality, and everything to do with politics and changing fashion.[33] Gentlefolk were admittedly subject to the weaknesses of all humans—suspicion of anything exotic or unfamiliar, a temptation to view and do things as they had been done and viewed, affection for their locality above other localities, condescension toward those who differed from them. But this was not all there was to them. They did struggle to add a richer dimension to their lives. We should therefore guard against elevating weaknesses into fatal flaws.

An early critic of gentlefolk was George Santayana, a Spanish Catholic who taught at Harvard from 1889 to 1912. He detested the "genteel tradition" of Americans and especially of New Englanders, which embraced beliefs and standards that kept faith with their past and were not his own. Therefore, he said, these "genteel" people were "a hundred years behind the times." He found the writings of Hawthorne and Emerson to have "a certain starved and abstract quality." Culture was dominated by women and therefore was "passive, delicate, apart from the on-going business of society." The fondness of New England's gentlefolk for music also came in for condemnation: "Music and landscape make up the spiritual resources of those who cannot or dare not express their unfulfilled ideals in words. . . . When a genteel tradition forbids people to confess that they are unhappy . . . imagination is driven for comfort into abstract arts. . . . To understand oneself is the classic form of consolation; to elude oneself is the romantic. In the presence of music or landscape human experience eludes itself." To him, music was "a mental complication which may be an index to other psychological facts connected with it genetically, but which has no valid intent, no ideal transcendence, no assertive or cognitive function." Music "understands nothing: it is a buzzing labour in the fancy which, by some obscure causation, helps us to live on."[34]

Santayana's inimical statements about "genteel" Americans were quickly echoed by Vernon Parrington and other writers on American literature.[35] (Not far behind were the writers on America's musical culture, like Gilbert Chase and Wilfred Mellers, who convicted the New England composers of genteelness, and their music of pretentiousness and servile emulation of various outmoded Teutonisms.) Yet these gentlefolk were neither countrified, unsophisticated, nor incapacitated when thinking about matters outside of their region; to call them provincial is false. The music lovers among them did not pretend to a snobbish status based on superior taste, nor show false delicacy and excessive refinement; this sort of genteelness is more appropriately seen in the socially exclusive and fashion-conscious sets in no way connected with honest gentility. They were open to new experiences, and art music was a new and exhilarating experience to them. They could not comprehend every musical composition and might reject what they could not comprehend. But rejection was not always due to bigotry. First exposure to an unusual style might also account for rejection. Given repeated exposure, acceptance often ensued, as it did with the music of Wagner, Berlioz, and Strauss.

What did gentle people see in high culture? "Culture," wrote Thomas Wentworth Higginson, at one time the editor of the Atlantic, "is the training and finishing of the whole man, until he . . . pursues science and art as objects of intrinsic worth." The cultured man "places the fine arts above the useful arts" and "is willingly impoverished in material comforts, if it can thereby obtain nobler living." If reactionary, the impulse is unhealthy and morbid. If healthy, "it simply keeps alive the conviction that the life is more than meat; and so supplies that counterpoise to mere wealth which Europe vainly seeks to secure by aristocracies of birth."[36] Gentlemen like Higginson espoused artistic cosmopolitanism, seeking beauty wherever they could find it—in Greek statuary, French illuminated manuscripts, Persian rugs, and German symphonies. By so doing they hoped to broaden the appreciation of the arts beyond the vernacular and provincial. They tried to set examples for the remaining populace, inviting the masses "to reach upward toward perfection, obtain a sense of the importance of standards of conduct, knowledge, and art unrelated to private advantage. Thus, the masses would understand the importance of quality independent of quantity."[37]

Some gentle people had been aesthetically weak in their youth, like Charles Eliot Norton, the Harvard scholar, who "had the stiff New England brain which (naturally) had never come in contact with the fine arts in childhood, but had learned them as a grown man learns French." German culture usually informed musical taste, as it did that of the historian George Bancroft. (Amy Fay says he had splendid aesthetic judgment and a passionate fondness for "good music.") Once won over to art music, such persons wished to experience it at every opportunity. Celia Thaxter, living in seclusion on the Isles of Shoals, welcomed the visits of William Mason and John Knowles Paine and the opportunity of hearing them play piano sonatas, especially Beethoven's. She lived for "music, pictures, poetry, and conversation," declaring, "If people do not enjoy what they find [when visiting her], they must go their way; my work and the music will not cease." On 10 September 1878, she wrote to a friend: "I missed my mother so I know not which way to turn. But heaven sent down here a musician, who played Beethoven to me morning, noon, and night the livelong summer, and cured my sick soul as a splendid tonic cures a sick body. Mr. and Mrs. Paine, from Cambridge,—Professor Paine . . . came for a week and stayed six and more; and though he did not intend to play, and I never asked him, he found out how much it was to me, and played to me hours every day." She called on the Paines during the period when John Knowles Paine was working on the highly important music to *Oedipus Tyrannus* and describes her experience that evening: "I am in the midst of the awful and thrilling music of the Oedipus Tyrannus, and it curdles my blood; we are all steeped in it, for J.K.P. goes on and on composing it all the time, and the tremendous chords thrill the very timbers of the house."[38]

Celia Thaxter was also aware that, even as she and her friends grew in their fondness for the arts, they represented the end of an era, a closing off of the society of which they were a part. She wrote to Annie Fields in 1892, "Dear Annie, has not Death been busy? Everybody is gone. Bryant, Longfellow, Lowell, Whittier, Browning, Tennyson! even dear Sam Longfellow has joined that mute procession, too. What an empty world it grows!"[39] This was also the problem of the New England composers, who came on the scene when the society that sustained them was fading away.

Concerned people like those cited above labored to maintain an environment in which artistic activity had meaning and merited doing. Their encouragement bolstered the efforts of the New England composers. They advanced a type of cultivated reasoning that distinguished what native composers, painters, architects, and sculptors were creating as cogent artistry, and they demonstrated how artistic contributions filled some important requisites for a society with any pretension to civilization.

A FURTHER EXAMINATION OF NEW ENGLAND'S MUSIC LOVERS

Another encouragement to composers was the increase in the audience for art music brought about in part by the contention that such music was beneficial to the spirit, proper for enjoyment, and an activity in accord with the aspirations of all human nature. Intellectual leaders regarded art composers and other serious artists as benefactors of mankind and therefore encouraged their endeavors. They persuaded audiences to give composers a hearing, performing groups to play their new works, colleges and music conservatories to find them employment, and private individuals to engage them for music lessons. Even before the Civil War, the Unitarian leader William Ellery Channing, of Boston's Federal Street Church, was preaching to workers about self-culture and the care they owed to themselves, "to the unfolding and perfecting" of their natures. Emerson lectured on the avoidance of the "trivial and sordid." He wanted every individual from whatever walk of life to set forth "in quest of Culture," in order to hear "the voice of the Eternal" in his heart.[40]

After the Civil War, several New England writers came to believe that the arts could achieve viability in America only if linked to a significant portion of the public and the workings of democracy; otherwise they would forfeit the broader human connections necessary for their maintenance. Furthermore, as Harvard's president, Charles William Eliot, concluded, in an 1895 address entitled "The Happy Life": "Every American had the right to enjoy the sensuous and spiritual pleasures", including music, that gave "health, strength, and life itself." Attempts to divide pleasure into what was animal or moral, unworthy or worthy, he saw as doomed to failure. Such attempts had been made in the past. However, drawing a line between pleasures, saying one was bodily, another intellectual, and still another moral, had proved "manifestly impossible." Musical enjoyment could come from all three. The "high degree of that fine pleasure which music gives" might not be within every reach; yet almost all could achieve it. Every individual found that musical enjoyment came from both the physical and the mental sensations of sound. In a civilized society, the experiencing of distinguished musical works should be open to every person who wished to hear them and had the intelligence to cultivate fine music, whatever his or her social and economic status.[41] Not surprisingly, when Eliot assumed the presidency of Harvard, he threw his support behind Paine and the offering of music courses to benefit all students.

In the postwar decades we find the father of the novelist George Cable coming to Northampton, Massachusetts, and conceiving the idea of "Home-Culture Clubs," directed by volunteer teachers, through which the laboring classes might "improve" their lives. Mill and other laborers, shop and office clerks met in private homes to build social relationships, find spiritual enrichment, and learn about literature, art, music, science, and history. By 1896, the ninth year of the movement, around sixty such clubs existed in Massachusetts, and a lesser number in other states.[42]

Men and women were told that a cultivated taste for music was not a gift of nature but could be acquired by anybody. This was the observation of an editorial published in the Boston *Musical Herald*, for January 1890. The unnamed editors (among the editors were Louis C. Elson and Eben Tourjée) claimed that every human ear was susceptible to the charms of sound, its regularity, symmetry, and agreeable vibrations. But nature could take a person only so far. Natural appreciation required the aid of education and of constant and careful listening at concerts to achieve maturity and complete appreciation.[43]

A surprisingly large number of men and women did begin to attend concerts with some consistency after the Civil War. To be sure, even the popular Boston Symphony Orchestra had its down years. However, note the observation Henry Lee Higginson, the orchestra's founder, made to its music director, Wilhelm Gericke, in the spring of 1889, on the hall being "so crowded" on concert evenings that "many listeners of all ages sit on the steps and stand in the aisles each week and each year." Moreover, "they do not come there to please Mr. Gericke or me; they do not come twenty miles to show their good clothes; they come to hear music, and they listen attentively. . . . That audience is not from the Back Bay or from any particular set of people. They are town folks and country folks, and they come to hear the music at the hands of Mr. Gericke and his Orchestra."[44]

Writing to Bayard Taylor in 1866, Thomas Bailey Aldrich was already noticing a genuine appetite in Boston for the serious works of creative people.[45] When Aldrich wrote his letter, the work of the art composers of the New England group was still in the future. Nevertheless, he indicated the kind of encouraging climate they could expect—that is to say, encouraging when compared to any other American city. The former Clara Doria, a trained English musician who married Henry Munroe Rogers and settled in Boston, looked back in 1919 on the "old Boston" she had known in the 1870s, a place where "people were valued for what they *were* and not for what they *possessed.*" Boston then was "the hotbed of literature, art and science in America." People aspired "to be familiar with and to appreciate the better things." When she visited Boston in 1873 to sing the part of Donna Elvira, in *Don Giovanni*, she discovered Boston's "very advanced" musical taste. Amateur singers were avidly taking up the lieder of Schubert, Schumann, and Franz. She saw for herself how Boston had "outstripped New York in musical appreciation."[46]

Because some Bostonians zealously cultivated the arts, they became the subject of biting satires, like the one entitled "The Girl He'll Wed," published in the pamphlet *Hood's Sarsaparilla Book of Wit & Humor*:

I shall wed a fair aesthetic
  Quite regardless of expense,
All I ask is that she's utter,
  And in all things quite intense.
Limp of course, and lank she must be,
  Clad in minor tones of green,
Consummately soulful earnest,
  Must she be, my queen.
We shall feast on lilies daily,
  Quaffing drafts of beauty fair,
With a dish of ferns on Sunday,
  Or a peacock's feather rare.
Thus shall flow our lives forever,
  Like two gently gurgling rills,
Breathing poesy and too-too,
  And her dad shall foot the bills.[47]

A "Boston Letter" pubilshed in the New York *Musical Courier* of 1890 (and possibly written by James G. Huneker, the New York music critic and associate editor of the *Courier*) proclaimed that the Boston public was the most musical in America. New York was "inferior to Boston" not in the number of its concerts, the letter noted, but "in the quality of the audiences." Boston's music lovers displayed "unflagging interest in everything musical and their true and unaffected enthusiasm" was immediately apparent. Bostonians turned out for concerts even in bad weather. Three years later, the *Musical Courier* published comments that Horatio Parker made to Henry Krehbiel. New York audiences, said Parker, regarded "first-class musicians" as entertainers and secondary to "any other worker in art or science." In contrast, audiences in western cities gave serious musicians "more proportionate consideration," and Boston outstripped even western cities in this respect.[48] Parker undoubtedly had in mind his own status and that of other composers in the two cities. No wonder the composers examined in this study preferred to work in Boston, except when tempting teaching positions called them to other cities.

Of course, not all members of Boston's music public had a thorough understanding of new works. To a considerable extent, a majority of them found it easier and more prudent to rely on the responses of musically trained and experienced critics than on their own responses to new music, including that of the New England group. If guaranteed that a native work was accepted by Boston's cultural leaders, they could discard their inhibitions and allow their own enthusiasm to take hold. Yet composers needed the backing of these many listeners, for through their very numbers they could determine a trend and increase the chances that untested compositions would get a hearing. The composers knew that any chamber-music audience they might write for would normally number no more than two hundred listeners. If the Handel and Haydn Society performed a choral work, the audience might number as few as six hundred attendees. On some evenings, a half-full house might greet the singers. Symphony concerts usually had larger turnouts. Yet, they too experienced bad years, when subscriptions were down and few people purchased tickets at the door.[49] But at least composers knew that performing groups did exist that were capable of presenting works in all categories save perhaps opera, audiences did attend concerts with some consistency, and people could be found to perform or listen willingly to their offerings.

Not to be discounted were the clubs that provided companionshp and encouragement to native composers, like the Tavern Club, whose meetings George Chadwick attended. This club, "formed for the enjoyment of music and good-fellowship," had Higginson as its president for twenty years. All sorts of musical celebrities came to dine, drink, play billiards (Paderewski enjoyed playing the game here when he visited Boston), and make music. Although the club was open to men only, such was its fame that Lilli

Lehmann once insisted: "I want to go to the Tavern Club." And she "went, sang, and . . . danced, taking with her a few choice spirits."[50]

Helen Howe describes her father, M. A. DeWolfe Howe, as belonging to the Tavern Club and friendly with Chadwick. She tells of an evening at the club when her father, who played the piano by "ear," made music only to hear Chadwick rib him with: "You certainly know your way around the key of G." Thomas Russell Sullivan tells of another evening, the "Annual Narrenabend" at the Tavern Club, which produced an original operetta (music by Chadwick, libretto by Arlo Bates) "called 'A Quiet Lodging.' The whole night went gaily. Around seventy men were present, all in costume. The most successful get-up was that of Frank Sturgis, who came as Paderewski."[51] In the novel *The Chippendales*, Robert Grant describes a fictitious Sphinx Club, which seems modeled after the Tavern Club. Members were "artists, writers, musicians, men of science, . . . doctors, and a certain number of unlabelled spirits who were chiefly good fellows. . . . To foster and protect the arts, to protest against Philistinism and humbug, and to let down the barriers between soul and soul was the bond which held them together."[52]

There was also the famous Saturday Club, whose older members included Emerson, Holmes, Lowell, Longfellow, Dana, and Norton, and whose younger members included music lovers like Fiske, Henry Lee Higginson, and Edward Newton Perkins. Although some members had only a slight affinity for music, all agreed on its importance for a civilized community. Most of them dependably turned out for musical events like the premiere of *Oedipus Tyrannus*, with music by Paine. Annie Fields testifies to Longfellow's love of music, especially opera: "He was always ready to hear 'Lucia' or 'Don Giovanni,' and to make a festival time at the coming of Salvini or Neilson. . . . He easily caught the gayety of such occasions, and in the shadow of the curtains in the box would join in the singing or the recitative of the lovely Italian words with a true poet's delight."[53]

Of course clubs existed whose main function was to foster the performance of music, like the Boylston Club, Apollo Club, and Cecilia Society, sponsors of choral music, and the Euterpe Society, which sponsored chamber music. The Harvard Music Association had funded symphony concerts prior to those of the Boston Symphony.

Many Boston homes were receptive to music and musicians, and wealthier families had spacious rooms built to accommodate concerts and dancing. Mr. and Mrs. Montgomery Sears were noted for their musical evenings. Maude Howe Elliott's diary for 26 April 1890 reads: "In the evening music at the Montgomery Sears'. Very lovely. Ernst Perabo and the Adamowski quartette. Mr. Sears a perfect host, the musicians at their best." Thomas Sullivan was at the Sears home one evening in 1892 (the night before, he had listened to a song recital at the home of William Apthorp): "Music and more music!—this time at the house of Mrs. Montgomery Sears, who had the better part of the Symphony Orchestra, with Nikisch to lead. Paderewski gave the host a pleasant surprise by appearing suddenly and asking leave to play, which he did in his best manner."[54]

Many a home musicale was anything but stiff. Clayton Johns states that the Apthorps had unique Sunday evenings with six to eight people coming to dine, including at least one important musical guest, such as Paderewski or Melba. Mrs. Gardner and the musical director Gericke always attended. Members of the "younger set" were invariably invited. "Later in the evening," Johns recounts, "beer and cigars lent a Bohemian air to the occasions. Mrs. Apthorp appeared carrying a large pitcher of beer in one hand, beer mugs handing from each finger of her other hand." They ate, drank, made music, and, after midnight, danced. Johns also remarks on the evenings at the home of Mr. and Mrs. Dixey, who "didn't entertain in a large way, but . . . gave charming dinners of ten or a dozen, frequently. Mr. Dixey was a lover of music and Mrs. Dixey loved all things beautiful; they entertained artists, musicians, and the beau monde. Let me recall one evening when Lilli Lehmann was the chief guest. Her sister Marie and Van Dyck were there, also the Gerickes and others." After dinner, Lehmann, accompanied by Gericke, sang from Wagner's *Tristan*. "As the company was getting a little too serious, Lilli asked for a broom. Astride the broomstick she sang and acted the witch's dance from *Hänsel und Gretel*. Hilarity then knew no bounds. Staid matrons and maids joined in the dance. I remember one imitated a can-can."[55] The most famous musical evening of all were those given by Mr. and Mrs. Jack Gardner, first in their Beacon Street house and later in Fenway Court. Louise Tharp writes that Mrs. Gardner's music room "was unique because used more for music than for dancing."[56]

One must stress that, despite the unconfident majority and the exclusive, fashion-enslaved set, Boston had enough genuine music enthusiasts so that local composers felt encouraged. They could hope for understanding from more than one or two persons. Although infrequently named in journals and letters of the period, local composers did perform at musical evenings in several homes and at times included their own works. Unfortunately, the keepers of diaries and journals were overawed by the eminent foreign musicians whom they met and neglected to mention Boston's homegrown musicians. Moreover, when weighed against the prestige garnered through cultivation of noted foreign celebrities, American composers were second choices when invitations to affluent homes went out. Even hosts with some dedication to native artistry were tempted to modify their views if one or more celebrities were in town. They might have felt that local composers would always be there to fill the hiatus between visits by the outsiders.

Surprising is the number of Bostonians trained in music, some extensively enough so that they could make a modest claim to being composers. Others, less intensively trained, were capable of understanding musical notation and following a performance with score in hand. For example, individuals like Charles C. Perkins and John Fiske of the Harvard faculty, though engaged in other professions, knew enough about music to compose a few compositions of their own. The former, a patron of the Handel and Haydn Society, produced a string quartet, a trio, and violin pieces; the latter, a supporter of Paine, composed an ambitious mass.[57] And of course there were other music lovers on the Harvard faculty. They constantly attended concerts, promoting now one, now another, musical cause. Several were capable musicians.[58]

It was not at all unusual to see music lovers going to concerts with scores in their hands. Charles Flandrau states that, as a Harvard freshman, he attended "a wonderful concert . . . although I couldn't help wondering all the time why I was enjoying it. . . . I felt so lonely and homesick and as if I had wasted my life and broken my mother's heart, that I began to sniff; and the lady who was sitting next to me (she had a huge music book on her lap and was following every note with her finger and swaying from side to side like a cobra) turned and glared at me." After Paine's Second Symphony was published and the work was performed before local audiences, it was noted that many attendees listened with the score in their hands.[59]

THE NEW EXPERIENCE OF LISTENING

For devoted music lovers, however recent their discovery of music, the finest works introduced them to what they often described as the sublime. To have a composition evoke elevated emotion and awe through the magnificence of sound was their greatest hope. They felt that if the responsible composer gave his utmost, so also must the responsible listener. The composer, in turn, knew his work took value from the layers of meaning and the richness of pleasure his music conveyed to his circle of listeners, however small it was. These convictions may not coincide with those of some twentieth-century writers on music, but the lack of agreement does not make them any the less sincere. Literally moved to tears, Fiske often "had a good bawl" at a concert. James Fields said, "I would rather be a fine tenor singer than anything else in the world." Josiah Royce, philosopher and Harvard professor, confessed to music's prominent place in his emotional life, and once even wished to become a composer; of him, Daniel Gregory Mason said, "He had an intuition of the place of sorrow and tragedy in our lives, which [William] James, for all his delightful chivalry, somehow missed, and which made his philosophy plumb the depths." Celia Thaxter gave to musical compositions "her generous response, overflowing, almost extravagant in expression . . . [but] never half enough to begin to tell the new life they brought her." A Thaxter poem addressed to the tenor William J. Winck went:[60]

> Carry us captive, thou with the strong heart
> And the clear head, and nature sweet and sound!
> Most willing captives we to the great art.
> . . . .
> Sing, and we ask no greater joy than this,
> Only to listen, thrilling to the song.
> . . . .
> Borne skyward where the wingèd hosts rejoice.

Fields's and Thaxter's affection for music is seconded in Arlo Bates's novel about Boston, *The Pagans*. Bates had a thorough knowledge of Boston's artistic circles and was a friend of Chadwick, who gave a musical setting to many of Bates's poems and to Bates's operetta libretto, *A Quiet Lodging. In The Pagans Bates's fictional character Helen Greyson is* found singing for her friends: "There was a personal quality about the chant which made it seem like a direct appeal from the singer to the heart of each listener. It came to each as a spontaneous flowing of the singer's innermost self; a confidence made in mystic wise, sacred and inviolable, and setting him honored by receiving it forever from the common multitude of men. It was an appeal to some unspoken and unspeakable bond of fealty, which made the pulses throb and great emotions stir in the breast. Before hearing one would be stubbornly incredulous of the possibility of his being so deeply affected; afterward he would remember how he had been moved with wonder and longing." Later in the novel, another character describes art as embodying the aspirations and attributes of humanity, and a friend replies: "There are so few people who have imagination enough even to understand what one means by saying art is the only thing in the world worth living for. Why, art is the supreme expression of humanity; the apotheosis of all the best there is in the race."[61]

The Connecticut-born and Yale-educated poet Edward Rowland Sill once addressed a poem "To a Face at a Concert":

> When the low music makes a dusk of sound
> About us, and the viol or far-off horn
> Swells out above it like a wind forlorn,
> That wanders seeking something never found,
> What phantom in your brain, on what dim ground,
> Traces its shadowy lines?
> . . . .
>
> When the lids droop and the hands lie unstrung,
> Dare one divine your dream, while the chords weave
> Their cloudy woof from key to key, and die—
> Is it one fate that, since the world was young,
> Has followed man, and makes him half believe
> The voice of instruments a human cry?

He summarizes what many like him thought was the effect of music on them when he says that its expressive power did not stop with the feelings: "Inextricably bound up with every human feeling is a host of ideas associated with it in the mind." Music's "power of direct expression is almost limited to the emotions"; yet at the same time it "expresses different ideas to different people,—or to ourselves at different times,—according as the particular emotion is associated in experience with one set of ideas or another. The sonata which to an Alpine goatherd would express a thunderstorm among rocky peaks to a sailor might with equal distinctness express a tempest at sea. The larger and deeper the life experience of the listener, the more a symphony will mean to him in ideas; or the fuller his emotional development, the more it will mean to him in feeling,—always provided that it is a great work . . . to which he listens." Also from Sill comes the statement that art affirms life itself, that "great music adds the greatest total to our conscious existence." If music belittled or brutalized human nature, pleasure was low; if it enlarged it, pleasure was high.[62]

Tempering the music lover's passion for music was a dominant and pivotal certainty for both composer and connoisseur—the conviction that the creation of an artwork was a social activity having a much larger public in mind than a small elite. A composer could not exist within a narrow circle. It follows that not every one of his compositions had to have significant social consequence. He might intend the most absolute of his absolute music for the most select of listeners, but he still had to consider the larger audience and sympathize with the general social and cultural preferences of his time and place.[63] Most concertgoers were novices in listening. Their tolerance of a novel contemporary work, to which the experienced listener might give serious consideration, was minimal. Even Beethoven was a still half-digested novelty to them. Yet, the general American audiences for music were not necessarily inferior to those of Europe. For example, Mark Twain once remarked that a Boston audience consisted of four thousand critics. After a year spent in Europe, Parker gave a talk about his impressions and included disparaging observations about German audiences, and those of Munich in particular: "A concert, by a Spanish conductor, of Russian music, . . . showed the provincialism of the Germans, their inability to appreciate music which is laid out on lines unfamiliar to them! They seem quite unable to understand Tschaikowsky. The personal element enters very largely into the German's enjoyment of music. If one is well known and popular it makes little difference how well or badly things are done. For instance, I heard a performance under Zumpe of Tschaikowsky's B minor Symphony about as bad as possible. It would have left a New York or Boston audience perfectly cold, but the Germans became almost frantically excited because Zumpe conducted."[64]

Apthorp admitted that musicians, and he as a critic, found it difficult to put themselves in the place of nonmusicians. However, he had noticed that many a concertgoer, though knowing nothing about music, had a passable ear and more than a little acquaintance with good music. Such a listener persistently attended concerts, "not for the look of the thing, but because he likes it." Swept up and delighted by a symphony, he expressed a "perfectly sincere and real enthusiasm." Music hypnotizes and stimulates such a person, but he can't explain why, nor tell you what any work is all about.[65]

Catering to the listener were professional performing ensembles, most of them newly established and in a tenuous stage of their existence. Thus, instrumentalists, vocalists, and composers alike had to win over and educate their audiences. No government grants, no plethora of prizes, no abundance of commissions existed to back anybody's artistry and independence. In short, Boston might have been a better place than most for artistic survival, but conditions there were by no means ideal. Ignoring these realities would have jeopardized everything the composer was hoping to achieve. Fortunately, composers, connoisseurs, and members of the general audience more or less agreed on what meanings were to be derived from musical sound. For that time and place, when agreement was essential if native music was to begin its existence and continue into the future, they had to reach a consensus about the function of tonality, melody, and harmony, the ideas to be conveyed through musical tones, and the structures best suited to the integration of sounds and ideas. Whether Paine, MacDowell, or Parker, the composer hoped to create tones that could play upon the public's anticipation of what was to transpire in a work, either defeating, deferring, or gratifying expectations in pleasurable ways; one moment increasing tension; another, offering repose. The aim always was to design a piece that made intellectual sense and encouraged sympathetic reverberations in listeners' feelings. And the listener was often someone with conservative tastes, like those of William Foster Apthorp, who was leery of bold departures from the tried and true in music: "I am a man of my own time; I was born into it, I live in it—and in it alone. My time may be a hideous time, for aught I know—or care; but it is mine. The men of my time speak the language I best understand; they speak it fluently, and I catch their slightest innuendos without effort. Do I regret other times and ages? How can I? If I did, I should regret being myself!"[66]

Both pride in a native son and concurrence in what was intrinsically desirable in an oratorio won Paine an excited ovation from a Portland, Maine, audience of three thousand, at the premiere of *St. Peter*, in June 1873. This large gathering was astonishing for such a small town. Carried away by the music, John Fiske heard "a very great work—perhaps the greatest work in vocal music since Elijah," owing to its "exquisitely lovely arias and sublime choruses." Fiske heard Paine's First Symphony introduced by Theodore Thomas in Boston, January 1875, and describes the audience as giving it "the wildest applause that I ever witnessed at a concert." Paine must have felt gratified when he saw among the audience at Harvard's Sanders Theater, which had assembled to see the play *Oedipus Tyrannus*, such important personages as William Dean Howells, Alexander Agassiz, Julia Ward Howe, Henry Wadsworth Longfellow, Ralph Waldo Emerson, Charles Eliot Norton, and Oliver Wendell Holmes. Paine had composed an orchestral prelude and several choruses for the performance. The music received hearty endorsement. A more modest work, the Violin Sonata, first performed in May 1876, also delighted local audiences with its brilliance and drama.[67]

Even so, native composers still found general acceptance equivocal, one moment strong, another moment weak. After Paine's Mass in D was performed and had won acclaim in Berlin, well-wishers in New England tried to sell subscription tickets at a dollar apiece for a projected Boston performance on 12 April 1868. John Sullivan Dwight, James R. Lowell, Benjamin Peirce, Longfellow, and Apthorp supported the proposed performance but to no avail. Few tickets were sold; the concert was cancelled. A possible explanation lay in the composer's youth and lack of a local reputation. Yet, Chadwick was able to comment ironically a little over forty years later that he and others like him were grateful for the performances granted them by the Boston Symphony and for the local disposition not to put them "into a class by themselves as freaks and curiosities," since the American composer generally continued to be "the despised American composer."[68] When he said this, he knew full well that the Boston Symphony had not been that assiduous about scheduling local compositions, especially after their first presentation, and that the New England group of composers were already in the process of being forgotten, their music performed less and less often.

NOTES

1. William Treat Upton, *William Henry Fry* (New York: Crowell, 1954), 272–73.

2. Louis C. Elson, *The History of American Music*, rev. to 1925 by Arthur Elson (New York: Macmillan, 1925), 187–88.

3. Margery Morgan Lowens, in H. Wiley Hitchcock and Stanley Saide, eds., *The New Grove Dictionary of American Music* (London: Macmillan, 1986) s.v. "MacDowell, Edward."

4. Arthur Foote, "A Bostonian Remembers," *Musical Quarterly* 23 (1937): 41; *An Autobiography* (1946; reprinted, New York: Da Capo, 1979), 55. George Chadwick, "American Composers," in *The American History and Encyclopedia of Music* 8, *History of American Music*, ed. W. L. Hubbard (Toledo: Squire, 1908), 13; also see the item in the *New England Magazine Review* 6 (1916); 120–21. George W. Chadwick, *Horatio Parker* (New Haven: Yale University Press, 1921), 12. The Parker obituary that appeared in the *Boston Transcript*, 1906, quotes Parker as stating that John Knowles Paine was his mother's teacher in composition, his encourager in music when he first started as a musician, and his close personal friend over the years (Allan A. Brown Collection, scrapbook of clippings, **M165.8, Vol. 7, in the Boston Public Library).

5. Arthur Farwell and W. Dermot Darby, eds., *Music in America, Art of Music* 4 (New York: National Society of Music, 1915), 335.

6. Ibid., 344.

7. Steven Ledbetter, album notes to New World Records NW 339–2.

8. T. P. Currier, "Edward MacDowell As I Knew Him," *Musical Quarterly* 1 (1915): 14.

9. Isabel Parker Semler, in collaboration with Pierson Underwood, *Horatio Parker* (New York: Putnam's Sons, 1942), 200.

10. Van Wyck Brooks, "Foreword" to Helen Howe, *The Gentle Americans* (New York: Harper and Row, 1965), xv.

11. Howard Mumford Jones, *The Theory of American Literature* (Ithaca: Cornell University Press, 1965), 5; *Grove's Dictionary of Music and Musicians*, 2nd ed., Vol. 6: The American Supplement, ed. Waldo Selden Pratt (Philadelphia: Presser, 1926), 30.

12. For a discussion of the new popular-music culture that arose after the Civil War, see Nicholas E. Tawa, *The Way to Tin Pan Alley* (New York: Schirmer, 1990).

13. Richard Guy Wilson, "The Great Civilization," in *The American Renaissance, 1876–1917* (New York: The Brooklyn Museum, 1979), 11; see also Stow Persons, *The Decline of American Gentility* (New York: Columbia University Press, 1973), 99.

14. Henry Steele Commager, *The American Mind* (New Haven: Yale University Press, 1950), 10.

15. Howard Mumford Jones, *The Age of Energy: Varieties of American Experience, 1865–1915* (New York: Viking, 1971), 192.

16. *Musical Herald* 6 (1885): 164.

17. Carl Engel, "Views and Reviews," *Musical Quarterly* 18 (1932): 179; William Dean Howells, *Imaginary Interviews* (New York: Harper, 1910), 51; Daniel Gregory Mason, *Tune in, America* (New York: Knopf, 1931), 182.

18. Florence Efrench, *Music and Musicians in Chicago* (Chicago: Ffrench, 1899), 33, 34; Amy Fay, *More Letters of Amy Fay: The American Years, 1879–1916*, ed. S. Margaret William McCarthy (Detroit: Information Coordinators, 1986), 5–7; Theodore Thomas, *A Musical Autobiography* (1905; reprinted, New York: Da Capo, 1964), 104.

19. Boston *Musical Record* 1 (1978): 78.

20. Louis Moreau Gottschalk, *Notes of a Pianist*, ed. Jeanne Behrend (New York: Knopf, 1964), 157, 232–33.

21. Arlo Bates, *The Philistines* (Boston: Ticknor, 1889), 44; Sylvester Baxter, "Boston at the Century's End," *Harper's New Monthly Magazine* 99 (1899): 844.

22. [Price Collier], *America and the Americans* (New York: Scribner's Sons, 1897), 122–23; M. A. DeWolfe Howe, *Boston, the Place and the People* (1903; reprinted, New York: Macmillan, 1912), 233; George Templeton Strong, *The Diary of George Templeton Strong*, ed. Allan Nevins and Milton Halsey Thomas (New York: Macmillan, 1952), 4: 266–67.

23. Arlo Bates, *The Pagans* (Boston: Ticknor, 1888), 210; Bates, *The Philistines*, 80–81, 276; William Dean Howells, *Annie Kilburn* (New York: Harper and Bros., 1891), 49. See also Collier, *America*, 116–17.

24. Allan A. Brown Collection, scrapbook of clippings, **M304.1, Vol. 5, in the Boston Public Library, item dated 20 March 1885.

25. Ralph Waldo Emerson, *Letters*, ed. Ralph L. Rusk (New York: Columbia University Press, 1939), 3: 64, 84, 87.

26. John Fiske, *The Letters of John Fiske*, ed. Ethel F. Fiske (New York: Macmillan, 1940), 368; Daniel Gregory Mason, *Music in My Time* (New York: Macmillan, 1938), 43.

27. Foote, "A Bostonian Remembers," 38; Henry Morton Dunham, *The Life of a Musician* (New York: Mrs. Henry M. Dunham, 1931), 38. Dunham was born in Brookline, Massachusetts, in 1853, taught at the New England Conservatory of Music, and died in 1929.

28. John Sullivan Dwight, "Music in Boston," in *The Memorial History of Boston*, ed. Justin Winsor (Boston: Ticknor, 1881), 4: 437.

29. David Stanley Smith, "A Study of Horatio Parker," *Musical Quarterly* 16 (1930): 163. See also "The Contributor's Club," *Atlantic Monthly* 42 (1878): 769.

30. Louis C. Elson, *Modern Music and Musicians* (New York: University Society, 1918), 1:339.

31. The poem is quoted in Edwin Harrison Cady, *The Gentleman in America* (1949; reprinted, New York: Greenwood Press, 1969), 178.

32. Persons, *The Decline of American Gentility*, 1–2, 55.

33. See the significant article on this subject by John Rockwell, entitled "Paine and Chadwick Return to Favor," in the *New York Times*, 15 January 1989, sec. 2.

34. George Santayana, *The Genteel Tradition*, ed. Douglas L. Wilson (Cambridge: Harvard University Press, 1967), 13, 39, 51; George Santayana, *Character and Opinion in the United States* (New York: Norton, 1934), 113–14; George Santayana, George Santayana's *America: Essays on Literature and Culture* (Urbana: University of Illinois Press, 1967), 135.

35. See Douglas L. Wilson's Introduction to Santayana's *Genteel Tradition*.

36. Quoted in Lewis Perry, *Intellectual Life in America* (New York: Watts, 1984), 263–64.

37. John U. Nef, *The United States and Civilization*, 2nd rev. ed. (Chicago: University of Chicago Press, 1967), 128–29. See also Wilson, "The Great Civilization," 29, 32.

38. Celia Thaxter, *Letters of Celia Thaxter*, ed. A. F. [Annie Fields] and R. L. (Boston: Houghton, Mifflin, 1895), xv, xviii, 93; Annie Fields, *Authors and Friends* (Boston: Houghton, Mifflin, 1897), 247.

39. See, respectively, John Jay Chapman, *Memories and Milestones* (New York: Moffat, Yard, 1915), 136; Amy Fay, *Music-Study in Germany* (New York: Macmillan, 1896), 48; *Letters of Celia Thaxter*, 193.

40. Perry, *Intellectual Life in America*, 265.

41. Charles William Eliot, *American Contributions to Civilization and Other Essays and Addresses* (New York: Century, 1898), 249–53.

42. Lucy Leffingwill Cable Bikle, *George W. Cable, His Life and Letters* (New York: Russell and Russell, 1967), 186–89.

43. Unsigned editorial in the Boston *Musical Herald* 11 (1890): 1. Eben Tourjée was managing editor; Louis C. Elson, Stephen A. Emery, and George H. Wilson were associate editors.

44. M. A. DeWolfe Howe, *The Boston Symphony Orchestra* (Boston: Houghton, Mifflin, 1914), 151.

45. Ferriss Greenslet, *The Life of Thomas Bailey Aldrich* (Boston: Houghton, Mifflin, 1908), 81.

46. Clara Kathleen Rogers, *Memories of a Musical Career* (Boston: Little, Brown, 1919), 403, 417.

47. *Hood's Sarsaparilla Book of Wit & Humor* (Lowell, Mass.: Hood, 1881), 22.

48. New York *Musical Courier* 20 (1890): 25; the 1893 item forms part of the Allan A. Brown Collection, scrapbook of clippings, **M.165.8, Vol. 3, in the Boston Public Library, and is dated 5 April 1893.

49. Dwight, "Music in Boston," 432; H. Earle Johnson, *Hallelujah, Amen!* (Boston: Humphries, 1965), 125; Boston *Musical Times*, 4 January 1868, p. 7; William Foster Apthorp, *By the Way* (Boston: Copeland and Day, 1898), 2:75–79.

50. Clayton John, *Reminiscences of a Musician* (Cambridge: Washburn and Thomas, 1929), 68–69.

51. Howe, *The Gentle Americans*, 12–13; Thomas Russell Sullivan, *Passages from the Journal of Thomas Russell Sullivan, 1891–1903* (Boston: Houghton, Mifflin, 1917), 61–62.

52. Robert Grant, *The Chippendales* (New York: Scribner's Sons, 1909), 206–7.

53. Fields, *Authors and Friends*, 30–31.

54. Maude Howe Elliott, *Three Generations* (Boston: Little, Brown, 1923), 229; Sullivan, *Passages from the Journal*, 58.

55. Johns, *Reminiscences*, 69–71.

56. Louise Hall Tharp, *Mrs. Jack* (Boston: Little, Brown, 1965), 111–12.

57. John Tasker Howard, *Our American Music*, 4th ed. (New York: Crowell, 1965), 295; *The Letters of John Fiske*, 368.

58. Walter Raymond Spalding, *Music at Harvard* (1935; reprinted, New York: Da Capo, 1977), 188–89.

59. Charles Macomb Flandrau, *The Diary of a Freshman* (New York: Doubleday, Page, 1901), 103; John C. Schmidt, *The Life and Works of John Knowles Paine* (Ann Arbor: UMI Research Press, 1980), 140.

60. See, respectively, *The Letters of John Fiske*, 218–19; Daniel Gregory Mason, *Music in My Time and Other Reminiscences* (New York: Macmillan, 1938), 43–44; [Annie Fields], *James T. Fields* (Boston: Houghton, Mifflin, 1881), 258–59; Fields, *Authors and Friends*, 243.

61. Bates, *The Pagans*, 85–86, 253–54.

62. Edward Rowland Sill, *The Poems of Edward Rowland Sill* (Cambridge: Riverside Press, 1902), 88; *The Prose of Edward Rowland Sill* (Boston: Houghton, Mifflin, 1900), 144–47.

63. Much the same thing is said about American literature, in Jones, *The Theory of American Literature*, 13–14.

64. Van Wyck Brooks, *New England: Indian Summer, 1865–1915* (New York: Dutton, 1940), 8; Semler, *Horatio Parker*, 159.

65. Apthorp, *By the Way*, 1:117.

66. Ibid., 2:184–85.

67. *The Letters of John Fiske*, 223; Spalding, *Music at Harvard*, 154; Schmidt, *The Life and Works of John Knowles Paine*, 113–14, 147.

68. Schmidt, *The Life and Works of John Knowles Paine*, 76; *New England Conservatory Magazine-Review* 5 (1914): 67.

2

NOURISHING THE COMPOSER

In its formative stage, native art music, of course, required fosterage beyond people's attendance at concerts to insure continuous growth. At best, the size of audiences varied from year to year, even if the overall trend was to increased attendance. Besides, a larger mass of listeners did not of itself guarantee the success of native works. Another stimulus to creativity was the composer's, his society's, and its cultural leaders' interest in their shared intellectual and artistic history, and the ambition to contribute to and extend that history. Both conditions were satisfied in the Boston of the late nineteenth century. However, what monetary sponsorship there was came mainly from private, not governmental, sources.

Pride in Boston's civilization centered on the Puritan-derived legacy of intellectualism and moral rectitude, the moral-aesthetic philosophy of the Transcendentalists, and the literary tradition of Emerson, Hawthorne, Thoreau, Longfellow, Whittier, and others. Boston had orderly governance, free public libraries and schools, and exemplary higher-education institutions. In order to take pride in the present, said Charles Eliot Norton, social leaders had to encourage artists to higher and higher achievements, since artistic works were less an expression of solitary individuals, more an expression of a society's faith and loftiness of spirit. If America was great enough, its civilization would find artists ready to meet its needs.[1]

John Jay Chapman, a prominent Boston intellectual, praised the "little groups of sincere men" that he knew, who worked to form centers of thought, music, and painting. They strove to educate their fellow citizens to respect artists and saw the need for serious art and music, if only to counterbalance the effect of the raw, boisterous, unfamiliar American burgeoning about them. Chapman urged everyone to aid these groups and the native artistry they promoted.[2] More recently, David Shi points to the "prominent group of patrician intellectuals centered in Boston but represented in other parts of the country as well" whose tastes combined "conservatism and romanticism." Owing to "an abiding sense of public duty and a presumptive sense of moral and intellectual superiority," they acted as "custodians of culture" and preferred the "security of tradition" over revolt.[3]

In his novel *The Chippendales*, Robert Grant claimed that Boston in the second half of the nineteenth century was morally and culturally superior to and less mercenary than Boston in the early twentieth century. In the earlier period, he wrote, there were more "true Bostonians" who were never "happy without a burning cause." He praised those successful businessmen of the city whose generosity had made the existence of artists possible.[4] Several novels of William Dean Howells deal with the clash between the values of the older, gentler Boston, now fading away, and those of the less principled mercenary crowd, whose potency was increasing day by day. The latter thought the arts unimportant. Altruism was foreign to its nature; obliviousness to literature, painting, and art music, proof that one lived in the real world. For example, Howell's Annie Kilburn depicts a merchant, Mr. Gerrish, as a self-made man from whom patronage should not be expected: "I came into this town a poor boy . . . and I have made my own way, every inch of it, unaided and alone. I am a thorough believer in giving every one an equal chance to rise and to—get along; I would not throw an obstacle in anybody's way; but I do not believe—I do *not* believe—in pampering those who have not risen, or have made no effort to rise."[5] In Gerrish's view, native composers would have numbered among those who had not risen.

Mr. Gerrish's counterparts apparently were more in evidence in New York City. Witness Antonín Dvořák's complaint, in 1895, that the city's business people were hostile to high culture. When he offered a scholarship to a musically talented person, his offer was usually rejected because, even if that person came only on Saturday afternoons for lessons, it was reason for dismissal from a position. In addition, he said, the "creditable works" of American composers found no New York publishers; his own works had to be sent to Europe for publication. Was it any wonder that American composers were discouraged from continuing?[6]

As indicated earlier, as art music took hold, old-line Bostonians were sensing that their era was coming to an end, due to the influx of immigrants from Ireland, the Mediterranean area, and eastern Europe; the rise of a crude, money-driven class; and the spread of an assertive popular culture. Cultural leaders like Charles Eliot Norton were sounding warnings that, with the increase of poor, uneducated immigrants and wealthy Philistines, Boston and other cultural centers were threatened with spiritual barrenness, because of the tyranny of the majority and the indifference of the newly affluent. This combination of factors discouraged creative individuality and promoted mediocrity. The vulgarity of the uneducated and unrefined masses, he said, required parrying by the few who were more enlightened and educated. The masses were not to blame for what might take place culturally; rather, blame lay with the few who knew better and failed to lead the way toward higher spiritual standards, better education, improved cultural institutions, and increased encouragement of serious artists.[7] Norton's call to action mingles condescension with unease over what seemed imminent.

Paradoxically, some cultural sociologists have suggested that just such a period as the one described may see the expansion of the high arts. The Brahmins had accumulated their wealth and power and now had the leisure and the desire to exercise both in the interest of the arts. As yet, only their political power was on the wane. An examination of the information available to us indicates that the spur to New England's musical flowering was the desire for a reassertion of traditional values and a cultural upgrading of the city by means of high art, during this Indian summer of the old order.[8]

THE FOREIGN COEFFICIENT

Foreign-born musicians resident in Boston both helped and hindered the American composer. Certainly they stimulated interest in art music, albeit European oriented, and the institutions for its maintenance, thus preparing the ground for the New England group of composers. They acted from the first as performers, directors of orchestras and choruses, music educators, sheet-music publishers, and composers of songs and piano pieces. Among the earliest of these musicians was the organist William Selby, from England, a Boston resident of the 1770s. The von Hagens, a Dutch family arriving in the 1790s, concertized, published and sold sheet music, and taught. More significantly, Gottlieb Graupner, a German, in Boston about the same time as the von Hagens, labored hard and long to make art music viable—teaching, publishing music, and, in 1809, founding the Boston Philo-Harmonic Society for the performance of serious orchestral music. He was also a cofounder, in 1815, of the Handel and Haydn Society. The Englishman George Webb came to Boston in the 1830s to teach at the Academy of Music and to direct the rather mediocre orchestras of the academy, the Music Fund Society, and the Handel and Haydn Society. Charles Zeuner, the German organist, composer, and teacher of theory and composition, was elected president of the Handel and Haydn Society in 1838.

Starting in the 1840s, noted European musicians concertized in the city, among them the violinists Ole Bull and Henry Vieuxtemps, the singer Jenny Lind, and the orchestra conductor Louis Antoine Jullien. Then, from 1848 on, many Germans settled in Boston, having fled from the unrest occasioned by the futile democratic revolt in central Europe. They, and especially the professional musicians among them, were devoted to the art music of their homeland and desired to perpetuate it in the New World. Of great significance was the arrival in Boston of the Germania Musical Society, in 1849, an ensemble of skilled Berlin musicians whose playing set high performance standards. The band remained together until 1854. From it emerged Carl Zerrahn, responsible for a cycle of Boston Philharmonic concerts. Later he conducted another cycle of orchestral concerts sponsored by the Harvard Music Association and also directed the music making of the Handel and Haydn Society. He and Bernhard Listemann were the chief orchestral directors in Boston before the advent of the Boston Symphony in 1881, an orchestra made up entirely of Germans, including its director, George Henschel.

It is not surprising, therefore, that for Bostonians great art music meant the works of Mozart, Schubert, Beethoven, Mendelssohn, and Schumann. As interest in musical study increased, most students found their way to local German teachers. Inspired and influenced by these musicians, a few people went to Germany and Austria for further musical study and to sample the music-centered cultural life available there. In this fashion Bostonians with a taste for music became Germanophiles.

During the post–Civil War years, several Germans resident in Boston loomed prominently in musical affairs: Julius Eichberg, Otto Dresel, Franz Kneisel, Wilhelm Gericke, and Arthur P. Schmidt. Eichberg, in Boston by 1859, was a violinist, conductor, composer, and founder of the Boston Conservatory of Music, in 1867. Dresel, in Boston in 1852, was a pianist, teacher, and author of many articles on music that reflected his conservative outlook. Kneisel arrived in 1885 to serve as concertmaster for the Boston Symphony and soon formed the Kneisel Quartet, a godsend to American composers who wished their chamber works performed. Gericke conducted the Boston Symphony from 1884 to 1889, and again from 1898 to 1906, thereby premiering many of the orchestral compositions of the New England group. (Other Boston Symphony conductors were Arthur Nikisch, 1889–1893, and Emil Paur, 1893–1898.) Arthur P. Schmidt arrived in 1866 and by 1877 had established a music firm that published works by all six composers of the New England group—in particular, those by Foote and MacDowell.

These Germans not only got Bostonians to take their own art music and composers seriously but also encouraged recently arrived Germans to form a reliable nucleus of the audience for art music. They guided the education of future native composers and befriended the ones already composing. Through them, new native music was given local performances. This music often won their approval (and thus the approval of those Americans less certain of their judgments), especially if it met their stylistic criteria for excellence. Finally, they, and in particular Arthur P. Schmidt, had the music of native composers published in America or Germany. Schmidt's Boston publishing house had distribution agreements with many European firms; moreover, it pushed for performances in London, Paris, Leipzig, Vienna, and Berlin. Through Schmidt, Paine's Second Symphony became the first large score issued in the United States (1880), after a subscription drive defrayed expenses. In 1888 Schmidt published Chadwick's Second Symphony, making it the first large American work issued without a previous private subscription. Foote acknowledged the debt composers owed Schmidt: "When it is remembered that before Schmidt there had been published in this country no music other than such as was of comparatively small consequence, it is obvious that what he did was of far-reaching importance."[9]

One other German, not a Boston resident, who came to the aid of American composers requires mention, Theodore Thomas. In 1869 he formed his own fine orchestra, concertized in New York, and travelled to play in other cities. Three years after the orchestra disbanded in Chicago in 1888, Thomas became the first director of the Chicago Orchestra. He had an abiding interest in America's own art music and performed the works of the New England group. Of importance to American music was his giving the first performance of Paine's First Symphony, at the Music Hall in Boston, in January 1876. He then introduced it to New Yorkers. The excellence of his orchestra gave a strong impetus to the demand for a permanent professional orchestra in Boston. His superior performance of Paine's composition encouraged music lovers to take native artworks seriously.

Foreign influence also had a deleterious side. Musical emigrés could not help but honor the compositions of their own countrymen more than those of Americans. Moreover, a certain condescension was usually in evidence even when high praise was given an American singer, instrumentalist, or composition. This attitude was, of course, communicated to the people willing to spend money on music.[10] The preference for musical works from overseas, some of them mediocre, was obvious throughout the post–Civil War decades, whether among Bostonians, New Yorkers, or Chicagoans.

John Knowles Paine was bitterly aware that his works needed the endorsement of Europeans in order to gain American approval. Horatio Parker complained that opera was a foreign-dominated enterprise. He saw American money poured into it so that American audiences could hear foreign singers supported by foreign instrumentalists sing foreign operas in foreign languages, with little left over for American musicians, and said: "One is tempted to say that a knowledge of our language is a hindrance rather than a help in gaining admission to the opera here [New York City]." Chadwick cast a jaundiced eye on competitions for original works, saying that if a competition was open only to Americans, the entries would be too few to make the contest worthwhile; if open to all, then foreigners would take every prize, since invariably the judges were themselves foreigners and none was impartial.[11]

Writers on music and newspaper critics had urged the administrators of the Philadelphia Centennial Exposition of 1876 to schedule the performance of a major work by Paine or to commission a new one from him. Instead, the people in power gave Richard Wagner five thousand dollars for an embarrassingly substandard march. As a sop to the undervalued Paine, the directors approved his writing of a centennial hymn. (Another New England composer, Dudley Buck, contributed *The Centennial Meditation of Columbia.*) When Paine retired in the spring of 1905, the *Boston Transcript* (31 May 1905) was still able to comment that his works were more often played and better known in Europe than in the United States. Amy Fay, writing in the *Musical Courier*, spoke of Paine's major effort in his later years, the unperformed but "beautiful opera *Azara*," and felt that Harvard's retirement gift to him would have been more appropriate had it been a subscription raised for the opera's production rather than the silver service the school gave him. Of this opera, Henry Finck states that, though Paine must have enjoyed writing the ambitious work, he got nothing else out of it: "I made personal appeals to Emma Eames and Geraldine Farrar to interest themselves in the rôle of Azara, and they were not deaf to my appeals; but nothing came of it. A guarantee fund of $10,000 was discussed. We got up a petition to Conried [Heinrich Conried, born in Austria, was manager of the Metropolitan Opera House] signed by Carl Schurz and many other eminent men, and that manager seemed favorably inclined, but nothing was done. After Paine's death his widow had the full score printed by Breitkopf & Härtel in Leipsic . . . at a cost of $2,000. No use; 'Azara' has never been sung and probably never will be."[12]

THE AMERICAN PROMOTERS OF NATIVE MUSIC

The role of patron is necessary but difficult, wrote Daniel Gregory Mason, a composer of the generation that followed the New England group. A benefactor of artists needs tact, an ability to see another's point of view, and a greater love for art than for artists. Otherwise he would be a patronizer, "substituting a feudal relation of lord and vassal for the democratic one of the cooperation of equals variously endowed for the realization of ends desired by all."[13] Mason would have approved the encouragement of American musicians through the medium of the musical at-home, even though substantial monetary support did not usually go with it. Clara Kathleen Rogers had gained a high reputation as a professional singer before her marriage to Henry Munroe Rogers and had won respect as a song composer. After marriage, husband and wife devoted themselves to the private cultivation of music. We learn from her that their musical evenings were in part intended to help aspiring young American musicians, by giving them a hearing before people of influence. She mentions as attending her at-homes the musicians Benjamin Lang and Julius Eichberg, the music critics John Sullivan Dwight and William Foster Apthorp, the several music directors of the Boston Symphony, the writer Julia Ward Howe, and the composers George Chadwick, Arthur Foote, and Edward MacDowell. Louise Moulton and her husband held similar evenings, to which came intellectuals, academics, novelists, musicians, and, of course, composers in the New England group. They welcomed "the socially unknown guest"; the Moultons' sympathies "had little relation to social standing."[14]

Celia Thaxter, already mentioned as a friend of John Knowles Paine, helped advance MacDowell's music. William Mason praises the setting for the summer music making at Appledore, her home on the Isles of Shoals, with "doors wide open to the sun and salt breezes, the people sitting in the room and grouped on the piazza, shaded by its lovely vines, the beautiful vistas of gaily colored flowers, sea and sky beyond." Appledore in the 1890s was the center for Thaxter's vacationing friends, among them music lovers, musicians, artists, and writers. MacDowell introduced his *Sonata Tragica* there; with listeners' reactions at first reserved, but after the work's repeated playing, very positive, the work eventually became a favorite of most of those in attendance. Later, MacDowell played the *Sonata Eroica* at Appledore to a highly appreciative audience. Mason ends by saying: "This incident [MacDowell performing his newly composed sonatas] is related to illustrate the remarkable effect of musical surroundings and the great advantage of living in a musical atmosphere. Here were people of intelligence and culture who, under adverse circumstances would not have appreciated the beauty of these intellectual works, but who after closer association were led to perceive their beauty and who learned to love them."[15]

The advancement of Paine's career owed a great deal to John Fiske, philosopher and historian on the Harvard faculty. Their close friendship began in 1864. Fiske took the rough edges off Paine's social manners, introduced him to a select circle of friends (such as William James, Chauncy Wright, and William Dean Howells), supported his position on the Harvard faculty, and wrote appreciative articles about his music. We hear of Paine accompanying Fiske and his children in strolls around Spy Pond, of his conversations on Darwinian theories of evolution with intellectuals in Fiske's library, and of his attendance at and participation in Fiske's frequent musical evenings.[16]

Some professional American musicians worked hard to advance native music. For example, the noted Philadelphia-born singer David Bispham claimed credit for the first English performance of Horatio Parker's *Hora Novissima*, at Worcester; he showed the score in 1898 to Hans Richter, director of the Birmingham Festival, and the eventual result was the Worcester performance. Another famous singer, Emma Eames, who grew up in Bath, Maine, championed the songs of Amy Beach, performing them everywhere. (She illustrates the observation Henry Finck attributes to Arthur Foote: "Mr. Foote thinks—and here I again agree with him—that the popularity of songs depends very largely on their being taken up by concert-singers.") The respected Benjamin Lang, teacher, conductor, and pianist (also the father of the composer Margaret Ruthven Lang), was convinced of Arthur Foote's talent and influenced him to abandon a business vocation in favor of music. As a conductor, Lang introduced many American compositions, one of them Chadwick's *Viking's Last Voyage*. As for MacDowell, the famous Venezuelan concert pianist Teresa Carreño took up his cause, playing his works in the Americas and during her European concert tours. MacDowell's Second Piano Concerto, dedicated to her, was one of her featured numbers.[17] Louise Homer provides an example of how encouraging it was for a composer to find a sympathetic performer devoted to his or her cause. She befriended Horatio Parker, and when his opera *Mona* was to be mounted at the Metropolitan Opera, she devoted herself to mastering the title role: "Her passionate desire to make a success of this work was most touching. It occupied her thoughts, almost exclusively, for several months."[18]

On occasion, money was forthcoming. When Horatio Parker was a youth living with his parents in Auburndale, a few miles out of Boston, a Mr. Burr supplied him with the funds needed to travel to Germany for his musical education. Although Parker's granddaughter could not identify the benefactor beyond his name, Mr. Burr's assistance was of the utmost importance to Parker's career. Interestingly, J. Montgomery Sears, after meeting MacDowell in Boston, offered the composer substantial financial help so that he could free himself of all teaching duties in order to compose an opera. MacDowell was moved by the offer but turned it down because he did not wish to write on order and feared the opera he might produce would not be a good one.[19] Nevertheless, the actual advancement of money to support a composer or commission a work remained rare indeed during the fifty years or so after the Civil War.

Perhaps the best-known benefactor of the arts in Boston was Isabella Stewart Gardner. Her sponsorship of the musical compositions of the Alsatian composer and violinist Charles Loeffler is generally known. (Loeffler joined the Boston Symphony in 1882 and remained in the Boston area until his death in 1935.) Gardner's home was constantly awash in music, most of it European and played by Europeans, to be sure, but some of it American and, when feasible, played by Americans. Arthur Foote both played and heard his own music performed (like his Trio in B-flat, opus 65) at the Gardner home. Less known is Gardner's aid in the formation of the Manuscript Club of Boston, begun in January 1888 to help local composers receive a thoughtful and supportive hearing of their music. Among the compositions performed were Foote's Orchestral Suite in E, opus 12, and Parker's Quartet in F for Strings, opus 11. Regrettably, after a year, enthusiasm for the club lessened and it was dissolved.[20]

Another organization, the Music Teachers National Association, founded in 1876, has continued into the twentieth century. Among its founders was Chadwick, who at that time was teaching at Olivet College, in Michigan. Although the members' principal interests centered on music education, they also wished to advance the cause of American composers through performance of their music. For example, for its eighth annual meeting, in Cleveland in 1884, the association presented the first known all-American concert, with songs, piano pieces, and chamber works by Paine, Chadwick, and Foote. The next year, members heard Paine's Violin Sonata, among other works. The principal organizer of these concerts was Calixa Lavallée, a Canadian composer and pianist who had settled in Boston at the beginning of the 1880s. Foote attended meetings of the organization during the eighties and praised its fostering of American music: "Two things of value came from my interest in the society. First, I thus became acquainted with most of the best musicians not living in New York or Boston, thereby broadening my ideas, and doing away with a certain provincial conceit that we are apt to have here. Second, through their concerts came the first real chance of a hearing of my compositions in large form. At that time . . . opportunities for a hearing being hard to get. To these concerts I thus owe the beginning of what reputation I may have."[21]

Composers' reputations could be made to grow or diminish through the critical reviews of the surprising number of music commentators active in the city of Boston. Most of these writers had musical training, conservative tastes, and an affinity for German music. Their reports, published in newspapers and magazines, were avidly read and discussed by the music public, a large proportion of whom were practicing amateur musicians. The first significant local critic had been Joseph Tinker Buckingham (1779–1861), whose reviews appeared during the first third of the century in the *Polyanthos*, the *New-England Galaxy*, and the *New England Magazine*. No American art composers to speak of existed during his time.[22] Then came John Sullivan Dwight, influential editor of *Dwight's Journal of Music*, published from 1852 to 1881. In the years when Paine, Chadwick, and Foote were trying to establish themselves, his favorable comments on their works—seeing their merits, praising their sound, and urging their claims upon the public—had wide sway.[23] As these composers were quite aware, Dwight believed in musical orthodoxy and disfavored innovation. He loved the music of Bach, Mozart, and Beethoven and disliked operatic works (save for those by Gluck, Mozart, and Beethoven), program music, and concertos emphasizing virtuosity. Most contemporary compositions left him cold. According to William Apthorp, Dwight's "naïveté of perception, his ever youthful enthusiasm, his ineradicable power of enjoyment, held out unimpaired" until his death in 1891.[24] Dwight wrote enthusiastically about Paine's First and Second Symphonies when they were premiered. His negative reaction to Paine's programmatic *Symphony*

Fantasy—Shakespeare's Tempest in D minor, opus 31, was predictable. When Theodore Thomas conducted the *Tempest* on 2 November 1877, Dwight understood it as a postclassical, overly romantic symphonic poem after the manner of Liszt and wished Paine had written a concert overture in the traditional sonata-allegro structure instead.[25]

During the years when the New England group was most active, several Boston writers on music constantly called attention to them and their compositions. The public respected these writers, and their views on native efforts at composition were taken seriously. Fortunately for the composers, much of what they wrote was positive. Benjamin Edward Woolf's writings appeared in the *Saturday Evening Gazette*, the *Boston Globe*, and, in 1894, the *Boston Herald*. Louis C. Elson wrote for the *Musical Herald*, the *Boston Courier*, and the *Boston Advertiser*. William Foster Apthorp's writing appeared in the *Boston Evening Transcript*, the *Atlantic Monthly*, the *Sunday Courier*, and the *Boston Traveller*; he also was responsible for the program notes of the Boston Symphony from 1892 to 1901. Howard Malcom Ticknor was for a time an assistant editor of the *Atlantic Monthly*; his articles appeared there, and also in the *Boston Advertiser*, the *Boston Globe*, the *Boston Herald*, and the *Boston Journal*. Henry Taylor Parker wrote principally for the *Transcript*. Philip Hale's commentaries appeared in the *Home Journal*, the *Boston Post*, the *Boston Journal*, the *Musical Courier*, the *Boston Herald*, the *Musical Record*, and the *Musical World*; he took charge of the program notes for the Boston Symphony concerts from 1901 to 1934. The number of writers and publications issuing commentaries testifies to the strong hold art music had on the attention of Bostonians. The extraordinary number of volumes of newspaper and periodical clippings that contain their writings on the New England composers, now a part of the Boston Public Library's Allan A. Brown Collection, proves how consistently these writers kept native music before the public over the years.

In Chicago, the most eminent writer on music was the Bostonian George P. Upton, and after him, W.S.B. Mathews. The two men wrote appreciatively about the New England composers, making them known to Chicagoans. In New York, there were Henry Krehbiel, William James Henderson, James Gibbons Huneker, Henry Finck, and Richard Aldrich. Both Finck and Aldrich had studied under John Knowles Paine at Harvard. The activities of the New England group were reported on with some frequency in New York publications.[26] Huneker and Finck (along with Lawrence Gilman, who belonged to the next generation of New York critics) were champions of MacDowell's music.

OBTAINING A LIVELIHOOD

Composers could not support themselves through the sale and performance of their compositions, nor through the largess of affluent patrons. For income they had to turn to teaching, directing ensembles, and keyboard performance. Typically, they first set themselves up as private music teachers; as their reputations grew, more and more students came to them for lessons in theory, composition, and keyboard playing. For example, when Parker returned from Germany, in 1885, he and another young composer, Arthur Whiting, opened a studio on Boston's Tremont Street. Their reputations being negligible, no students appeared. Parker had to accept the offer of an organist's position in Brooklyn and a teaching post at St. Paul's School in Garden City, Long Island, especially since he wished to get married.[27] On the other hand, Foote survived the meager returns of his first years and soon was deriving a respectable income from his studio.

A majority of the New England group of composers eventually found positions at colleges or conservatories of music. Fortunately for them, openings began to appear for music instructors in already established institutions and in newly founded schools of music. Daniel Gregory Mason noted that teaching at a college or conservatory of music promised a steady means of income, free summers, and sabbatical years: "Hence the wise composer of thoughtful tendency will accept the academic life—despite his natural irritation at the persistence with which the press will consequently call all his work 'academic'."[28] In 1862 Paine, supported by the Harvard Musical Association, had succeeded in getting Harvard College to make him an instructor in music. President of the college at that time was Thomas Hill, grandfather of the future composer Edward Burlingame Hill. In 1869 Charles William Eliot replaced Hill as president and immediately strengthened Paine's position by granting him an M.A. degree. Six years later, he approved Paine's elevation to a full professorship, thus setting a precedent for other prestigious institutions of higher learning. Eliot's father, while mayor of Boston, had worked hard to promote music in the public school system. He himself also decided to aid music: "When I became president of Harvard University there was no organized department of music in it and it was not customary in New England for highly educated, long-trained men to adopt the profession of music. There were many amateurs but few professional devotees. . . . I knew how fine an element in culture music was, and I did my best with admirable supporters to develop a department of music at Harvard University, hoping that the influence of that department might spread through all the walks of life."[29]

Paine took his duties seriously. The *Harvard University Gazette*, on 1 June 1906, summarized his life at Harvard by stating that from the beginning he regarded music teaching as a sacred duty and strove to familiarize the college community with the best music. For years he supplemented his teaching by a series of pianoforte lecture-recitals of the works of the great masters. These recitals, "given in the lecture-room of Boylston Hall, were always well attended by students, to many of whom they furnished the first opportunity to hear classical music."[30] His composition students included Arthur Foote, Daniel Gregory Mason, Edward Burlingame Hill, Frederick Shepherd Converse, and John Alden Carpenter; students devoted to musical history and literature were Henry Lee Higginson, Henry Finck, Richard Aldrich, M. A. DeWolfe Howe, Archibald Davison, Olin Downes, Hugo Leichtentritt, and Owen Wister.

Julius Eichberg founded the Boston Conservatory of Music in 1867. Its principal mission was to train instrumentalists, especially violinists and singers. In the same year, Eben Tourjée founded the New England Conservatory, modeled after similar institutions in central Europe; five years later, he established the College of Music of Boston University. In addition to his Harvard teaching, Paine also taught at the New England Conservatory and the College of Music. On 28 October 1872, when Paine gave the inaugural lecture for the College of Music, he had occasion to remark of the rest of the United States: "In Europe, music has held an honorable position for centuries in the principal universities, and numerous royal establishments of music have been founded to provide for the wants of the profession. A doubt seems to have existed in this country as to the worth of music as a branch of liberal education, judging by what has *not* been done by institutions of learning in America. We would almost be constrained to believe that our educated and influential classes, including even scholars and scientists, have held a small opinion of the importance of music as a means of the highest culture, and have been somewhat ignorant, I fear, of music as an intellectual, as well as aesthetical and spiritual source of good."[31]

After Chadwick returned from studying in Germany, in 1880, he began teaching privately (Parker was one of his students), but soon he was engaged to teach at the New England Conservatory, whose director he was to become in 1897. Under Chadwick, the school developed into a mature conservatory, with a complete theory and composition department, a strong repertory orchestra, and a thriving opera workshop. Allen Langley, one of his students, states that Chadwick "admired nothing without force, form, and solid backbone. He had small respect for 'youth-neurosis,' the self-indulgence that gloats over a minor discovery, all the futility of passing preoccupations in composition. . . . He kept us level-headed by honest criticism."[32] Among his composition students were Horatio Parker, Frederick Shepherd Converse, Edward Burlingame Hill, Daniel Gregory Mason, Arthur Farwell, Arthur Shepherd, and William Grant Still. (Note the future composers who studied with both Paine and Chadwick.) During the nineties, Chadwick also acted as music director of the Springfield and Worcester festivals in Massachusetts.

Parker returned from Germany to teach in two New York religious schools and the National Conservatory of Music and to direct the musical activities of three New York churches. In 1893 he became organist and music director of Boston's Trinity Church, a post he retained until 1902. The year after the Trinity appointment, he was invited to Yale University as professor of music; by 1904 he was the dean of Yale's School of Music. Chadwick says Parker "organized and conducted a symphony orchestra, which became an indispensable laboratory of the department, since it furnished the necessary experience for composers, conductors, singers, and players who were studying in the school." A fuller description of Parker's contribution to education comes from H. E. Krehbiel, who states that he brought high dignity to the chair in music by joining the musical activities of the university with those of New Haven through a series of orchestral concerts and a reorganized choral society, both conducted by him, and through taking the lead in the construction of a splendid concert structure, Woolsey Hall.[33]

On his return from Germany, MacDowell lived in Boston where he privately taught piano and composition, gave piano recitals, and appeared with chamber ensembles and the Boston Symphony; in 1896 he left the city for a professorship at Columbia University. Nevertheless, he continued to concertize with some frequency in Boston, where he had close friends and his music was admired. His teaching experience at Columbia underlines a danger some composers had to contend with when they became academics. As "M.M.M." (otherwise unknown) explained, in *Music in America*: "Mr. MacDowell, either because of his temperament or the limitations imposed by the university on his work, did not find the position so congenial as Dr. Parker has done at Yale. Instead of being inspired by teaching to greater feats of composition, Mr. MacDowell seemed hampered, and, to the great loss of American music, produced fewer and fewer of those fine works which cause him to be acclaimed as the greatest of American composers."[34]

Arthur Foote's principal occupations were the private teaching of organ, piano, and composition; the post of organist at Boston's First Unitarian

Church; and the directing of and participating in chamber-music concerts. Amy Beach became well known as a concert pianist in Boston and in tours of America and Europe, performing in solo recitals or with orchestras.

Although the occupations of all these composers had to do with music, the demands made on their time and energies often left little of either for creativity. In order to compose music, they looked forward to vacations during the summer months and to holidays during the other three seasons. Sabbatical leaves from teaching were devoted to writing and to travel to Europe every now and again so that they might witness what was going on there musically. Daily, they tried to drive themselves to write a little in the evening. Yet, we frequently read about the physical and mental exhaustion that resulted from their jobs and left them hardly able—or unable—to compose music. At the same time, a worrisome thought must have recurred in the minds of these composers: Would anyone really care if they stopped writing music altogether? The wonder is that, despite everything, they persisted as creative artists.

THE PERFORMACE OF AMERICAN ART MUSIC

One additional but all-important factor necessary to the creation of art music is the possibility of performance and the nature of the performing medium. During the ensuing discussion, we must keep in mind that a nation's musical culture resides usually in its native musical compositions. For the most part, musical institutions—symphony orchestras, opera companies, chamber ensembles—and solo recitalists are the vehicles through which a nation's musical culture is made known to a present generation of music lovers and transmitted to a future one. Too often in the past, Americans have thought of institutions like the Metropolitan Opera and the several large metropolitan symphony orchestras as representing American culture, when in truth neither their attitudes, personnel, nor repertoire really represented America and their disdain of American works curbed the maturing of a native music.

When William Billings (1746–1800), Boston's first native composer, appeared on the American scene, only a modicum of musical training was available to him, and the performing groups for which he could write consisted of the amateur choristers who enrolled in singing schools or sang in the choirs of churches. Most of his compositions were settings of psalm or hymn texts, simple in construction and easy to sing by an unaccompanied chorus. Around eighty years later, the New Orleans–born and Paris–trained composer Louis Moreau Gottschalk (1829–1869) was producing piano composition after piano composition, since he himself was a pianist and the people likely to perform his music were pianists. Some compositions were virtuosic, intended for his own playing; others were easier, more sentimental pieces aimed at the amateur musician. During his concert tours, he carried with him sets of orchestral parts for a few works, just in case an instrumental ensemble was available; otherwise, even these pieces were performable on one or two pianos. William Fry (1813–1864) and George Frederick Bristow (1825–1898) tried writing ambitious works—symphonies, operas—and attempted to get them performed, especially in New York. They spent their entire adulthoods battling for recognition, trying to convince the performance groups that they should be taken seriously as composers. What performances they won were grudgingly given.

From 1879 to 1909, for example, the number of performances allotted to American compositions by the New York Philharmonic remained near zero, according to Howard Shanet. As the twentieth century progressed, the New York orchestra grew less American, writes Shanet, and apparently more worthy of praise from the fashionable Europhile concertgoers. Note how, when speaking to Otto Kinkeldey, in 1902, MacDowell complained that his New York surroundings lacked "a musical atmosphere" and that up until that time the New York Philharmonic had played only two of his works, each of them only once, an astonishing observation from an American composer of widespread fame and, since 1896, a resident of that city.[35] When Parker lived in New York, most of his compositions done locally were choral ones intended for amateur singers, because such musicians were most ready and willing to perform what he wrote. The two most significant of these were *Hora Novissima*, composed for the Church Choral Society of New York, and *The Legend of St. Christopher*, for the Oratorio Society of New York. Both are oratorios calling for orchestral accompaniment. One ambitious work premiered in New York was his opera *Mona*. The Metropolitan Opera mounted it in 1911; the action was exceptional.

Performance is the nourishment that sustains a composer's creative existence. Such nourishment was available in New England, and in Boston in particular. This should not be taken to mean that Bostonians passionately desired new works; rather, the local musical societies were receptive enough to reassure Boston's resident composers and bolster their desire to create new works. As is usually the case, the compositions they produced had to conform to what the existing musical establishments could manage. Most composers turned out more than a few choral works and organ pieces in order to meet the needs of the many local Protestant churches. Moreover, amateur choral societies abounded in the Boston area, all of them interested in adding new compositions to their repertoire. Among the outstanding ones were the Handel and Haydn Society, founded in 1815; the Apollo Club, in 1871; the Boylston Club, in 1873; and the Cecilia Society, in 1877. As Dwight observed, after the Civil War a prominent feature of the Boston cultural scene was "the springing up and prosperous continuance of so many vocal clubs, composed mainly, but not entirely of amateurs."[36]

The Handel and Haydn Society was one of the finest choral groups in the country, though not always flawless when it performed. Its reputation was good enough for Thomas to invite its then five hundred members to appear at his New York festival, expense free, in 1873. A New York newspaper reported: "They represent all classes of society—ladies from Beacon street, merchants from State street, shop girls, young lawyers, clerks, mechanics. Their opportunities for study and practice are no better than ours; yet we believe that most of our connoisseurs will be amazed when they find how far the Boston singers are in advance of the highest achievement of any similar organization in New York. They will not only teach our societies how to sing an oratorio, but they will teach our audience how to enjoy one."[37] Nevertheless, its direction was German, under Carl Zerrahn until 1898, save for two years under Benjamin Lang. When in 1898 a new director was to be appointed, Reinhold Herman, an obscure German, was selected over Chadwick. Fortunately, the Handel and Haydn Society did schedule some large native works, including Paine's *St. Peter* and *The Nativity*, Parker's *Hora Novissima* and *Morven and the Grail*, and Beach's *Mass*.

The Apollo Club began life with fifty-two active members. Within a few weeks, five hundred gentlemen joined as associate members and Benjamin Lang was chosen as the conductor, a position he retained until 1901. For the fifteen dollars each associate member paid, he received four tickets, thus securing a potential audience of two thousand persons. The club put on works for chorus and solo voice with keyboard and less frequently with orchestra, least often for orchestra alone.[38] Some works presented were Paine's *Tempest*, *The Summons to Love*, *Phoebus Arise*, and *The Birds*, and Foote's *Farewell to Hiawatha*. The concert of 29 April 1885 included Paine's music to *Oedipus Tyrannus*, Chadwick's Introduction and Allegro from his Second Symphony, and Foote's *If Doughty Deeds*. A reporter comments on that event: "The American muse has at last been provided with board and lodging. The concert of the Apollo Club . . . was a great stride in the right direction. It gave a programme composed entirely of the works of Boston musicians, and as some of these are the leading composers of the country the concert stood out as a representation of American music. The utter callousness in this matter, which has characterized the series of symphony concerts this season found a tacit reproof in the intrinsic merit of the Apollo programme. If our composers only knew that they can obtain a hearing for their best works there will be a great impetus given to American composition. Not every one can have the patience . . . [to] compose great works without seeing any chance of their performance."[39]

The Boylston Club started life as an all-male chorus devoted to light music. Then Lang took over its leadership, expanded the chorus's membership to include women, and scheduled the performance of serious choral works, among them Paine's *Realm of Fancy*. Lang also guided the Cecilia Society when it was formed as a mixed chorus meant to perform with a local orchestra. At first that orchestra was the one supported by the Harvard Muscial Association; later it was the Boston Symphony. This ensemble, directed by Lang, would premiere Foote's *Wreck of the Hesperus*, in 1888.

From what has been said about Lang, it is obvious that American directors, more than foreign ones, were likely to support native creative efforts. This was certainly true of Chadwick during the years he directed Boston ensembles and was responsible for the Springfield and Worcester festivals. For example, around 1886, he wrote to Parker saying he had a "first rate" chorus in his charge and would like to do Parker's *King Trojan*, though he feared the singers might find it too demanding. Yet he wished to try and asked for the orchestral parts.[40] Four years later Chadwick conducted Parker's *Kobolds*, a cantata for chorus and orchestra, at the Springfield Festival.

On occasion, a foreign-born director proved sympathetic to American works. Thomas has already received mention in this regard. In the early 1900s, another German, Carl Stoeckel, led the Norfolk, Connecticut, festivals of the Litchfield County Choral Union, which boasted a large chorus, an imported orchestra made up of members of the New York Philharmonic, and soloists when needed.[41] Parker's *Star Song*, *King Gorm the Grim*, and *The Dream of Mary*, works for singers and orchestra, were presented here. Also done were Chadwick's *Noel* and *Land of Our Hearts*, for chorus and orchestra, and his purely orchestral *Aphrodite*, *Tam O'-Shanter*, and *Anniversary Overture*.

When Paine completed his Second Symphony, he was fortunate to have it performed in March 1880 by two orchestras: first, by Bernard Listemann and the Boston Philharmonic; second, by Carl Zerrahn and the orchestra of the Harvard Musical Association. Both ensembles utilized the available local instrumentalists; their playing was less than perfect. Then the next year the permanent and completely professional Boston Symphony Orchestra gave its first concert, on 22 October, at the Music Hall and supplanted all other orchestras in the public affection, owing to its superior competence and interpretation.[42]

The Boston Symphony was a gift to the city from the music patron Henry Lee Higginson (1834–1918), who authorized the recruitment of the finest central European players for its membership and who paid its yearly deficit during much of his lifetime. Joseph Lee describes Higginson's decision to establish an orchestra to rival any in Europe as requiring courage and a sense of adventure, since most people considered his aim presumptuous, if not absurd. Lee says further: "His desire in it was not to do people good or to educate them, but to give them something of the great happiness that he himself had always found in music."[43]

The Boston Symphony, to its credit, did perform most of the orchestral compositions written by the New England group—symphonies, overtures, suites, symphonic poems, concertos, and the like. Philip Hale, in the *Boston Herald* of 14 January 1906, catalogs the American works played by the symphony from 22 October 1881 to 6 January 1906. The list is an incredibly long one. Regrettably, the great majority of the compositions were done only once. Extraordinary therefore are the five performances of Chadwick's *Melpomene* Overture and the three of Paine's Prelude to *Oedipus Tyrannus*.[44] That some music lovers might have wanted to hear more native compositions is hinted at in a valentine sent to the first conductor of the Boston Symphony, George Henschel, on 16 February 1884:

> Let no more Wagner themes thy bill enhance
> And give the native workers just one chance,
> Don't give the Dvorák symphony again;
> If you would give us joy, oh, give us Paine![45]

Interestingly, on 1 March, the symphony did give the public Paine, his Second Symphony.

At no time, however, was getting an orchestral work premiered—or once premiered, repeated—easy. Composers had to court and cajole conductors, or request the intervention of powerful intermediaries, in order to win a performance. The process was time-consuming, enervating, and sometimes demeaning. During a year when MacDowell ceased writing for orchestra, he was asked why he preferred to compose for piano. MacDowell replied: "It's one thing to write works for orchestra, and another to get them performed. There isn't much satisfaction in having a thing played once in two or three years. If I write large works for the piano [he had just completed the *Sonata Eroica*] I can play them myself as often as I like." Furthermore, MacDowell complained, he found it difficult to have a new score simply tried out by a friendly conductor, as was possible in Europe.[46]

As for native chamber music, Boston was fortunate to have the outstanding Kneisel Quartet, whose members did play the works of the New England group: Paine, Chadwick, Foote, Parker, and Beach. (MacDowell was not interested in writing in this medium.) It and other fine local chamber players encouraged an outpouring of chamber works: violin sonatas, violin and piano pieces, cello and piano pieces, string quartets, trios and quintets for piano and strings, and so forth. As with orchestra conductors, the heads of chamber ensembles might be derelict in scheduling American works. Early in 1886, Horatio Parker and George Chadwick tried hard to get Franz Kneisel to perform a Parker composition, but to no avail. A highly irritated Chadwick wrote to Parker, on 8 April 1886: "Kneisel gave for an excuse for not playing your Quartet that so many people wanted to hear the Brahms Sextette that he was obliged to put it on the programme to the exclusion of the great American work."[47]

NOTES

1. Kermit Vanderbilt, *Charles Eliot Norton: Apostle of Culture in a Democracy* (Cambridge, Mass.: Belknap, 1959), 205.
2. John Jay Chapman, *Memories and Milestones* (New York: Moffat, Yard, 1915), 13.
3. David E. Shi, *The Simple Life: Plain Living and High Thinking in American Culture* (New York: Oxford University Press, 1985), 156–58.
4. Robert Grant, *The Chippendales* (New York: Scribner's Sons, 1909), 192–93, 210.
5. William Dean Howells, *Annie Kilburn* (New York: Harper and Bros., 1891), 86–87.
6. Antonín Dvořák, "Music in America," *Harper's New Monthly Magazine* 90 (1895): 430–31.
7. Vanderbilt, *Charles Eliot Norton*, 207–8.
8. See Vytautas Kavolis, *History on Art's Side* (Ithaca: Cornell University Press, 1972), 38. Van Wyck Brook's *New England: Indian Summer, 1865–1915* (New York: Dutton, 1940) has as its subject this last period of tranquility before the turbulent modern age took over.
9. Arthur Foote, *An Autobiography*, with an introduction and notes by Wilma Reid Cipolla (1946; reprinted, New York: Da Capo, 1979), 51–52; Arthur Foote, "A Bostonian

Remembers," *Musical Quarterly* 23 (1937): 41; George W. Wilson, program notes for the concert of the Boston Symphony, 6–7 February 1891.

10. In 1938 Elliott Carter was still able to state anything American in serious music was synonymous with "novelty." Even though many compositions by European composers of secondary rank were frequently heard, those by the New England group and later composers continued to be novelties, rarely heard and subject to condescension. See Elliott Carter, "Vacation Novelties, New York," *Modern Music* 15 (1937–38): 96–97.

11. John C. Schmidt, *The Life and Works of John Knowles Paine* (Ann Arbor: UMI Research Press, 1980), 129; Isabel Parker Semler, in collaboration with Pierson Underwood, *Horatio Parker* (New York: Putnam's Sons, 1942), 160–61; Victor Yellin, "The Life and Operatic Works of George Whitefield Chadwick" (Ph.D. diss., Harvard University, 1957), 83.

12. Schmidt, *John Knowles Paine*, 116–17. Both the *Transcript* and the *Musical Courier* items are contained in the Allan A. Brown Collection, scrapbook of clippings, *M165.8, Vol. 6, in the Boston Public Library. For the Finck quotation, see Henry T. Finck, *My Adventures in the Golden Age of Music* (New York: Funk and Wagnalls, 1926), 79–80; the two singers mentioned, Eames and Farrar, were American.

13. Daniel Gregory Mason, *Music as a Humanity* (New York: Gray, 1921), 59.

14. Clara Kathleen Rogers, *The Story of Two Lives* (Boston: Plimpton Press, 1932), 30; Lilian Whiting, *Louise Chandler Moulton, Poet and Friend* (Boston: Little, Brown, 1910), 124–25.

15. William Mason, *Memories of a Musical Life* (New York: Century, 1901), 253–56.

16. John Spencer Clark, *The Life and Letters of John Fiske* (Boston: Houghton, Mifflin, 1917), 1:206, 418–20; 2:83.

17. William Kearns, "Horatio Parker and the English Choral Societies," *American Music* 1 (1986): 21; Adrienne Fried Block, in H. Wiley Hitchcock and Stanley Sadie, eds., *The New Grove Dictionary of American Music*, (London: Macmillan, 1986) s.v. "Beach, Amy Marcy (Cheney)"; Henry T. Finck, *Songs and Song Writers* (New York: Scribner's Sons, 1900), 233; David Ewen, *American Composers* (New York: Putnam's Sons, 1982), s.v. "Foote, Arthur William"; Stephen Ledbetter, in *American Grove*, s.v. "Lang, B(enjamin) J(ohnson)"; Louis C. Elson, *The History of American Music*, rev. to 1925 by Arthur Elson (New York: Macmillan, 1925), 182–83.

18. Sidney Homer, *My Wife and I* (New York: Macmillan, 1939), 217.

19. Semler, *Horatio Parker*, 40; T. P. Currier, "Edward MacDowell As I Knew Him," *Musical Quarterly* 1 (1915): 26.

20. Morris Carter, *Isabella Stewart Gardner and Fenway Court* (Boston: Houghton Mifflin, 1925), 112–13; Honor McCusker, *Fifty Years of Music in Boston* (Boston: Trustees of the Public Library, 1938), 40; Rogers, *Two Lives*, 187–88.

21. Foote, *An Autobiography*, 32; Sumner Salter, "Early Encouragements to American Composers," *Musical Quarterly* 18 (1932): 78–79.

22. See Nicholas Tawa, "Buckingham's Musical Commentaries in Boston," *New England Quarterly* 51 (1978): 333–47.

23. George Willis Cooke, *John Sullivan Dwight* (Boston: Small, Maynard, 1898), 223.

24. William Foster Apthorp, *Musicians and Music Lovers* (New York: Scribner's Sons, 1894), 279.

25. Maude Howe Elliott, *Three Generations* (Boston: Little, Brown, 1923), 41, 42–43; Cooke, *John Sullivan Dwight*, 216–17; Schmidt, *John Knowles Paine*, 121–22.

26. The Allan A. Brown Collection also contains clippings of articles and reviews written by the New York critics, especially when their subject was a composer of the New England group or a performing group from Boston.

27. Semler, *Horatio Parker*, 69–70.

28. Daniel Gregory Mason, *Music in My Time and Other Reminiscences* (New York: Macmillan, 1938), 331.

29. Finck, *My Adventures in the Golden Age of Music*, 75.

30. Quoted by H. E. Krehbiel, in *Grove's Dictionary of Music and Musicians*, 2nd ed. (1926), s.v. "Paine, John Knowles."

31. John Knowles Paine, "Inaugural Lecture of the Department of Musical Composition, History, and Aesthetics in the College of Music of Boston University," 28 October 1872 (n.p., n.d.).

32. Allan Lincoln Langley, "Chadwick and the New England Conservatory of Music," *Musical Quarterly* 21 (1935): 52; also see Henry Morton Dunham, *The Life of a Musician* (New York: Mrs. Henry M. Dunham, 1931), 116; Steven Ledbetter and Victor Fell Yellin, in H. Wiley Hitchcock and Stanley Sadie, eds., *The New Grove Dictionary of American Music* (London: Macmillan, 1986), s.v. "Chadwick, George Whitefield."

33. George Whitefield Chadwick, *Horatio Parker* (New Haven: Yale University Press, 1921), 14; H. E. Krehbiel, in *Grove's Dictionary of Music and Musicians*, 2nd ed. (1926), s.v. "Parker, Horatio William."

34. Arthur Farwell and W. Dermot Darby, eds., *Music in America, The Art of Music* 4 (New York: National Society of Music, 1915), 267.

35. Howard Shanet, *Philharmonic: A History of New York's Orchestra* (Garden City, N.Y.: Doubleday, 1975), 110, 180, 194–95.

36. John Sullivan Dwight, "Music in Boston," in *The Memorial History of Boston*, ed. Justin Winsor (Boston: Ticknor, 1881), 4: 452.

37. H. Earle Johnson, *Hallelujah, Amen!* (Boston: Humphries, 1965), 117–18.

38. Unidentified clipping reviewing the Apollo Club's 151st concert, of 6 May 1896, in the Allan A. Brown Collection, scrapbook of clippings, **M304.1, Vol. 5, in the Boston Public Library.

39. Allan A. Brown Collection, scrapbook of clippings, **M304.1, Vol. 3, in the Boston Public Library. In pencil at the top of the clipping is written "*Courier.*"

40. Semler, *Horatio Parker*, 88.

41. Ibid., 196.

42. Dunham, *The Life of a Musician*, 53; Yellin, "The Life and Operatic Works of George Whitefield Chadwick," 61.

43. Joseph Lee, "Henry Lee Higginson," in *Later Years of the Saturday Club, 1870–1920*, ed. M. A. DeWolfe (Boston: Houghton Mifflin, 1927), 250–51, 254.

44. Allan A. Brown Collection, scrapbook of clippings, **M165.9, Vol. 6, in the Boston Public Library.

45. M. A. DeWolfe Howe, *The Boston Symphony Orchestra* (Boston: Houghton, Mifflin, 1914), 98.

46. Currier, "Edward MacDowell As I Knew Him," 43.

47. Semler, *Horatio Parker*, 84.

3

ARTISTIC FRAMES OF REFERENCE

Every society with windows open to the surrounding world must eventually come to terms with any more sophisticated, complex, and subtle culture that constantly impinges upon it. To expect the society to retain a simpler native identity in all its purity is unrealistic. The challenge for such a society is to digest the sophistication, complexity, and subtlety of another culture without eliminating its own identity. For late-nineteenth-century art music in the United States, more often than not, this process involved, first, an assimilation of what was foreign, which, for reasons suggested in the last two chapters, usually meant German culture; second, an increasing infusion of indigenous elements into the otherwise extraneous characteristics of American-produced compositions, and, in time, an articulation of a new synthesis, identifiably indigenous however indebted to an outside civilization. The New England group was deeply engrossed in this course of development, contributing to it, debating its pros and cons, and hoping to create compositions made in America, by and for Americans.

Their compositions show keen awareness of the richness of life's varied properties—physical, mental, emotional, imaginary, and spiritual. Thus Foote's assertion that "the object of the artist should be to tell us in music . . . the truths of life and the beauty and sublimity of life which we, with lack of genius, fail to grasp."[1] We discover MacDowell cherishing the sight of a derelict farmhouse near Peterborough, New Hampshire, and portraying it in one of the *Woodland Sketches*, Paine debating the nature of human destiny with Fiske and his friends and then setting forth his own interpretation in *Oedipus Tyrannus*, the emotional Beach revealing glimpses of inner turmoil in her Piano Quintet, Chadwick ingenuously envisaging in his works a hobgoblin's antics or Tam O'Shanter's rickety ride, and Parker yearning for moral wholeness in the idealized Heaven of *Hora Novissima.*

Looking back at the parents and ancestors of the composers, we find few family paintings, photographs, and writings telling us how they looked, what they thought, and how they behaved. Yet the patrimony they transmitted to their descendants had distinction: moral uprightness, a resolute sense of mission, a tenacious dedication to achieving their goals, and a fervid ambition to win the esteem of their peers. Ever present was a stern conscience that bid them to fulfill all obligations to God and community arising from the positions they occupied. Most New Englanders of the first half of the nineteenth century were not in conflict with their society; nor were the composers descended from time. They had an affection for their New England land, which they worked with diligence. They respected a person capable of competent work exhibiting fine quality. From the beginning of their settlement in the New World, New Englanders tried to capture their aspirations, however tentative and sometimes primitive, in poetry, painting, literature, and music. We can point to Anne Bradstreet and her *Several Poems*, published in Boston in 1678; John Singleton Copley and his paintings of the 1760s, *Paul Revere* and *Boy with a Squirrel*; Samuel Adams and his polemical pamphlets that helped achieve political independence; Nathaniel Hawthorne and the tales in *Mosses from an Old Manse* (1846) and the novel *The Scarlet Letter* (1850); and Timothy Swan and the grave warmth of the sacred music in his *New England Harmony* (1801). These were all part of the heritage of the New England group of composers.

In the discussion that follows, one must remember that these composers would never have rejected a past that meant so much to them. Whatever learning they acquired in Europe, it would be layered onto a granite foundation built during two hundred and fifty years of American and New England history. The musicians embodied first the values of America's northeastern seaboard, which found things Germanic sympathetic and therefore absorbable. Romantic tendencies as much native as Germanic were the conveyance of emotions and ideals through music and the belief in music's transcendent power to transmute these emotions and ideals into universal experiences. When W.S.B. Mathews of Chicago named the American composers of front rank in the year 1892, he declared that only those composers whose works demonstrated the highest ideals were worthy of such a designation. Significantly, he turned to Paine for help in the classification and came up with the names of all of the New England group save for Beach, whose recognition was in the future, and he included one additional name, Dudley Buck, of Connecticut.[2]

Horatio Parker insisted that the composer had to draw his inspiration from far within his artistic consciousness. He aimed to realize to the best of his ability the ideals that he honored. He endeavored to express them through music that invoked sympathetic feelings in the public that came to listen.[3]

BACKGROUNDS OF THE COMPOSERS

That these six composers embarked on musical careers reveals singularity of purpose and individuality, traits common to other New Englanders of the time. They seem anything but the submissive "go along and get along" dullards that the English writer Wilfrid Mellers makes them out to be.[4] Very few other nineteenth-century Americans had the courage to take this particular direction, however strong their interest in music. These six composers' abiding desire as students was to possess what they saw as the genuine musical masterpieces bequeathed them by composers of the previous two hundred years, which meant acquiring the proficiency needed to comprehend the bequest. These native musicians held that a composer worthy of the name examined all music of the past and knew and eveutually came to terms with much of it, exactly as writers had to know and come to terms with past literatures. To achieve this, they had to master melody, harmony, rhythm, and musical forms.[5] They sympathized with the conclusion of New England's contemporary painters and sculptors, that "the art of the past could provide useful sources for the development of a national American art. While the reliance on sources or authority would be important, what would be produced would be a unique American art."[6] They desired, as Foote once wrote, to understand the world of thought and emotion within them and to express it externally and to discriminate between what was permanent and essential and what was accidental and vanishing. In addition, they had to refuse to countenance whatever suggested "the material and imperfect."[7] One can see in Foote's words the composer endeavoring to deliver America's music from the superficiality that he felt burdened it and to justify his effort. He and the other composers undertook to forge a large body of American art music into impeccable structures that answered the needs of the enlightened Americans of their day and that, they hoped, would also function as convincing guides to the people informing America's cultural tomorrow:

"We are entrusted with the task of forming the taste of the next generation whether we will or no," said Parker. Moreover, "It is our duty to do so."[8]

Of the six composers, Paine was born into the most musical family, although they all grew up with musical sounds from their early childhood. Paine's grandfather had built one of the first church organs made in Maine; his father, Jacob Paine, was director of a band in Portland, Maine, and operated a music store; his uncle was a music instructor; and his sister Helen, a contralto vocalist, taught voice and piano. No barriers were placed in the way of the young Paine's music studies. He worked with Hermann Kotzschmar in Portland, composed a string quartet at sixteen, and then accepted a sum of money from his sister and gave three subscription concerts in order to get together the funds needed to go abroad. He left for the Berlin Hochschule für Musik in 1858. For three years, he studied organ with Karl Haupt and composition with Friedrich Wiepricht.[9] Early on, he revealed a capacity for hard work and an intense desire to master his craft thoroughly, characteristics of all six composers while students. During the learning years and throughout his adult life, Paine did not strike those who delighted in his music as being an imitation German. On the contrary, when he visited London, in 1879, his close friend John Fiske "took great pleasure in introducing these good friends [Mr. and Mrs. Paine] to his London friends as representative Americans."[10]

Paine, like the other New Englanders, was most earnest about the studies to which he had committed himself. Why did he go to Germany for further schooling? Because Germans had thought about music with seriousness, as evidenced in their writings; their teaching was thorough, as evidenced in the graduates of their music schools; and they composed at the highest level of craft and creativity, as evidenced in the works of Bach, Mozart, Beethoven, Mendelssohn, and Schumann. Chadwick would have agreed with him. In a lighter moment, both men might have read with amusement the comment by Peter Dunne Finley's Mr. Dooley, in *Mr. Dooley in Peace and in War* (1898): "An Anglo-Saxon, Hinnissey, is a German that's forgot who was his parents. . . . I'm wan iv th' hottest Anglo-Saxons that iver come out iv Anglo-Saxony."

Some of Chadwick's uncles and aunts, like his parents, had training in the old psalmodic singing styles of New England, which they learned in the homegrown singing schoools. His father, while supervising his insurance business in Lawrence, Massachusetts, also taught singing; and his older brother gave him his first piano lessons. Yet, his father opposed a music profession for his son. Before George had completed high school, his father forced him to go to work as a clerk in his insurance office. The son proved obstinate and self-reliant. He rebelled against parental authority at the age of twenty-one, taught music privately, and continued his music education at the New England Conservatory. He then went to teach at Olivet College, in Michigan, in 1876. The next year, with barely enough money to get him there, he boldly embarked for Germany and music lessons, first in Berlin under Karl Hauptmann, then in Leipzig under Karl Reinecke, and finally in Munich under Josef Rheinberger.[11]

Parker's father was an architect; his German-born mother had studied music in Munich, was versed in Latin and Greek, wrote English verse, taught piano, and was the organist at an Auburndale church. Parker's first music lessons were with his mother. Chadwick gave him his first lessons in composition. Chadwick says he found the young Parker to be rebellious in the face of rules but diligent in his studies. On Chadwick's advice, Parker went to Munich in 1882 for music study under Josef Rheinberger. He found his teacher to be thorough and dry. In 1893 the New York *Musical Courier* reported him as saying that he wished he had also gone to France for study. Nevertheless, he came back to the United States with a thorough understanding of his profession. As he once had occasion to say: "There is a popular notion that a composer sits down and waits until a great idea occurs to him. Nothing can be more erroneous. If he has great ideas it is because he has spent many years of unremitting toil in learning how, when, and where to find them, and just what to do with them when they are found."[12]

Amy Beach had proved musically gifted before reaching her second birthday. Her mother, a capable singer and pianist, was her earliest music teacher, beginning her daughter's instruction when Amy was only six. Amy proved to have a phenomenal memory and musical precociousness. She quickly illustrated the observation made by Amy Fay about the "New England principle of teaching young women independence and looking out for themselves from the first," a thinking for one's self not allowed Germany's young women. Fay further observed: "The best plan is the old-fashioned [New England] one, viz: Give your children a 'stern sense of duty,' and then throw them on their own resources." Amy Beach gave her first public piano recital at the age of seven and played a Moscheles concerto with orchestra at the age of sixteen. She never went abroad to continue her studies, but instead she worked for a while on piano with Ernest Perabo and on harmony with Junius W. Hill, in Boston. Carl Baermann had a hand in her piano instruction; Wilhelm Gericke, in her composition studies. These mentors should be kept in mind when reading her statement, made years later: "My instruction in orchestration, composition, counterpoint and fugue has been acquired alone, without a teacher, through the faithful study of standard treatises. . . . In addition, [there was] the analysis, practical and theoretical, of the orchestral scores and other great works of the great masters, both at home and in the concert room."[13] She did indeed fully cover the musical field in her independent studies, even making her own translations of music treatises by Hector Berlioz and François Gevaert.[14]

Only two out of the six composers had no clear-cut musicians in their families. Arthur Foote's father was editor of the *Salem Gazette*, and his sister, who raised him after the death of his mother, was a writer. As Foote once stated: "I had no especial musical inheritance or surroundings." His introduction to music came when he began piano lessons with a Salem teacher, Fanny Paine (no relation to John Knowles Paine), at the age of twelve. Foote says: "At thirteen I began to take notice and to find that music was to be a real thing in my life—my ambition having previously been to become a locomotive engineer!" He did not go to Germany, but instead he entered Harvard and studied with Paine. In 1875 Foote received an M.A. in music (the first granted by any American university). Throughout his life, Foote cherished the area around Boston for its "tradition and cultivation." Just before he died, he reflected on his long career and said that life in the 1890s and the early years of the twentieth century had been "simple and easy, and is a pleasant thing to look back upon in these restless, anxious days [of 1937]."[15]

MacDowell's parents were not especially musical, but his mother did begin him on piano at the age of eight. He studied with various piano teachers in New York and then left for Europe with his mother, working with Antoine-François Marmontel in Paris, then with Siegmund Lebert in Stuttgart and Louis Ehlert in Wiesbaden. He finally ended up in Frankfurt, where he took lessons in piano from Karl Heymann, composition from Joachim Raff, and counterpoint and fugue from Franz Böhme.[16] Of all the teachers that the Americans studied under, Raff was by far the finest composer; he was able to inspire MacDowell's creativity by his example. Not limiting his teaching to the music of past masters alone, he imparted an admiration for the highly romantic music of Franz Liszt to his American protégé.

These six composers neither forgot while in Europe, nor dismissed afterwards, their love for their own homeland. As Marian MacDowell said of her husband Edward, even when he was away in Germany for several years, he continued to feel an "immense, honest enthusiasm for his own country that characterized his whole mature life." He grew especially fond of Peterborough, New Hampshire, "haunting its hilltops, once covered with farms wrested from the wilderness by those who first settled this country. To him there was something quite as poignant and interesting in the days passed on those hills as in the days passed on some Italian hilltop on which stood the ruins of an old castle." MacDowell enjoyed exploring the New England countryside and grew excited when visiting those spots connected with American history. Assuredly, America to him "was not a bare and arid tract," culturally speaking.[17] The comment is especially significant because he was away in Europe longer than any of the other composers, there from the age of thirteen to the age of twenty-nine, and he was a New Yorker by birth.

All of these musicians realized that the path they had chosen to follow, because unconventional, was filled with pitfalls. To study music and become a professional writer of ambitious art compositions was an unheard-of direction to take. No precedent existed for supporting such a person. As Parker explained in 1911: "The many rewards of a serious composer are slender at best, and most precarious, especially in this country. . . . One who aspires to compose must therefore be prepared to content himself with little beyond his work. The exaltation which attends the continued pursuit of beauty should be his. The communion and fellowship of the great masters of music should comfort and encourage him, but he must seek his rewards in spiritual and not in material things."[18]

Throughout their lifetimes, these composers recognized that they did *not* actually reflect their American society as a whole or completely accept its precepts. They, after all, did become composers in opposition to the given wisdom of the time. They had entered a profession that would deny them rich financial compensation for all their striving. They were, from the point of view of the millions of profit-directed Americans of their era, almost useless members of the community, who supplied luxury goods of no specifiable value. Perhaps in one regard they were of some worth—in the area of American-European cultural competition. In those moments when the bolstering of native prestige seemed advisable, they were touted as local champions. Their hour of ascendancy, however, soon passed, especially when the appeal of novelty wore off. They then took on secondary importance and experienced neglect. Nevertheless, they persisted in originating a body of artistic music that allowed the United States to stand beside European nations as a serious contributor to Western musical culture.

Finally, the significance of women in the composers' lives remains to be discussed. Of great importance to their start in music were the mothers of Parker, MacDowell, and Beach. Of at least equal importance were the wives of the men, and the husband of Amy Beach, in sustaining their spouses during their adult lives. Doctor H.H.A. Beach, a Boston surgeon much older than his wife, encouraged Amy to develop her talents as a composer and provided the home conditions to sustain her artistic efforts. His attitude and actions were extraordinary for the era.

Paine's wife, the former Mary Elizabeth Greeley, daughter of a Portland merchant, esteemed her husband as a man, writes Henry Finck, although she had no great understanding of his music. She fended off the outside world during the hours he was free to compose and uncomplainingly made do with the small salary he earned. She fought his battles, especially with those members of the Harvard faculty who wished no music taught at the university, mothered his students, and labored to get his music performed and published. Mrs. Paine, in turn, according to John Alden Carpenter, was revered by her husband and his students.[19]

Parker met his future wife, the music student Anna Poessl, in Munich. When they married and came to the United States, she remained sunny and dependable, relieving her husband of the day-to-day chores, certain that the creation of his musical works was all-important. Their daughter says of her childhood: "How often we would come flying into the house, full of enthusiasm over something to be greeted by Mother standing guard. 'Hush,' she would say, 'your father is working.' Her absolute selflessness, devotion and understanding never wavered for an instant. Father and his work came first, last and always."[20]

Marian MacDowell, the former Marian Nevins, had been her husband's piano student in Frankfurt before she became his wife. She recognized the sensitive, visionary nature of her husband's genius and carefully nurtured it. She provided strength when he met frustration in Europe as he sought a permanent teaching position, when money proved scarce and living was hand-to-mouth during the early days of their marriage, and when nervous excitement later threatened to get the best of him during his tribulations at Columbia University. After Edward's death, she earned money by giving concerts of his music and welcomed donations so that the Peterborough home he had loved could be transformed into the MacDowell Colony, a retreat for creative people of every description.

Wives like those just named, and Amy Beach's husband, aided the cause of American music by providing circumstances that made creativity possible for their spouses. Otherwise, these composers might easily have been distracted by the cross-grained people that they encountered and the demands of teaching, family life, and household matters.

THINKING ABOUT MUSIC

It was not easy for these American composers to determine the musical style in which to write. They knew that their decision would have consequences both for themselves and possibly for American art music. In the end, they created their own musical identities through a succession of choices for which few American guides existed. The composers were not born into an environment of inherited criteria for writing a symphony, a string quartet, or a grand opera. Thus, the necessity for making choices that included European musical styles was unavoidable. "The fact that the composers of Paine's generation and those immediately following him did not discover typically American paths is no cause for wonderment," comments Howard Hanson. "Their inspiration, their musical sustenance, was drawn almost entirely from Europe. The United States of that period had little to offer them from the musical standpoint in the ways of encouragement or assistance. The path of the pioneer . . . is a difficult one, and it has always amazed me that such a vital force as that typified by Paine's music could exist in the comparatively barren soil and almost hostile climate of that period."[21]

True to their New England inheritance, the composers disciplined themselves against excessive individuality and temperamental excess. Firm convictions, consistently held, guided their thinking. They set themselves the task of balancing the ear's desire for sensuous sound-colors, the mind's demand for rational forms, and the imagination's inclination toward unexpected and random fancies. Music's beauty to them resided in achieving an equilibrium among all three. For example, Paine thought that the more prominent the melody, the more subjective were the emotions expressed. Yet, the more equally melodious the simultaneously sounding parts, the more the demands of harmony had to be heeded and subjective expression lessened. Yet, "what is lost in subjective expression is compensated for by architectural beauty of form. The highest aim of art is to avoid *extremes*; to unite the individual and the general, the real and the ideal, in harmonious form and expression."[22]

The ideal of musical balance and the avoidance of extremes hints at classicism, as does the emphasis on self-discipline and control over one's material. But the application of these principles varied from composer to composer: more strictly on the part of Paine and Chadwick, more flexibly on the part of MacDowell and Beach. And as Paine and Chadwick continued to write, their tendencies were toward the romantic: an increase of emotionally over rationally conceived passages, a greater disposition to follow feeling and fancy over the demands for systematic thinking and tidy forms, an increased experimentation with music of programmatic meaning over that of abstract intent.

In any event, the term *classicism* is vague, warns Douglas Moore, who had been a student of Horatio Parker. (And certainly it was unclear when applied to Parker and his fellows.) Moore's explanation of the term provides a useful approach to understanding the New Englanders' attitude toward music making. To the six composers, and to Moore, the term denoted a style "characterized by a fine sense of roundness of form, equilibrium of means of expression and content, discipline of mind, and an absence of any vulgar or sensational effects, especially the overemphasis of emotional content." Yet, when the composers constructed their works "with highly developed skill," they did not stress form "at the expense of emotional values. On the contrary [they] . . . were deeply interested in human problems, and their compositions glow with warm human feeling."[23]

The use of dissonance and consonance necessitated the careful adjustments. An older composer, such as Paine, was more disposed to employ dissonance as Beethoven, Mendelssohn, and Schumann had employed it, although Paine's usage grew freer in time. Younger composers, like MacDowell and Beach, made more liberal use of escape tones, unresolved appoggiatura chords, and nondominant seventh and ninth constructions. Introduced in moderation, these dissonances gave pleasure, offset the threat of monotony from too much consonance, and produced a sense of forward movement. So long as dissonance remained a secondary element, it provided an interesting diversity in sound, did not interfere with the impression of unity, and had aesthetic merit.[24] An elderly Foote commented, in 1937, on the twentieth century's rejection of triadic harmony and consonances as frames for dissonance in favor of polytonality and "linear" counterpoint, saying: "Dissonance and consonance seem to me to be complementary: while music entirely consonant soon becomes monotonous, that which is constantly dissonant without the relief of consonance is not only tiresome, but, worse than this, unpleasant."[25]

Melody, for all the composers of the New England group, was more romantic than classical in its longer phrases, arching lines, songlike character, and affective implications. Paine's melody can sound Schumannesque; MacDowell's seems more individualistic. Every now and again, a broad paean sounds forth that has links with New England's psalmodic and hymnic traditions. At other times, the lyricism mirrors American folk song or the New Englander's Celtic or Anglo-Saxon musical heritage.

Often, these two sources of inspiration are indistinguishable. Every now and again, and with Chadwick in particular, a tune resembles popular song—the sentimental ballad or the perky minstrel ditty.

Rhythms rarely show any probing for novel effects. They occasionally owe something to dance: the meter and rhythmic phrasing of the Boston waltz, the minstrel walk-around, the American march, for example. A syncopation or some rhythmic quirkiness will suggest an American provenance. With Foote, old dance rhythms permeate some musical suites that look back to the Baroque period. Otherwise, if influences must be found, one looks to central European practices for precedents.

When Paine composed his First Symphony in the early seventies, his rhetoric was principally that of Beethoven. However, already apparent in this work, especially in the middle movements, were a romantically inspired use of warm orchestral colors, an idiomatic exploitation of the individual characteristics of instruments for expressive purposes, and a sure-handed manipulation of the glowing sonorities that typified the music of the post-Beethoven years. The orchestral music of the other five composers is even more explicitly a result of these romantic procedures. All the composers, including Paine, sooner or later had to acknowledge the expanded knowledge of orchestral procedures evidenced in compositions by Wagner, Liszt, and Strauss. Beginning in the mid-eighties, one discerns an interest not only in late Germanic musical models, but also in those supplied by Berlioz, Tchaikovsky, and Dvořák.

Formal structures, especially in abstract pieces and concert overtures, normally follow tradition: binary and ternary forms, rondo, sonata, sonata-rondo, prelude and fugue. The tonal applications pertinent to each form are for the most part also observed: cogent modulations from tonic major to dominant major or tonic minor to the relative major. When a third-key reference is made, it is either to the subdominant or the submediant minor. Also found, however, are the more extended postclassical usages: sudden key change from tonic major to the lowered submediant major, for example. Transient and more permanent modulations to distant keys are freely introduced, pervasive chromaticism is not uncommon, and unexpected enharmonic interpretations of ambiguous harmonies like those of the diminished-seventh and the augmented-sixth chord persuade the listener that the piece firmly belongs in the latter part of the nineteenth century. Individual formal structures independent of tradition do occur in conjunction with program music other than the concert overture. These works may be designated as symphonic or tone poems, ballads, or simply character pieces, as in Foote's *Four Character Pieces after Omar Khayyám.* Recurring motives and the cyclic reintroduction of distinctive ideas are not uncommon in works made up of several sections or movements.

These composers wrote symphonies, concertos, concert overtures, suites, tone poems, masses, oratorios, cantatas, variations or preludes and fugues for organ, piano or piano and violin sonatas, string quartets, piano quintets, brief character pieces given evocative titles for piano or piano plus another instrument, art songs, and operas. Paine steered clear of out-and-out program music, although the *Tempest*, a freely structured tone poem based on the Shakespearean play, is a major effort. He, Chadwick, and Parker liked composing for chorus, vocal soloists, and orchestra, and their works include oratorios and operas. Although Foote also wrote cantatas for voices and orchestra, he was never happier than in those moments when he could allow one or more instruments to sing out a long melody with supportive but subordinate accompaniment, as in his Violin Sonata and his *Night Piece* for flute and string quartet. MacDowell reveled in program music, although few of his works follow a detailed nonmusical plan; an evocative title usually suffices. Three MacDowell compositions reveal an abundance of extramusical references: the tone poems *Hamlet and Ophelia*, *Lancelot and Elaine*, and *Lamia*. No such references are made in his two piano concertos. Like Beach, he enjoyed writing for solo piano: witness his four piano sonatas, each given a title serving to call forth a proper emotional response; witness also the romanticized imagery of the many short keyboard pieces gathered into collections with such names as *New England Idyls* and *Sea Pieces*. Beach, in addition to her character pieces for piano, contributed a grand mass, a symphony, a piano concerto, examples of chamber music, and a large number of songs. Her "Ah, love, but a day" and "The year's at the spring" were two of the most well-liked art songs at the turn of the century. In short, between them the six composers tried out all the ways of writing music that had been cultivated up to their own time and left consummately constructed American models for future composers to study.

Howard Hanson wrote in 1943 of the debt that he and composers like him (he names Douglas Moore and Quincy Porter) owed the New England group and works like Paine's *Oedipus Tyrannus* and Chadwick's *Tam O'Shanter*. Their music, Hanson noted, came out of a scholarly Anglo-Saxon tradition that put a premium on high technical standards and controlled and restrained expression—sometimes urbane, often good-humored, direct and honest.[26]

Moreover, the compositions of these composers retained a humanistic intent, states Howard Mumford Jones, in his discussion of the musical developments that occurred between 1865 and 1915: "If it [their music] could in no sense be 'realistic,' it could at least carry on a grave tradition, noble and sympathetic. Contrast, whatever the merits of the two styles, MacDowell's *Sonata Tragica*, intended to express grief . . . with the *musique concrète* of our time, which, whatever it expresses does not express general emotion and scarcely mathematical relationship. If we insist (and we do) that art in some sense mirrors its own epoch, the five decades . . . must surely be allowed to express themselves and not some later time—allowed also to create a style satisfactory to those who used it without anticipating a style that was not to be dominant until a half a century after the Battle of the Marne."[27]

WHETHER TO BE ORIGINAL, OR "AMERICAN"

The question of originality, or an American identity, as related to the music of the New England composers requires some discussion, if only to understand their point of view, which was so different from that of the twentieth-century modernists. The commentary that follows may possibly lead to a better insight into and sympathy for their music. The six composers did not desire independence from their social system; liberty meant room for artistic development within their society, in accord with the goals they had set for themselves. They wanted freedom to ferret out meritorious musical symbols consonant with America's civilization at its finest, thus allowing them to continue, as their contemporary, the architect Jay Wheeler Dow, put it, "to belong somewhere and to something, not to be entirely cut off . . . as stray atoms."[28] Furthermore, the composers knew that unheard music was like unviewed pictures and unread novels. They wanted to be heard; yet, they desired people to listen willingly. Realists, they knew that not everyone wished to attend concerts of serious art music and that not more than a few who came to listen had a genuine understanding of the composer's art. As Parker said, the public's thoughtful approach toward performer and composer stimulated both. However, artistic music would not necessarily please everybody. So the stimulation had to come from the intelligent listeners among the public. Parker recognized that many auditors underwent a "passive suffering of music," which was "not the way [for a composer] to acquire merit or understanding. Merely to let music trickle in and out of one's ear is not a more permanently profitable pleasure than that of drinking soda-water, or having one's back scratched. Nothing remains, for effort is needed."[29]

The composers actively shaped their styles to achieve coherence. They chose not to arrive at a style that sounded singular and far removed from an audience's expectations. In this regard, Vytautis Kavolis's observations are perceptive. Kavolis, a sociologist, points out that one should not assume all artistic values and the resultant styles (like those of the New England group) are passive reflections of a society. On the contrary, the formation of style relies on an active principle, which "consists in the establishment of coherence among the elements of perception embodied in a work of art." Style conceived in this way "is a necessary condition of art's existence." Kavolis realizes that assumptions like his have been questioned by a few twentieth-century aestheticians and "a good many fashionable avant-garde artists." Nevertheless, most psychologists bear him out and see stylistic "patterning in perception as a generic human characteristic." In these ways artists establish affinities among the countless components of a shared human experience. The task of art, he concludes, is to integrate social reality and personal emotions. Failure to meet this basic societal need betrays "a faulty conception of the sociocultural functions of art."[30]

The New England group opted out of the "grand scramble to dodge the obvious way of putting things," the striving "to create an entirely new vocabulary" to the detriment "of form and substance," that was going on in Europe at the turn of the century, said Parker in a talk delivered in 1902. Disconcerting was the "continual effort in the direction of individualism and protest on the part of the composer against being confounded with his fellow men." Richard Strauss's music, for example, now resembled "a shriek for the recognition of his own personality." Such tendencies were "anti-pathetic to our character. . . . We can admire but we need not imitate them." For American composers, "the old vocabulary will do very well if one has but new ideas," he continued. "Not that I object to addition to our means of expression—but the new vocabulary must always remain a means and never become an end of expression."[31]

Empty experimentation and the pursuit of the latest styles for their own sakes were not for these composers. Their primary objective was to write music that mattered to them and their public because of its persuasive power and perceptible significance. There was no sense that the established methods of composing music had been exhausted.[32] After all, these musicians were a part of the New World, where art music was not yet indigenous and its performance still novel. Everything sounded fresh, and listening was never tedious. They felt that they could speak contemporaneously and vitally using the techniques bequeathed them by those acknowledged to be master composers. When they composed, it was as if they were dynamically reliving the history of the last hundred years of music for the first time. They were convinced that if they could but write honestly and unaffectedly, what was original in their music would show through. For their age, they offered power and originality. Writing about concert life in New York at the death of MacDowell, in 1908, Richard Aldrich states that MacDowell, Paine, Parker, and Chadwick, above all other American composers, had made major contributions to American music, with strong and singular works.[33] James Russell Lowell observed that originality should be allowed to take care of itself and not become an absolute that one courted assiduously. "Nobody could take a patent out on it," he declared. Today's new invention, someone would remember as having heard before. The painter William Morris Hunt pithily advised his Boston students: "Chase your shadow!—but *don't run after originality.*"[34]

That these composers were not hostile to new musical experiences is evidenced again and again. The young Paine's aversion to Wagner is frequently referred to by writers; his slow appreciation of Wagner as he grew older is ignored. For example, a letter signed by Paine, Foote, Lang, Apthorp, and George L. Osgood, and sent as part of a notice dated 8 May 1883, requested Gustav Kobbe to give two lectures on Wagner while he visited Boston. He complied. Twenty years later, Foote and Chadwick are found inviting people to the home of Miss Susan H. Wainwright, on 2 April 1903, in order to hear music of the Ojibway Indians presented and discussed by F. R. Burton.[35] Horatio Parker, in 1899, told Vernon Blackburn of his deep feeling for Puccini's *La Boheme*, which he considered great music. A few years later, Chadwick spoke of his admiration for Stravinsky's music and praised Stravinsky's mastery of instrumentation, rhythm, and mood.[36]

At first, Foote's preferences were conservative, he says, and his models, were Mendelssohn, Schumann, and Chopin. But he tells us that he did not remain frozen in that earlier era. He did keep an open mind, listened to and studied all the contemporary compositions that came his way, including the advanced ones, and often modified his thinking as he matured. Much as he tried, however, he could never accept as a matter of logic and sound judgment those radical innovations that repudiated all the conventions and instead opted for unrelenting discord and antilyrical angular melody. We must respect his integrity when he writes: "It is not easy to keep an open mind for changes and new developments, especially when they fly in the face of all that one has cared for. But we should pray not to become so hardened in traditions as not to be honest toward what may seem to be new and perhaps not of value. It must be confessed, however, that since 1910 a severe strain has been put upon one's willingness to be hospitable to new ideas. There has been, beyond doubt, a sweeping away of a lot of rubbish, such as the uncompromising doctrines as to consecutive fifths, cross-relations, etc.; our ideas as to key-relationships have been broadened (chiefly through Wagner); our feeling about form has become more elastic; knowledge of the orchestra is infinitely greater, and so on."[37]

The true contemporaries of the New England group were not the innovators Schoenberg and Stravinsky but the traditionally oriented Brahms, Saint-Saëns, Tchaikovsky, Verdi, Elgar, Puccini, Dvořák, and Grieg. The last two were national composers, expressing the traits of Bohemia and Norway, respectively, through use or emulation of folk tunes and dances and programmatic references to their country's geography, history, and literature. Mrs. Jeanette Thurber, wife of a wealthy New York grocer, even succeeded in getting Dvořák to come to New York, in 1892, so that he could take charge of her National Conservatory of Music and found an American school of composition.[38] Mrs. Thurber had apparently followed her own inclinations and paid little heed to native composers then active in the United States. Dvořák's arrival was the signal for heated controversy in the American art-music world over whether anything distinctively American and utilizable in serious compositions did indeed exist and whether native composers, to be worthy to be called American, had to be conscious nationalists. In the few years that Dvořák resided in the United States, he made various pronouncements about the distinctive qualities of Afro-American and American Indian music and praised the songs of Stephen Foster. However, in works of his reputedly inspired by the New World, he shows no real assimilation of these qualities, remaining mostly Bohemian in his style.

MacDowell immediately rebutted the nationalists, saying that the use of folk song and dance identified the composer not for what he was but for what he was clothed in. In Dvořák's Symphony "From the New World," MacDowell found the composer masquerading in "Negro clothes cut in Bohemia." He heard little that was really American in the work. He suggested instead that, to achieve distinction, the native composer must "arrive at . . . the youthful optimistic vitality and the undaunted tenacity of spirit that characterizes the American man. This is what I hope to see echoed in American music."[39]

Horatio Parker, who had taught at the National Conservatory of Music and knew Dvořák personally, saw the pursuit of nationalism as a chimera. Whether Dvořák's Symphony "From the New World" or Puccini's opera

The Girl from the Golden West, no amount of New World coloration could make a work American. An indisputably American composition had to be conceived in America, by an American, and "executed in the spirit which must inform all creative artists of whatever nationality." References to Indians, Negroes, or cowboys alone could not make a work American.[40]

Bostonians regarded Dvořák's statements about achieving an American identity through use of music by African Americans and native Indian Americans as naive and pretentious. The Boston *Home Journal*, reviewing the season of 1892–93, stated: "We were allowed to gaze upon Antonin Dvořák, the Bohemian composer, who was imported to this country that he might teach ambitious Americans the art of writing American music, a task to which the process of extracting sunbeams out of cucumbers is a joyful job." Warren Davenport, in 1893, said he knew nobody who was convinced that the "New World" Symphony sounded American. He quotes the New York *Musical Courier* statement that it could as easily be heard as Scandinavian or Celtic. He also noted that the symphony was written by a Bohemian, conducted in New York by a Hungarian, and played by Germans in a hall built by a Scotchman; he concluded: "About one third of the audience were Americans and so were the critics." Davenport saw music as universal, not national. Neither Dvořák nor any one else could confine it "to some groove that may be labelled 'American music.' We shall have numerous American composers in the near future and they will be recognized and encouraged when Americans and not Germans control our musical affairs, but it is easy to prophesy that their models of composition will be the recognized forms that have served in displaying the genius of the composer, whatever his nationality."[41]

Paine considered himself to be a universal, not just an American, composer. Chadwick commented: "Music, in a broad sense, is cosmopolitan and universal; more or less nonsense is talked about a national school of music. The Californians are inheritors of the musical arts of the ages, just as we in New England are." Once asked by John Tasker Howard whether she resented being called an American composer, Mrs. Beach replied: "No, but I would rather be called a composer."[42]

In 1913 Oscar Sonneck, the great American-music scholar, wrote of the European prejudice against American composers, which influential Americans had accepted. Even America's best composers, said Sonneck, were considered "weak dilutions and imitations of an inferior European article." America's "only noteworthy contribution to music has been 'rag-time,' " according to this point of view. Not only was this not true, Sonneck countered, but we have "perceptibly American composers." He claims that

MacDowell's music, for example, has a New World atmosphere and that he could make out a similar case for the music of several other American composers. Moreover, the use of folk songs will not by itself give a work an American identity. Dvořák's "New World" Symphony is "a beautiful outburst of Bohemian homesickness with Afro-American ingredients," nothing else. Composers can employ whatever national music they wish, but they must add something of themselves—living in and identifying with America—to produce music identifiably American.[43]

The New England composers recognized the difficulty of speaking about an indigenous music representative of the entire United States. They knew they were neither of Indian nor African descent and felt uncomfortable about donning what seemed to them to be a false mantle. Yet, occasionally they did try, though always disavowing any claim to authentic ethnicity: MacDowell's *Indian Suite* and the "Br'er Rabbit" from his *Fireside Tales* are two examples. What native musical inheritance had come down to them could be traced back to Anglo-Celtic sources, and these had a greater influence on their idiom: overtly, in works like Chadwick's *Tam O'Shanter*, Foote's "Irish Folk-Song," MacDowell's Piano Sonata No. 4, *Keltic*, and Beach's *Gaelic Symphony*; more subtly in countless other works. These American musicians might possibly have had some awareness of several other distinct musical subcultures in the United States—Mexican, French Creole, Dutch, "Dutch" German, and Quebecois being the most obvious. Possibly they had an inkling of the more recent musical contributions made by Italian-Americans and Jewish-Americans from eastern Europe.[44] One cannot blame the composers for deciding that to distinguish any characteristically "American" idiom along racial or cultural lines was futile save when a composer wished intentionally to summon up an American ethnic subgroup, as Chadwick had done in the opera *The Padrone*, set in a locality corresponding to Boston's Italian North End.

Amy Beach introduced Gaelic, Eskimo, Balkan, and other national tunes into her pieces. In doing so, she never dreamed she was writing anything approaching national music: "She merely adapted for her own purposes melodies she happened to like. With her, nationalism was something subtler than using Indian or other tunes found in America—Americanism was something that could not be acquired by thinking about it."[45] All members of the New England group would have agreed with this statement.

The six composers were leery of the more recent popular-song types as a source for an American art music. On occasion a composer like Chadwick would allude to the antebellum Stephen-Foster type of sentimental ballad or minstrel song, since these in turn had connections with the Anglo-Celtic musical tradition with which they were already comfortable. However, they were much less likely to find useful the more recent trend in popular music toward coon song, cakewalk, and ragtime, for they were aware of the low-down origins of these pieces and their tendency to make their strongest appeal at the lowest social levels. We do have evidence that a couple of the composers were privately entertained by some of this new popular music. Of them all, Chadwick was the most inclined to introduce its rhythms and melodic twists into his compositions, but cautiously. On the whole, the six composers thought that the characteristics of popular music had their place in pieces intended for simple entertainment and immediate sensory gratification but had a diluting effect on music intended to be serious, sophisticated, and expressive of humanity's highest ideals and profoundest experiences. They were also trying to establish an American art music, in contradistinction to an American popular music, and wished not to confuse the two. At any rate, they had the good sense to leave alone what they felt uncomfortable with.

Because they had deep convictions about America, not Europe, being their hereditary ground, physically and spiritually, they could not help but portray the spirit of the people and the land they called their own.[46] Sonneck states that composers like MacDowell, Chadwick, and Parker might derive from the German, but they would have found it unfair if one looked for only the German in their music, since they were also "cultivating music *after their own* fashion," valid for their own America.[47]

Cultural politics in the twentieth century have encouraged writers on American culture to deride the New England group of composers and all other creative people working in the Boston area during the post–Civil War decades. Paris, Boulanger, and Stravinsky had become the new focuses for aspiring young composers, many of them of non-Yankee origin. R. H. Ives Gammell's comments on the way New Yorkers denigrated the Boston painters of this time parallel the criticisms of the New England composers made by Gilbert Chase, Aaron Copland, and Wilfrid Mellers: "[New York critics and artists] relegated the Bostonians to the wings. . . . They were ridiculed for their cult of beauty and condemned for their knowledgeable workmanship which a rising generation of art students was being taught to despise as academic. Sneered at as the Genteel School by a new group of art writers . . . the Boston painters were shoved into a temporary oblivion."[48] Perhaps the six in the New England group would have responded to the criticism as James Russell Lowell did. In a letter to F. H. Underwood, dated 12 May 1872, he said: "Don't bother yourself with any sympathy for me under my supposed sufferings from critics. I don't need it in the least. If a man does anything good, the world always finds it out, sooner or later; and if he doesn't, why, the world finds *that* out too—and ought to."[49]

NOTES

1. Arthur Foote, ed., *Theory of Music* (London: Squire, 1908), 237.

2. See "American Composers of the Front Rank," *Music* 2 (1892): 491–92.

3. Horatio Parker, "Contemporary Music," in *Modern Music and Musicians*, ed. Louis C. Elson (New York: University Society, 1918), 3:519.

4. Wilfrid Mellers, *Music in a New Found Land*, rev. ed. (New York: Oxford University Press, 1987), 25–27. Some silly writing appears in these pages about these composers' "hearts" not being those of "a lonely hunter" and their turning their backs "on the wilderness," whatever that means. Does Mellers really believe that the mature Paine was a "Bracebridge Hall" composer and thought Wagner's music to be subversive, that all of Chadwick's music is cosy, and that MacDowell is a "Rip van Winkle" composer? If so, then he only proves he knows Washington Irving's writings far better than he knows the views and music of the New England group of composers.

5. Horatio Parker, ed., Introduction to *Music and Public Entertainment* (Boston: Hall and Locke, 1911), xv.

6. Richard Guy Wilson, Part 1, "The Great Civilization," in *The American Renaissance, 1876–1917* (New York: Brooklyn Museum, 1979), 12.

7. Foote, *Theory of Music*, 230–31.

8. Isabel Parker Semler, in collaboration with Pierson Underwood, *Horatio Parker* (New York: Putnam's Sons, 1942), 75.

9. George Thornton Edwards, *Music and Musicians of Maine* (Portland: Southworth, 1928), 122–23; John C. Schmidt, *The Life and Works of John Knowles Paine* (Ann Arbor: UMI Research Press, 1980), 29; Walter Raymond Spalding, *Music at Harvard* (1935; reprinted, New York: Da Capo, 1977), 150–51.

10. John Spencer Clark, *The Life and Letters of John Fiske* (Boston: Houghton, Mifflin, 1917), 2:144.

11. Louis C. Elson, *The History of American Music*, rev. to 1925 by Arthur Elson (New York: Macmillan, 1925), 170–71; Steven Ledbetter and Victor Fell Yellin, in H. Wiley Hitchcock and Stanley Sadie, eds., *The New Grove Dictionary of American Music* (London: Macmillan, 1986), s.v. "Chadwick, George Whitefield."

12. George Chadwick, *Horatio Parker* (New Haven: Yale University Press, 1921), 5–6; [H. E. Krehbiel?], New York *Musical Courier*, 5 April 1893, in the Allan A. Brown Collection, scrapbook of clippings, **M165.8, Vol. 3, in the Boston Public Library. The last quotation is from Parker, Introduction to *Music and Public Entertainment*, xv–xvi.

13. David Ewen, *American Composers* (New York: Putnam's Sons, 1982), s.v. "Beach, H.H.A., Mrs"; Adrienne Fried Block, in *American Grove*, s.v. "Beach, Amy Marcy (Cheney)"; Otto Ebel, *Women Composers* (New York: Chandler, 1902), 13–14. Amy Fay, *Music-Study in Germany* (New York: Macmillan, 1896), 82.

14. Elson, *The History of American Music*, 297.

15. Arthur Foote, *An Autobiography*, with an introduction and notes by Wilma Reid Cipolla (1946; reprinted, New York: Da Capo, 1979), 26; Arthur Foote, "A Bostonian Remembers," *Musical Quarterly* 23 (1937): 37; Wilma Reid Cipolla, in *American Grove*, s.v. "Foote, Arthur (William)."

16. Margaret Morgan Lowens, in *American Grove*, s.v. "MacDowell [McDowell], Edward (Alexander)."

17. Marian MacDowell, "MacDowell's 'Peterborough Idea,' " *Musical Quarterly* 18 (1932): 35–36, 38.

18. Parker, Introduction to *Music and Public Entertainment*, xvi.

19. Henry T. Finck, *My Adventures in the Golden Age of Music* (New York: Funk and Wagnalls, 1926), 80; M. A. DeWolfe Howe, "John Knowles Paine," *Musical Quarterly* 25 (1939): 261, 266.

20. Semler, *Horatio Parker*, 178.

21. Howard Hanson, "American Procession at Rochester," *Modern Music* 13 (March/April 1936): 24.

22. John Knowles Paine, "Inaugural Lecture of the Department of Musical Composition, History, and Aesthetics in the College of Music of Boston University," 28 October 1872 (n.p., n.d.).

23. Douglas Moore, *From Madrigal to Modern Music* (New York: Norton, 1942), 97–98.

24. George Lansing Raymond, *The Genesis of Art-Form* (New York: Putnam's Sons, 1893), 249.

25. Foote, "A Bostonian Remembers," 44.

26. Howard Hanson, "Twenty Years' Growth in America," *Modern Music* 20 (Jan/Feb. 1943): 97–98.

27. Howard Mumford Jones, *The Age of Energy* (New York: Viking, 1971), 18–19.

28. Wilson, "The Great Civilization," 45; see also Charles Horton Cooley, *Human Nature and the Social Order*, rev. ed. (New York: Scribner's Sons, 1922), 423.

29. Semler, *Horatio Parker*, 199–200.

30. Vytautis Kavolis, *History on Art's Side* (Ithaca: Cornell University Press, 1972), 161–63.

31. Semler, *Horatio Parker*, 163–65.

32. See Rupert Hughes, *Contemporary American Composers* (Boston: Page, 1900), 145–46. In *Music, the Arts, and Ideas* (Chicago: University of Chicago Press, 1967), 106–8, Leonard B. Meyer states that a style is dead only when nobody finds it significant or understandable; it remains vital so long as artists continue to discover an "unrealized conceptual-expressive potential in it." When experienced audiences find a work significant and satisfying, it has vitality. "The notion of 'exhausting' a style is largely a culture-bound concept, stemming from beliefs in the importance of originality and in the value of individual expression—beliefs important in [recent] Western ideology but by no means so in all cultures or in all epochs."

33. Richard Aldrich, *Concert Life in New York, 1902–1923* (New York: Putnam's Sons, 1941), 209.

34. Letter sent to James B. Thayer on 8 December 1868, in *Letters of James Russell Lowell*, ed. Charles Eliot Norton (New York: Harper and Brothers, 1894), 2:9; William Morris Hunt, *Talks about Art* (London: Macmillan, 1878), 43.

35. In Arthur Foote, scrapbook of clippings, **ML46.F65, Vols. 1 and 3, part of the Allan A. Brown Collection, in the Boston Public Library.

36. William Kay Kearns, "Horatio Parker and the English Choral Societies, 1899–1902," *American Music* 4 (1986): 30; item in the *New England Conservatory Magazine-Review* 6 (1916): 119.

37. Foote, *An Autobiography*, 57, 105–7.

38. John Clapham, *Antonín Dvořák* (New York: St. Martin's, 1966), 17–18.

39. Lawrence Gilman, *Edward MacDowell* (New York: Lane, 1909), 84–85.

40. Semler, *Horatio Parker*, 76, 234–35.

41. Allan A. Brown Collection, scrapbook of clippings, *M122.5 and *M433.5, in the Boston Public Library.

42. Schmidt, *The Life and Works of John Knowles Paine*, 29; George Whitefield Chadwick, in the *New England Conservatory Magazine-Review* 6 (1915): 39; John Tasker Howard, *Our American Music*, 4th ed. (New York: Crowell, 1965), 319.

43. Oscar G. Sonneck, *Suum Cuique: Essays in Music* (1916; reprinted, Freeport, N.Y.: Books for Libraries, 1969), 137–39.

44. For a discussion of the musical subcultures of ethnic groups arriving in America after the Civil War and their influence, see Nicholas E. Tawa, *A Sound of Strangers* (Metuchen, N.J.: Scarecrow, 1982).

45. Howard, *Our American Music*, 322.

46. See Lazare Saminsky, *Music of Our Day; Essentials and Prophecies* (1939; reprinted, Freeport, N.Y.: Books for Libraries, 1970), 150.

47. Sonneck, *Suum Cuique*, 11–12.

48. R. H. Ives Gammell, *The Boston Painters, 1900–1930*, ed. Elizabeth Ives Hunter (Orleans, Mass.: Parnassus Imprints, 1986), 3.

49. *Letters of James Russell Lowell*, 2:79–80.

4

JOHN KNOWLES PAINE (1839–1906)

Like other Americans who achieved prominance in the post–Civil War years, John Knowles Paine escaped from obscurity largely through his own effort. Vernon Parrington might well have included Paine among the people like Whitman, Twain, and Melville "thrown up . . . out of the huge caldron of energy that was America." Everywhere "were thousands like them, self-made men quick to lay hands on opportunity" or "ready to seek it out if it were slow in knocking, recognizing no limitations to their powers, discouraged by no shortcomings in their training."[1]

Paine had to be obstinate. Given the state of cultivated music in his youth, to be obstinate was to endure. He refused to remain in Portland, Maine, and find conventional work. Instead, he elected to pursue his first love, music, going abroad to redress his musical shortcomings and then to Boston to advance his vocation. Neither lack of money nor lack of precedent dissuaded him from a music career. When he found Harvard College ripe for music instruction, he mustered the aid of well-wishers to win an instructorship, then a professorship. He fought to improve the academic status of music, though powerful opponents, like the historian Francis Parkman, opposed him. Parkman, a member of the Harvard corporation, which was responsible for the supervision of all matters related to the operation of the university, "ended every deliberation of that body with the words '*musica delenda est*'; and . . . when the College was faced with a need of funds, was always ready with a motion to abolish the musical department."[2] Paine worked for acceptance as a composer, but he also assumed the momentous task of counseling the talented young composers who started their instruction with him and helping them to begin their own careers.

Daniel Gregory Mason complains that, when he was Paine's student, he found him despotic in disallowing compositional freedoms like unprepared dissonances, which, Mason claims, stemmed from creative excitement. Probably Paine felt Mason needed to develop his wings before he undertook to fly, a feeling common to other noted composers who were also teachers.[3] Apparently, his teaching was thorough and his classroom manner dry. Henry Dunham states that Paine occasionally used profanity in class, which proves him to have been quite human. Clayton Johns found his teacher's criticisms severe but just. Later, he and Paine became intimate friends. Emma Eames says that Paine often invited his more interesting students home for supper; she met Henry Finck and Celia Thaxter there. Walter Spalding speaks of Paine's sensitive nature, which sometimes made him irritable; but Spalding also attributes to him a "warm and loving heart, a strong sense of humor," and a sense of honor in his dealings with people. The composer Frederick Shepherd Converse attests to Paine's "genial and kindly soul" and his encouragement of a student's good ideas and enthusiastic support in working them out. Converse saw Paine take naive pleasure in his own music, playing and discussing works in progress (he mentions *Azara*) with students.[4]

Contemporary writers testify to his significance as a composer. When Thomas performed Paine's First Symphony in Philadelphia, in August 1876, an unnamed correspondent in *Dwight's Journal of Music* reported that the symphony was heard alongside a work by a native son, William Fry. Fry, the writer says, is a fine melodist but not a great composer. Paine, in contrast, had set American art on a level with that of other nations. His music contains agreeable themes, rich instrumentation, and unforced, healthy ideas. The First Symphony is "unquestionably the best large orchestral work yet produced by any native composer." By 1893 the Chicago writer W.S.B. Mathews was convinced that Paine was "a composer of the very highest rank among those in America and the world at large." Rupert Hughes, in 1900, commented: "The most classic of our composers is their vernerable dean, John Knowles Paine. It is an interesting proof of the youth of our native school of music, that the principal symphony, 'Spring' [no. 2], of our first composer of importance, was written only twenty-one years ago. Before Mr. Paine there had never been an American music writer worthy of serious consideration in the larger forms." When Paine began his career, wrote Louis Elson, "he stood alone." As he neared the end of his career, there were "at least three men,

Chadwick, MacDowell, and Horatio W. Parker, who might dispute the field with him."[5] The testimony of writers of the time confirms his contemporaries' high estimation of Paine and their inclination to regard every premiere of a large Paine composition as a milestone in American culture.

PAINE'S STYLE

At a time when the writings of Mark Twain and William Dean Howells, the paintings of Winslow Homer, and the sculptures of Daniel Chester French were introducing a new view of Americans, Paine was producing his Mass in D, the *St. Peter* oratorio, and his two symphonies. By the 1880s, he was considered the foremost herald of his age's newly fledged art music. He avoided writing music of banal or hollow substance that taxed one's attention with needless notes. Orchestral brilliance and the sensuous appeal of harmony inserted without regard for its musical function were not for him. Critical of himself, Paine commenced writing a major work with careful forethought, possibly troubled by the obligation he felt to approximate the accomplishments of the greatest composers and aware of the watchful eyes of severe judges like John Sullivan Dwight. He wished to invent themes that allowed lengthy development and at the same time retained melodic attractiveness.[6] He worked slowly. His total output is not extensive. John Lathrop Mathews visited Paine in 1896 and saw him at the piano playing something "with a decidedly oriental flavor [*Azara*?]." Asked how he went about composing, Paine replied; "Why, I have an idea—and jot down a sketch of it. Then bit by bit it grows and gets plainer and I increase my sketch, until at last I have the thing complete. Then when I feel in the mood I sit down to it and write the full score."[7]

In his first-movement sonata forms, the melodic subjects are constantly elaborated in new interpretations of the basic material. The object is to keep the ideas fresh and attractive. Developments sound natural. Erudition is hidden. Tunefulness interchanges regularly with climactic utterances or energetic rhythms, thus providing requisite contrasts. Reprises restate the original themes without ambiguity. The slow movements resemble *ballades*, elegiac or nuanced with the tender yearning of a *romanza*. The dance movements avoid the rugged jocularity of the Beethoven *scherzos*, in favor of greater charm and light effervescence of spirit. Finales sum up the expressive argument for the entire work. They tend to be broader in sound and less intricate in detail than the initial movement.

Although he grew more flexible later, Paine at first felt little urge to explore the radical innovations of his era. He eschewed the concentrated and miniaturized expression found in Wolf's songs, the complex sound-world of Wagner's operas, and the ecstatic extravagance of Liszt's and Strauss's tone poems. Yet, it would be unfair to conclude that he rejected this music entirely. He incorporated into his own style what was congenial but never went after innovation for its own sake. The young Paine, it is true, did spurn Wagner's ideas and compositions. By the 1880s, however, he was changing his mind. In a letter to Finck, dated 31 January 1882, he writes: "I want to take this opportunity to say that my opinions regarding Wagner and his theories have been modified since you were in College [class of 1876]. I consider him a great genius who has had a wonderful influence on the present day." In another letter to Finck, dated 25 March 1900 and written while Paine was working on the opera, *Azara*, he wrote: "You will find that I have entered upon a new path in all respects—in form, thematic treatment, instrumentation, etc. All dramatic composers must learn from Wagner, yet I have not consciously imitated him in style, etc." A month later: "I have followed throughout the connected orchestral rhythmical flow, and truth of dramatic expression characteristic of Wagner."[8]

Paine's style is given to large statements, solidly built and realizing their effect cumulatively over an entire section of a movement. He capably accomplished the creative tasks he set for himself. He can favor Beethoven, Mendelssohn, and Schumann in his earlier works, Brahms and Wagner in the later ones. His utterances are Augustan, like those in Beethoven symphonies, making them stirring and authoritative documents. Yet, he is no mere follower. An auditor conversant with his music is persuaded that individuality shows through, an expressive style of his own, representative of an artist solid in his convictions.[9]

A nationalistic stance did not attract him. He said of composers: "They are great because they are *individual*, not because they are local or patriotic. . . . It is barely possible that we may at some time have a representative American school. But I doubt it very much. The time for such a thing is past. We have now not national, but international music, and it makes no difference whether I compose here or in St. Petersburg, so long as I express myself in my own way."[10] The distinction as he saw it was not between the music proper to America and that proper to Europe. Rather it was between the appropriate abode of the serious artist, the milieu of cultivated music, and that of the more prosaic popular music meant only for entertainment.

In Paine's works, phrases are smooth, melodies stand out, and counter-melodies sound unforced. Rhythms are sturdy, tonal areas well differentiated, passing modulations frequent, harmonic motion logical, orchestrations germane, climaxes compelling, and structures unified. The vivid harmonic hues of Romanticism may combine with the contrapuntal techniques of the Baroque. Paine's best works, writes Richard Aldrich, "show fertility, a genuine warmth and spontaneity of invention, and a fine harmonic feeling, as well as a sure touch in instrumentation."[11]

When Paine became forty-three years of age, commentators were already dividing his output into three periods. In 1882 Elson mentioned a first period (the time of Paine's Mass in D), when Paine's works were romantic and genial, which revealed Paine's true nature. Elson also spoke of a second period, coincident with the *St. Peter* oratorio, when Paine's compositions sounded drier and more constrained. Perhaps, Elson surmised, Paine felt the dignity of his learning and labored under it. Lastly, Elson said, came the third period, centered on the *Spring* Symphony and the music to *Oedipus Tyrannus*. The virtues of the earlier periods were now integrated. Learnedness remained, but it served the composer. Paine's reputation had grown: "As many as thirty performances of his works have taken place this season," Elson stated.[12] The opera *Azara* was in the future at the time of Elson's comment.

RECITAL AND CHAMBER MUSIC

Paine composed few songs. Perhaps he could not generate a sustained interest in an idiom of small compass, which focused on intensely personal feelings that a text made explicit. In 1879 the publisher Oliver Ditson issued four songs as opus 29: "Matin Song" (B. Taylor), "I Wore Your Roses Yesterday" (C. Thaxter), "Early Springtime" (T. Hill), and "Moonlight" (J. von Eichendorff). In 1885 the publisher Arthur P. Schmidt announced four more songs as having come out, opus 40: "A Bird upon a Rosy Bough" (C. Thaxter), "A Farewell" (C. Kingsley), "Beneath the Starry Arch" (H. Martineau), and "Music When Soft Voices Die" (P. Shelley). Interestingly, the title pages of the first three songs of opus 40, while they list all four of the songs, give the prices of only the first three. The last song, to Shelley's poem, has not been found and was possibly never issued. Three more songs exist in manuscript. In general, these compositions are eloquent, sensitive to the accentuations of the English language, apt for the voice, and supported by a pertinent but unassuming piano accompaniment. No great technical proficiency is demanded from the vocalist and pianist. Most of them are brief. "A Farewell," one of the briefest, is nineteen measures in length. The music usually has a serenade-like quality to it. The melodies are delightful. Paine shuns deep psychological probings and intensely impassioned disclosures.

"Matin Song" was widely popular. It was first sung in public, in January 1877, by the English singer Clara Doria (later Rogers). During Paine's lifetime it often figured in recital programs. William Treat Upton, who praises its spontaneity and charm, finds the music remarkable because twelve of the measures have different rhythms, yet all sound natural.[13] A strophic composition, the vocal line comprises two phrases, the first eight measures, the second nine measures long, the piano adding a two-measure postlude. The tune unfolds with a gentle waltz-like lilt, over a simple, chordal quarter-note accompaniment. No modulations take place save for a fleeting one before a half-cadence. Though unpretentious, it shows skill and proficiency.

Paine's contemporaries also praised "I Wore Your Roses Yesterday," "Moonlight," and "A Bird upon a Rosy Bough." One song, "Early Springtime," excited surprise because it was uncharacteristic of Paine's usual manner of writing. "Most curiously original" is how Rupert Hughes described it at the turn of the century.[14] Here Paine chose to set a serious prose text by the Reverend Thomas Hill. Twice the music goes from the key of C-sharp minor to E major, and the solo-piano conclusion ends on the dominant of C-sharp minor. The listener will find the work dignified and may find its quality inconsistent.

In Berlin, Paine had studied the organ with the outstanding organist Karl Haupt. Returning to America, he became organist at Boston's Old West Church and gave recitals that featured Bach's and sometimes his own music. Paine's own organ compositions are secondary, mostly early works: preludes, fugues, fantasies, and concert variations. Many are based on a familiar melody, such as his variations on "Old Hundred," on "The Austrian Hymn," and on "The Star-Spangled Banner," and the fantasy on "Ein Feste Burg." An expert on American organs and organ literature, Barbara Owen states that American composers developed their own unique idiomatic style of organ music owing to relatively small halls with less reverberation and drier acoustics than those of Europe, the modest instruments usually at their disposal, and the sorts of occasions requiring organ music. Organ pieces formed a part of recitals, to be sure, but were also heard in American homes, a number of which contained organs. Organ compositions were also utilized as preludes, interludes, and postludes in the Protestant church service. Owen finds Paine's organ preludes to be attractive.[15]

As attractive and workmanlike as they can be, Paine's organ compositions rarely venture beyond the conventional. Procedures beholden to Baroque practices are maintained from work to work within a genre. To give one instance, in Concert Variations upon "Old Hundred" (1861), [16] Paine begins by introducing the tune *maestoso*, as a plain chorale. Variations 1, 2, and 3 use the melody as a *cantus firmus*, first in the highest, then in the lowest, and last in a middle voice, each time against three lines of figural counterpoint à la Bach. The most interesting variation, number 4, proceeds with measured dignity as the melody itself is expressively altered. The piece concludes with a four-part fugue, then a restatement of the chorale against running sixteenth-note passages in the bass. Paine's organ pieces are pleasant but not very memorable.

Paine was, of course, also a pianist. Yet, he did not write extensively for the piano. A couple of the works, among the few he composed, are impressive; most are enjoyable; all are minor efforts. After the early eighties, his interest in creating them flagged. One significant difference between them and the organ works is that their style is entirely of the Romantic period. If a mentor must be found, then he is Schumann, not Bach. By around 1860, Paine, still a student, had written two piano sonatas, one of them now lost. Then, in the mid-sixties, he issued *A Funeral March in Memory of President Lincoln.*[17] The piece is in a safe style, properly melancholic but similar to many such marches inspired by the *Marcia Funebre sulla Morte d'un Eroe* of Beethoven's opus 26 piano sonata. The A A B A structure is that of many American popular songs. Nevertheless, the music has nothing "American" about it. A better work is his opus 11 of 1868, *Vier Character-Stücke für Piano-forte*. A writer who heard them in 1872 praised their "genuine . . . at times almost startling originality." He also found them rather unpianistic.[18]

With the *Romance*, opus 12 (1869), Paine extends his harmonic vocabulary and speaks with some boldness.[19] The form is ternary. It opens on a VI^6 and quickly makes transient modulations to III and II. As it unfolds, it never firmly establishes a tonality until the last four measures of the first section. Rhythms change every one or two measures. A wide keyboard range is used, from EE-flat to g'''. Despite the markings of *dolce* and *cantando*, febrile tautness prevails throughout the first section and belies the term *Romance*. Slightly disjointed, the music leaves the impression that Paine is still probing for an appropriate pianistic style. If anyone's manner of writing comes to mind, it would be Schumann's. Yet, the opening phrase of section B does suggest that of the slow movement in Paine's First Symphony, and its contours will recur in other of Paine's compositions.[20]

Four Characteristic Pieces, opus 25, appeared in 1876: a "Dance," "Romance," "Impromptu," and "Rondo Giocoso."[21] They reveal an increasingly romantic disposition and imagination and emotions from tender to fervent. In every way the numbers are fully realized creations, certainly more assured than opus 11. The opening of the "Dance" (3/4 time) again resembles that of the slow movement of the First Symphony, whose premiere occurred early in 1876. A fondness for phrases of various length, often on the odd-numbered side, forecasts Paine's mature style. The second number is filled with appropriately songlike melody. Transient modulations take place, but they are securely under control. The expression is delicate, personal, and contemplative; only in the middle does the strength of feeling grow, and there only slightly. No great drama or passion intrudes. The "Impromptu" is in the vein of Schumann's Novelettes, opus 21. It swings with an easy motion that charms the ear. The "Rondo Giocoso," an affable piece, bears an 1893 copyright and the label "new edition." These are fine pieces, well above the ordinary and worth hearing today.

In the Country, opus 26, consists of "ten sketches for the piano."[22] Each piece bears an evocative title: "Woodnotes," "Wayside Flowers," "Under the Lindens," "The Shepherd's Lament," "Village Dance," "Rainy Day," "The Mill," "Gipsies," "Farewell," "Welcome Home." The woodnotes have fittingly birdlike trills in the melody; the flowers show Mendelssohnian delicacy; the lindens are depicted in descending arpeggiations and syncopated melody; the lament sorrows in A minor and through diminished-seventh chords and biting cross-relations; the dance has a sprightly skip to it;[23] the rainy day elicits a mood of fleeting sadness (its music resembles Schumann's "Albumblatt No. 2" from his *Bunte Blätter*, opus 99); the mill has a millrace whose running water is translated into sixteenth-note figures in the left hand. Paine does not attempt to introduce anything "gypsy" into "Gipsies," except perhaps for the conspicuous melodic augmented second in measure 25. The ninth number, the farewell, is touching, and the welcome joyous. All ten pieces satisfy. They dwell in a make-believe world, without strong feeling or outbursts of elation. Each piece explores one atmospheric mood, captured in a germane melodic-rhythmic motive that dominates the entire work. In each, Paine knows exactly where he is going and how to get there.

Romance, opus 39 (1883), departs from the one figure–one mood approach of opus 26 and is so decidedly eloquent that it brings Liszt to mind.[24] The piece conveys mounting emotion, from the deceptively quiet opening theme to its impassioned and transformed recapitulation. *Ro-*

mance is one of Paine's most praiseworthy compositions for piano. Trifles in comparison are the *Three Piano Pieces*, opus 41 (1884), consisting of *A Spring Idyl*, *Birthday Impromptu*, and *Fuga Giocosa*. The last is based on the tune of an old baseball song, "Over the Fence Is Out, Boys."[25] Although it is prefaced with the indication *allegro scherzando* and is a witty piece, no abandoned hilarity appears, owing in part to the control necessitated by the fugul structure. Paine throws off his usual restraints but will not play the clown.

A *Nocturne*, appearing as opus 45 in 1889, completes the works for piano. There is nothing of Chopin about it. Paine may have written it before the opus 39 *Romance*, a claim made by John Schmidt and W.S.B. Mathews.[26] Elson reviewed it in the *Boston Musical Herald* and found it a little more difficult than John Field's nocturnes and not too sentimental. He calls it healthy music, free from the morbidity found "in many of the nocturnes today, yet affording opportunity enough to the musician to display sentiment and refined shading."[27]

Chamber music by Paine is sparse indeed. An early String Quartet in D major (1855), a Piano Trio in D minor (1874), a Violin Sonata in B minor (1875, revised 1905), a Romanza and Humoreske for cello and piano (1875), and a Larghetto and Scherzo for violin, cello, and piano (1877) lists all of it. None of these compositions saw publication in Paine's day. In all probability, most of the performances they received were during musicales in private homes, such as the one at Fiske's home in 1874, when an audience of about a hundred men and women heard the trio.[28] Newspapers and periodicals of these years would not normally have reviewed such performances, and our information about them is scanty. The quartet, a student work from his Portland days, discloses the novice learning how to handle sonata, dance, variation, and fugal forms. The trio shows him confidently directing his material, albeit melody, harmony, and rhythm remain relatively unadventurous. Nevertheless, the work manages to project conflict and ardor in the first movement, unadorned and elegiac lyricism in the second movement, and rather bumptious and occasionally urgent rhythms in the finale. The music has force and conviction, and it deserves performance.

In the next three works, Paine reveals a substantial flair for lyricism. Communication is direct. Motives are open-ended and lend themselves to a lengthy working-out. Contrasts are skillfully managed; seams in the structure are nicely concealed. Expression runs from calm to passionate. The music sounds inventive, individual, and captivating. He is undoubtedly a romantic composer, although with some classical leanings. The

Sonata for Violin and Piano in B minor was composed in 1875 and dedicated to Paine's friend Celia Thaxter. After several public performances through 1887, it remained unmentioned in newspapers and magazines until Paine revised it in 1905 and his new version was performed in March 1906, just before his death. When the earlier version was performed in May 1876, the audience proved enthusiastic, and the reviewer for a Boston newspaper found the first movement to be spirited and abundant in melody and the second movement's canonical *larghetto* to have "a grave and tranquil beauty." The finale, an *allegro vivace*, was excitingly fierce and dramatic, qualities "which also characterized the [first] symphony of Mr. Paine."[29] The New York critic H. E. Krehbiel, hearing it in November 1887, praised the beautiful writing but wished that the slow movement's principle theme had more warmth.[30]

The reworking of the sonata produced a more daring composition having subtler textures, increased chromaticism and dissonance, less orthodox harmonic progressions, and greater intricacy in chord construction, including the use of nondominant sevenths and altered chords. John Schmidt, to whom we are indebted for a fine study of Paine's life and works, states that the second movement, except for transposition from the key of D to E-flat, remained basically the same as before. The outer movements, both in sonata form, were altered a great deal. Their first themes are dramatic and aggressive; the well-contrasted secondary themes are lyrical or passionate in the first movement and scherzo-like in the third.[31] A polished piece of musical craftsmanship, yet also a vehicle for vital expression, the sonata's merits are similar to those of a chamber work by Brahms. Paine's thorough Germanic education does show through; however, the music is estimable by virtue of its own artistic qualifications.

Both the Romanza and Humoreske for cello and piano (1875) and the Larghetto and Scherzo for violin, cello, and piano (1877) deserve similar praise and can reward the open-minded listener.

CHORAL WORKS

Paine composed three choral works in the early sixties, two of them for Harvard: the simple but effective *Commencement Hymn* in C major (1862), to a Latin text by James Bradstreet Greenough; and *Domine salvum fac Praesidem nostrum* in D major, opus 8, for men's voices and orchestra, written for the inauguration of Thomas Hill as president of Harvard in 1863. The *Domine salvum* is a completely homophonic work, hymnlike and suited to its purpose. The third work, *Radway's Ready Relief* for bass solo and men's chorus (1863), is atypical for Paine. In this comical trifle written for friends, Paine inserts parodies on composers' styles, among them Handel and Beethoven, and calls for absurd flourishes in the last five measures. The text derives from a newspaper advertisement extolling the virtues of a patent medicine. After the piece had been heard only on private occasions for twenty years, the Apollo Club, under Lang, presented it to the general public in 1883. The reviewer for the *Advertiser* (26 April 1883) found it an ingenious and genuinely humorous seriocomic work, with "nearly all the chief forms of the most sedate composers . . . used in turn with droll effect." The soloist's "series of roulades is very comical." More comical is "the steady melodic sweetness and dynamic softness that characterizes the music which directly follows," sung to the words "The continued use of Radway's Ready Relief cured him." The closing phrases abound in runs and roulades and are sometimes fugal, sometimes canonic, but always to humorous effect. Comic heights are reached "with the help of some unexpected notes from the piccolo." A writer in the *Courier* (26 April 1883) explains that the work was held back from the public "for fear that it might be misunderstood or misemployed." Most of the public enjoyed the musical joke. On the other hand, one listener, after a performance by the Mendelssohn Club, said the singers "blotted" an otherwise fine program "with the words of Mr. J. K. Paine's song," which is "trash."[32] This hostile commentary underlines the sort of reception that Paine had anticipated and that might have deterred him from writing other compositions of a light nature.

None of the three compositions prepared the public for the Mass in D major, opus 10, for soloists, chorus, and orchestra that he may have begun at age twenty and did complete at age twenty-six (1865), an amazing accomplishment for a Protestant living in an outpost of Western art-music culture and lacking the help of American precedents. Like the solitary Mount Khatadan that looms high above the surrounding lowlands in his native state of Maine, Paine's Mass surpasses anything heretofore composed by an American. For guidance he looked to the choral works of Handel, Mozart, and Beethoven. However, the Mass is no imitation. It abounds in original details, achieving stirring expressive heights, and can convince the listener that the total statement is Paine's own. This major effort should be recognized as a notable contribution to Western musical culture. A presentation of three movements with organ accompaniment took place at Harvard in June 1866, before an enraptured audience. The tenor soloist had to repeat the "Quoniam"; the serenity of the "Dona nobis pacem" gladdened listeners. The first complete performance, conducted by the composer, made his reputation. It took place in Berlin, on 16 February 1867, before a large audience that included the royal family. Paine won praise for his taste, technical command, and musical sincerity. Not least important, the concert identified him in Europe and America as a composer of consequence. A critic or two faulted him for disunity in some passages, vocal music occasionally difficult to sing, not enough individual characterization in a few sections, and a need for more "poetic originality." Acclaimed were the "Dona nobis pacem" and the "Crucifixus."[33] When Paine returned to America, several well-known Bostonians tried to have the local Handel and Haydn Society perform the work in an April 1868 concert. Ominous for the future of native art music, the effort failed.

The Mass in D is in eighteen segments and requires an orchestra with woodwinds, horns, and trumpets by twos, three trombones, organ, timpani, and strings. This early work confirms several attributes of Paine's style. Tonalities are unambiguous. Long pedal points occur. Shifting accents and phrases varying in length, which break up the regular four- and eight-measure patterns, are common. Sonorities are carefully adjusted. Orchestration sounds full and knowledgeably handled. Ideas flow smoothly from one to another. Cadences are variously treated, with the perfect cadence often avoided. Concern for minutiae, contrast, and textural variety remains always to the fore. Accompaniments are carefully thought out and invariably help bring out the expression in the melody.

One nervous motive in the orchestra dominates the "Kyrie" throughout (Example 4.1).[34] Its repetition as a ground bass is typical of Paine's style. The "Kyrie" is a deeply felt supplication coming from less than assured penitents. The spirited "Gloria" is mostly loud and outgoing and nicely contrasts the entreaties of the "Kyrie." Temporary displacements of meter, changing accentuations, rapid upward-surging scales, and choral parts in lockstep rhythm drive home the message. The "Qui tollis," for alto solo and chorus, is a touchingly lovely *adagio* that achieves a poignant climax just before the recapitulation of the opening material. An affirmative "Quoniam" follows. Next the "Cum sancto spiritu" serves as a prelude to the exciting four-voice fugue on "In gloria Dei Patris." Here the Mass's first part ends.

The second part opens with a straightforward and resolute "Credo." Then begins one of the most moving sections of the Mass, an "Et incarnatus" for soprano solo and a "Crucifixus" sung as a slow fugue by a sorrowing chorus. A passage in the "Et incarnatus," measures 55 to 62 (Example 4.2), shows a typical evasion of a perfect cadence, here by an unexpected modulation into the key of the submediant. This brief soprano aria is almost operatic in its candid expression of personal sorrow. Also to be noted is the fugal subject on the words "Crucifixus etiam pro nobis," sung by the chorus. An augmented second between the second and third notes and a dissonance on the seventh note magnify the feeling of bottomless grief (Example 4.3). Afterwards, a jubilant "Et ressurexit" dispels the gloom.

Each segment that follows demonstrates the composer's skills and gifts. The conductor Gunther Schuller, who recorded the Mass in D on New World NW 262/663, finds the finest portions of the work in the closing "Benedictus," for quartet and chorus; the "Agnus Dei," for soprano-alto duet and chorus; and the "Dona nobis," for chorus. He speaks of Paine's supreme melodic flair, the syncopated and throbbing rhythms, the wealth of inspiration and of fresh ideas and harmonies. The emotional culmination to the entire Mass begins with the "Benedictus," which, Schuller says, at times resembles the music of Gustav Mahler. In particular, he points to the alternating 7/8 and 6/8 measures as startling and unheard of for the time. The "Agnus Dei" encompasses a world of drama, pain, and anguish. And the conclusion on the "Dona nobis" alleviates the grief and consoles the distressed.[35]

The oratorio *St. Peter* was Paine's next large choral work. He himself compiled the text from the Bible. He also used the melodies of three Lutheran chorales, after the examples of Bach and Mendelssohn. Indeed, works like Bach's *St. Matthew Passion* and Mendelssohn's *St. Paul* provided guidelines for many sections of the work. The assured handling of the chorus from complex fugal writing to plainly harmonized chorales owes much to these archetypes. However, instead of the traditional bass voice, the tenor voice is assigned the part of Jesus. Paine made this novel choice undoubtedly because he had chosen the bass voice as that of St. Peter. Moreover, Paine's expressiveness is less weighty and learned than Bach's and more gritty and robust than Mendelssohn's. His harmonic paraphernalia stem from his own time: the striking diminished-seventh chords, sudden modulations, eloquent tone painting via ambiguous augmented sixths and nondominant sevenths, suspense through deceptive cadences and dashes into distant keys, and so forth. Paine's individuality often comes through in the unexpected ways he handles his musical passages, ways that have few precedents in the styles of other composers.

The oratorio's piano score was published by Ditson in 1872, and the premier took place in Paine's birthplace, Portland, Maine, in 1873. The next year, the Handel and Haydn Society produced it in Boston. After seeing the Ditson score, a critic writing in the *Nation* (13 February 1873) found *St. Peter* dull and lacking in emotion and melodiousness. Paine's friend John Fiske rebutted in the *Atlantic Monthly* of April 1873, saying the critic had studied only the piano score and had a silly idea that an oratorio should amuse. On the contrary, Fiske wrote, Paine deserved praise for melodies more religious than sensuous and for music that goes beyond pleasing the average listener. "An artist does not work for years putting his whole heart, soul, and being into his work, merely to furnish people with an aesthetico-intellectual anodyne,—to give them music which they can passively enjoy without the exertion of thinking." Fiske lauds the music's lack of sentimentality.[36]

After the Portland performance, Fiske again appeared in the *Atlantic Monthly* (August 1873), commending the Portland chorus for singing better than Boston's Handel and Haydn Society and criticizing the inadequacy of the orchestra. He asserted that the high standards maintained throughout the work merited comparison with the oratorios of Handel and Mendelssohn. Note, however, how he qualifies this claim: "Concerning the rank likely to be assigned by posterity to St. Peter, it would be foolish now to speculate; and it would be unwise to bring it into direct comparison with masterpieces like the Messiah, Elijah, and St. Paul, the greatness of which has been so long acknowledged. Longer familiarity with the work is needed before such comparisons, always of somewhat doubtful value, can be profitably undertaken." The advice is wise and refreshing, especially from such a strong partisan of Paine.[37] The "longer familiarity" through future performances, unfortunately, was limited; the work was performed only once more, by the Handel and Haydn Society of Boston, in May 1874. Then, at long last, *St. Peter* was revived in a performance at Harvard's Sanders Theater, on 21 May 1989, with the Back Bay Chorale and the Pro Arte Orchestra under Gunther Schuller. To hear an actual performance allowed a better assessment of the work as a whole, since examining the score alone tends to stress the importance of individual segments without relating them to the effect on the ear of the entire composition. To this listener it came through as an outstanding contribution to oratorio literature, eminently listenable, especially in the First Part.

Paine divides the work into two parts: the first in nineteen numbers; the second in twenty. The oratorio's first section, entitled "The Divine Call," begins with an impressive orchestral introduction, which leads directly into the stately and affirmative first chorus, "The time is fulfilled." One hears effective calls to repentance and admonitions to receive God's glad tidings. Jesus tersely tells Simon and Andrew to follow him (no. 2). This in turn leads to a fine *de capo* air for soprano, "The spirit of the Lord is upon me" (no. 3). No 4, "We go before the face of the Lord," has a nice coloristic touch as twelve tenors and basses take the parts of the twelve disciples. Next comes the simply harmonized chorale "How lovely shines the morning star." In this fashion Paine proceeds from number to number, providing musical and expressive variety to sustain the listener's interest.

The next two large sections of the First Part involve Christ's life and message up to his betrayal by Judas, followed by Peter's denial of Jesus and subsequent repentance. These are also the most dramatic and fascinating segments of the oratorio. Especially thrilling is Peter's bold answer to Jesus' question "But who say ye that I am?" (no. 6). Peter answers with an emphatic octave leap downward from c′-sharp to c-sharp, then an upward skip from c′-sharp to e′ on "Thou art the Christ"; trombones add grandeur and solemnity to the affirmation. The most beautiful music in the oratorio comes after Peter's denial and the crowing of the cock, in the six numbers (14 through 19) that terminate the First Part. No 14 is an instrumental B-flat minor "Lament," in part cast as a dramatic recitative, in part a sorrowing arioso (Example 4.4). The lamentation becomes vocal when Peter sings the air (no. 16) "O God, my God, forsake me not!" also in B-flat minor (Example 4.5). Unexpected yet marvelous is no. 17, "Remember from whence thou are fallen," where the minor key gives way to B-flat major. Here a few women's voices, singing *a capella* and in chordal style, represent an angelic chorus. A harp plays fleeting arpeggiated interludes during the pauses (Example 4.6). The ensuing section for full chorus, "And he that overcometh shall receive a crown of life," provides a polyphonic contrast and underscores the divine promise. The pledge receives further clarification in the contralto air "The Lord is faithful and righteous to forgive our sins." A magnificent choral number, "Awake, thou that sleepest," is a fitting culmination to the fascinating First Part.

The Second Part, "The Ascension" and "Pentecost," is filled with contemplative music. The drama has vanished. Contrasts are fewer. Erudition sometimes supplants imagination. Consequently, the listener's attention may wander. Its effect is that of an overly prolonged Protestant church service. Yet, Fiske considered the Second Part the true climax of the oratorio. The opening chorus, "The son of man was delivered," he found deeply pathetic; he liked the inwardness and meditative qualities in the quartet "Feed the flock of God." He praised the Second Part's lyric emotion and intense spiritual exaltation.[38]

After the 1874 performance by the Handel and Haydn Society, a reviewer in *Dwight's Journal of Music* found the work earnest but stiff. Yet, he said, dramatic truth and power did exist. Some choruses were original, noble, and beautiful; he cited the excellence of three numbers from the First Part: no. 11, "Sanctify us"; no. 13, "We hid our faces from him"; and no. 19, "Awake thou that sleepest."[39] Writing at the turn of the century, Rupert Hughes was of two minds about the oratorio. He commended its power and dramatic strength, praising Peter's air "O God, my God, forsake me not!" He complained about the work's musical floridity and repetitions but praised Paine's "erudition and largeness," like "Händel at his best."[40] Other critics found *St. Peter* to be competently written, praiseworthy for sections of great depth and loveliness, showing fine contrapuntal talents, but nevertheless exhibiting more "ingenuity than inspiration."[41]

One more choral work from the seventies deserves mention, *The Centennial Hymn*, a strophic, usually one-note-a-syllable setting of a Whittier text, which Thomas commissioned for the opening of the Centennial Exposition at Philadelphia, in May 1876. However simple it seems, the direction of the *Hymn*'s melodic lines and harmonies reveals the hand of an able composer. Its serene, leisurely paced music ranks the *Hymn* high among occasional pieces of this type. Without question, it is superior to Wagner's *American Centennial March*, also composed for the exposition. A writer in the *Atlantic* states that he considered it foremost "among the many modern attempts at *original* compositions in this style. . . . The opportunity seems to us hardly to have given room for anything great. An opening hymn for the Centennial Exposition was required . . . and he has given us one such as we are persuaded few other men in the country could write."[42]

ORCHESTRAL MUSIC OF THE SEVENTIES

After completing *St. Peter*, Paine seems to have become concerned with his manner of musical expression. Youthful vitality had characterized his Mass. Yet, immediately after its premiere he may have felt an increased need for self-discipline. The expectations of music lovers had soared, and he felt the onerous responsibilitly of proving them justified. An element of circumspection infiltrated Paine's creative process and dampened his vitality. *St. Peter* was the result, a distinguished work but more constrained than the Mass. Auditors had not given it the unalloyed praise he had hoped for. From 1872 through 1875, he again labored to produce a work that would satisfy his enormous demands on himself and merit the acclaim of cultivated listeners. The result was the Symphony No. 1 in C minor, opus 23, whose premiere on 26 January 1876 was given by Thomas and his orchestera. Later Thomas conducted it in New York and Philadelphia.

Music lovers' expectations were completely met. The applause was vehement at the close of each movement. A report in the *Atlantic* went: "Whatever anxiety or lack of entire faith anyone may have felt beforehand must have been removed by the very first phrase, which with its rushing bass and powerful stroke of chords . . . proclaims at once the technical skill and boldness of design that belong only to masters of symphonic writing." The audiences also acclaimed the work's impeccably urbane *scherzo*, its transcendent *adagio*, and solemn *finale*.[43]

According to a statement in the *Saturday Evening Gazette* of 29 January 1876, the symphony was judged a great work, full of strength, vigor, refinement, and resourcefulness in its harmonic and orchestral effect. Paine surprised everyone with his symphony's "fluency of idea, freedom from dryness, apparent spontaneous flow of thought, and the graceful flexibility of style." A comment on the *Adagio* movement is surprising, because it refers to Paine, who supposedly hated Wagner: "It flows calmly and sweetly after the manner of those continuous melodies with which Wagner has made us so familiar and it has much of the rich sensuousness that marks that composer in his more placid moods."[44]

That the symphony overcame the compositional impediments evident in the oratorio was the conclusion of several writers. They found counterpoint more innovative, thematic procedures authoritative yet more exciting, and compositional techniques more flexibly applied. Where the oratorio occasionally contained awkward orchestrations, the symphony showed instruments handled with assurance. Paine had succeeded in sounding original with no hint of laboring to make an impact.[45] George Chadwick, in 1908, said the symphony gained Paine real recognition "as a romantic composer of high ideals and genuine imagination." It "at once attracted attention by its interesting melodic material, its masterly use of symphonic form and its sonorous orchestration." He testifies that this work (and later Paine's Second Symphony), far more than any previously written native symphonic works, motivated other composers to add to native symphonic literature. Chadwick then caustically asserts that the "simple and benighted music lovers of those days had not been taught by blasé critics that the sonata form was a worn-out fetich, that noble and simple melody was a relic of the dark ages, and that unresolved dissonance was the chief merit of a musical composition."[46]

Chadwick was alluding to the cultural politics being played out in the first part of the twentieth century, as composers of the Boulanger-Stravinsky persuasion damned those who developed their styles out of a Germanic matrix. The conductor Karl Kreuger noted, in 1973, that Paine was labeled "the pedant incarnate" and he and others of the New England group were downgraded so much that histories of American music only grudgingly mentioned them and performers denied their compositions a hearing. Yet, Kreuger discovered, when he programmed Paine's First Symphony for national broadcast, that "listeners' response was extraordinary indeed, alternating between astonishment that a native American could compose such a symphony and pride in his having done so."[47]

The symphony calls for woodwinds, trumpets, and timpani by twos, plus four French horns, three tenor trombones and bass trombone, and a large complement of strings. It commences *allegro con brio* on a powerful, dramatic, elemental idea, the main motive of a movement in sonata form. Music is stripped to essentials: a thunderous tonic chord in full orchestra, followed by a unison rush of eighth notes in the lower strings, and an upward spring of the first violins into another tonic chord in the full orchestra (Example 4.7).[48] Momentum builds, sweeping the listener along. In contrast, the subordinate theme in the relative major key is a gracefully lilting tune in the first violins (Example 4.8), though it is not without tinges of sadness. An amazing clarity of texture prevails throughout the movement, even when the force of the entire orchestra is brought to bear. The model that comes to mind for this movement is Beethoven's Fifth Symphony. Regardless, the model is not closely followed. Everything is transmuted through Paine's sensibility into an individualized assertion of his own perceptions.[49] One also hears rather Brahmsian passages; yet it must be remembered that Brahms's First Symphony was still in the offing.

The fast C-major second movement, in 3/4 time and ternary form, stands the place of a *scherzo*. Its affable jog-along opening theme and the flute solo that enters thirteen measures after letter A have a kinship to works of Schumann and Dvořák. The poetic French horn–clarinet linkup with the Trio demonstrates Paine's newfound understanding of orchestral colorations.

The *Adagio* in A-flat major is to be played *molto cantando e espressivo*. Certainly it is one of the loveliest and most moving movements that Paine had composed up to this time, and it constitutes the emotional peak of the symphony. Melodies are sensitively orchestrated and harmonized. Accompanying ancillary melodies add interest and enhance the expressiveness of the whole. A writer in *Dwight's Journal of Music* extols the entire symphony and particularly this movement for sounding "entirely free from common-place thought or expression" and praises its "fine shades of tone, corresponding, indeed, to the delicate tints of an expert painter, and producing in the mind a similar pleasure."[50] This we can hear in the elegiac opening in the violins and cellos (Example 4.9).

The Finale in C major has a vigorous, and at times festive, and at times regal quality. It forms a fitting end to the symphony and can leave today's auditors convinced they have heard a major musical pronouncement from a composer to be reckoned with.

In November 1876 Thomas presented another new work by Paine, the Overture to Shakespeare's *As You Like It*, opus 28, in F major. As they had done with the symphony, music lovers acclaimed it as a valuable contribution to musical literature. The reviewer in *Dwight's Journal of Music* found it beautiful and genial. Although the play dictated the musical moods, he said, it was not necessary to trace the play in the music, "because the composition could be taken as music alone—rich, varied, consistent, and symmetrically laid out. Some might sense the shady forests of Ardennes and the serious love plot in the expressive *andante* introduction. The *allegro vivace* that followed was full of hunting strains and other sounds of the woods. Gaiety prevailed, but with a touch of the 'winter wind' and of 'man's ingratitude.' "[51]

The pastoral clarinet solo that commences the introduction does in fact sound most romantic when heard against the warm harmonies of the strings and the second horn. Eloquence marks the tune's continuation in the high violins. The main body of the work fills out the expected sonata structure, although the subordinate theme is placed in the key of the mediant major, rather than the expected dominant. At the conclusion, one feels one has heard a cheerful, optimistic work filled with winsome themes and splendidly crafted in all of its sections. The overture is not closely identifiable with the play, yet it is worth hearing for its own sake without worrying about a program.

In the fall of 1877, Thomas presented Paine's first venture into the Lisztian camp, the symphonic poem *Shakespeare's Tempest*, opus 31, in four connected parts: Part 1, *allegro furioso*, depicts the storm; Part 2, *adagio tranquillo*, the calm and happy scene before Prospero's cell and the appearance of Ariel; Part 3, *allegro moderato e maestoso*, Prospero's tale; and Part 4, *allegro moderato e maestoso*, the happy love of Ferdinand and Miranda, an episode with Caliban and Ariel, and the triumph of Prospero's "potent art." The reviewer in the *New York Tribune* found the work original as a creation and authoritative in workmanship. Dwight, a conservative with no fondness for the Liszt-Wagner approach to music, complained about the exaggerated praise given it in the newspapers and wondered about the worth of the realistic allusions: "Then, among passages of grave or tender beauty, where indeed we could think of Prospero and of Miranda, there were salient phrases like Wagner's *Leit-motive*, to say this is Ariel, Trinculo, Caliban, etc. Ariel's motive we confess we thought not worthy of so delicate a sprite. It was a pert little fillip on the piccolo, and by most was recognized as Ariel." He wished Paine had written an overture instead.[52] Fiske hastened to defend it, saying that the work showed freedom and originality but also orderly thematic treatment and lucid structures, which negated Dwight's reservations.[53]

Paine revised the score, and the revision was played several times. An 1885 performance was reviewed in the *Boston Transcript*: "We were heartily glad to hear Mr. Paine's 'Tempest' again. . . . Not because it is American music—that consideration, *per se*, leaves us quite cold—but because it is American music thoroughly worth hearing at a symphony concert." The reviewer noted with approval its engaging ideas, poetic fancy, and lack of triteness.[54]

The *Tempest* exists today only in its published, revised version.[55] It reveals the composer bent on exploring the possibilities of the new music of his day, especially the painting through tone promoted by Liszt and Wagner. Classicism is unequivocally in abeyance. The storm music of the beginning is sheer tonal depiction of a kind that must surely have offended Dwight. Mood is important; thematic exposure and elaboration, nil. The melodies given to Prospero in Parts 2 and 3 and to the lovers in Part 4, and the harmonies that support them, have a new lushness and chromatic emotivity to them. The perky brightness of the flute that depicts Ariel, twittering away in trills and sixteenth and thirty-second notes, is an appropriate foil. Caliban's awkward prancing in the bassoon seems more picturesque than uncouth, and this is the effect that Paine wanted, since his artistry excluded the crude and the primitive. The *Tempest* is a splendid composition that should not remain neglected.

On 23 April 1878 Bostonians heard Paine's Duo Concertante in A, for violin, cello, and orchestra, performed by Thomas. The audience warmly applauded the three movements. *Dwight's Journal* described the piece as elaborately and richly scored and abounding in bravura passages for the soloists. The *Adagio* was particularly melodious and charming and made a beautiful transition into the Finale's *allegro*.[56] After its initial performance, the composition remained ignored and unpublished.

The Symphony No. 2 in A major, "In Spring," was preceded and possibly encouraged by the "Spring" symphonies of Schumann and Raff. Although there are one or two resemblances to Schumann's style (particularly in the slow movement), Paine's work maintains its own integrity. Two different orchestras performed it in March 1880, in Boston, at a stage in Paine's career when his prestige had achieved its pinnacle. His style had fully matured; his romantic drift was more obvious than it had been in his First Symphony. Orchestral combinations and coloristic harmonies were adroitly deployed for affective purposes. Aldrich portrays Bostonians as driven to enthusiastic frenzy during its initial hearing: women's handkerchiefs waving, men's yells of admiration, Dwight's umbrella wildly snapping open and shut.[57] After hearing both performances, Dwight described the symphony as a long, elaborate, thoughtful work whose outstanding qualities made a profound impression on "a great majority of listeners." It swarmed with ideas, all springing from a few leading motives. Its nobility earned it a place "among the works of the masters."[58]

After the first hearing, the reviewer in the *Transcript* lauded the great power and exalted artistic character of the work. After hearing it again almost a year later, the reviewer wrote that the symphony grew in public favor and sounded more and more imposing with each new performance. He heard fresh musical ideas, inspiration, and elevated emotion. Three years later, it was again presented, and the *Transcript* reviewer singled out Paine's "peculiar individuality" for comment, stating that "at every turning one meets with something unexpected and out of the common run." The *Courier* critic at first complained of the symphony's length (a little over fifty minutes) and of tantalizing bits of melody that disappeared too quickly, although he did like the "peculiarly attractive" Scherzo and the noble, sonorous Finale. Four years later the *Courier* writer had come to appreciate the work, saying that a work of "loftier conceptions, more masterly treatment, more effective orchestration, it is impossible to imagine." The learning that "ruled the composer in his *St. Peter*, is now ruled by him."[59] Chicagoans, in 1892, thought it "the most important orchestral composition that has been issued from the pen of any American composer."[60]

Arthur P. Schmidt, assisted by Paine's admirers, found subscribers to underwrite the publication of the full score in 1880, a first for a large orchestral work by an American.[61] In 1889 Alfred John Goodrich printed a poetic title for each movement of the symphony; they may have come to him from the composer. Movement 1 was titled "Departure of Winter; Awakening of Nature"; Movement 2, "May-night Fantasy"; Movement 3,

"Romance of Springtime"; and Movement 4, "The Glory of Nature."[62] Perhaps because a few critics suspected he had absorbed some dangerous revolutionary tendencies from Liszt and Wagner, Paine suppressed any detailed description of the scenes he may have had in mind.

The instrumentation in this work is the same as in the First Symphony, except for the elimination of the bass trombone. The first movement commences with an *adagio* introduction in A minor. A germinal motive that will figure throughout the entire work is announced in the cellos and violas.[63] Possibly it represents winter; but it also leaves the impression of a yearning for spring (Example 4.10). Nature awakens to an *allegro ma non troppo* in A major as the main theme is announced. The germinal motive recurs with the subordinate theme (in the key of the lowered submediant) and plays a leading part in the rest of the movement. The second movement is a Scherzo in D minor and 3/4 time. A brusque, dancy tune with a sudden, attention-grabbing fillip of two eighth notes and a quarter note makes the sound more impish than elfin. The slower Trio in 2/4 time, however, does seem like a woodsy "May-night fantasy," as woodwinds supply a bucolic melody that hints at the germinal motive.

Compelling eruptions of feeling occur in the *Adagio* in F major, freely laid out as a rondo. A "Romance of Springtime" it may be, but it sings like a committed lover ardently wooing his beloved. A richness of melody heard in the *Tempest* reappears here. The germinal motive activates many of the melodic lines. The horn countermelody against the main melody in the divided first violins, beginning at measure 23, is especially enchanting. Passion achieves Tchaikovskian intensity with the syncopated theme in F minor, heard in measures 48 to 60 (Example 4.11).

The Finale, an optimistic *allegro giocoso* cast in sonata form, begins with a balletic gesture related to the main theme of the Scherzo. Variants of the germinal motive weave in and out of the fabric, their message a cheery one. The second theme is a hymnic song of thanksgiving with affinities to the germinal motive. When the hymn returns at the end of the movement, its lofty stateliness forms a fitting close to the entire work.

Rupert Hughes sums up contemporary opinions: "Paine's symphony, though aiming to shape the molten gold of April fervor in the rigid mold of the symphonic form, has escaped every appearance of mechanism and restraint. It is program music of the most legitimate sort, in full accord with Beethoven's canon, '*Mehr Ausdruck der Empfindung als Malerei.*' It has no aim of imitating springtime noises, but seeks to stimulate by suggestion the hearer's creative imagination, and provoke by a musical telepathy the emotions that swayed the nympholept composer."[64]

PAINE'S FINAL WORKS

In May 1881 audiences at Harvard's Sanders Theater attended performances of Sophocles' *Oedipus Tyrannus*, given in Greek and enhanced with music by Paine: an orchestral prelude, six choruses for male voices, and a postlude. At the height of his powers, Paine had turned to the musical depiction of a tragic king, unwitting slayer of his father and husband of his mother, who brings affliction on his people and ultimately must face a horror of his own making. The composer relinquished all thought of replicating ancient Greek music, feeling that the attempt would fail because of ignorance of how this music had really sounded and the probable unsuitableness of any essay at archaic sounds. He did believe that, through his own style, he could stimulate the imagination and encourage a livelier sympathy for the tragedy.[65] Charles Eliot Norton found the music "striking" but "too modern in quality to accord perfectly with the character of the play."[66] The great majority of writers who reported on these and later performances disagreed with Norton. The prelude and the second, third, fifth, and sixth choruses received the highest praise possible. That this composition, and particularly its prelude, excited great enthusiasm during the eighties and nineties finds corroboration in the numerous write-ups it received during these decades. Writers spoke of Paine's "individuality" and the work's "lofty, tragic sentiments," "strong imaginative appeal," and "an atmosphere . . . distinctly noble"; they described it as "a work ranking as a masterpiece."[67] On 18 November 1903, while Paine was visiting Germany, Berlin heard the prelude. Amy Fay states that an appreciative audience insisted on recalling the composer three times. Berliners presented him with a medal and diploma and treated him with great honor.[68]

The acclaimed prelude in C minor was often performed by itself at symphony concerts across the nation. It starts with a somber brooding phrase in the bass, then a clash of sound and declamatory expostulation in the full orchestra that foreshadow the anguish to come. An *adagio* in B major introduces the main theme (Example 4.12),[69] which recurs later, in the second chorus, on the words "Seeing neither past nor future, flutters now my heart with hope." A fiery eruption of the orchestra interrupts it. An *allegro moderato* in C minor begins with a variant on the main theme, to which is added a relentless marching bass line (Example 4.13) that will return in the sixth chorus, "O race of mortal men! How as nothing-worth I regard you." A weighty climax results. Then the *adagio* version of the melody returns in C minor, and again the orchestra erupts. Gradually the music becomes resigned, and the close symbolizes Oedipus's submission to his fate. The music has intense eloquence and persuasive strength. Many contemporary music lovers regarded the composition as an illustration of American culture at its best.

After completing *Oedipus*, Paine composed several cantatas, some hymns for official celebrations, and incidental music to Aristophanes' *The Birds*. In particular, the cantata *Phoebus Arise*, opus 37 (1882), for tenor soloist, male chorus, and orchestra, written for the Apollo Club, won praise for its "exquisite flavor of long-since," it "climaxes, which are never timid," and its "sensuousness of color."[70]

His last orchestral composition was a symphonic poem, *An Island Fantasy*, completed in 1888 and published in 1907 with the title changed to *Poseidon and Amphitrite: An Ocean Fantasy*.[71] This absorbing idyll was inspired by two paintings of the seashore at Summer Island, in the Isles of Shoals, by J. Appleton Brown, one serene and sunlit, the other stormy. Romanticism conquers classicism. Resplendently lustrous sounds prevail. Paine delineates moods of nature. The structure is that of a free rondo, with an introduction presenting motives that will return in the main body of the work and two different accounts of the primary melody. Wisely, Paine has refrained from commenting on his extramusical intentions. Unfair was Daniel Gregory Mason's accusation that the composer was unable to depict the real ocean and the real island; in other words, that he had failed to employ his compositional techniques for illustration.[72] What Paine really was trying to do, using the paintings and his memory of the islands as springboards, was to give expression to his own insights about reality as clarified in his imagination. Beethoven's comment on the score of his *Pastoral* Symphony, that it was "more an expression of feeling than of painting," is as pertinent here as it is for Paine's Second Symphony.

One final major work came from Paine, the three-act opera *Azara*, which he labored on from 1833 to 1898. The libretto, by the composer, derives from an early thirteenth-century French *chante-fable*, the love romance *Aucassin and Nicolette*.[73] The Boston Symphony presented its ballet music, the three Moorish dances, in March 1900. Ephraim Cutter, Jr., gave the opera an incomplete concert performance with piano accompaniment at Chickering Hall in 1903 and at his home in 1905. A concert performance with cuts in the music, but with orchestra, was given by the Cecilia Society under Lang in 1907. Paine went to New York during the summer of 1903 to try to get the Metropolitan Opera to mount it. Over the next several years several prominent musicians tried to convince Conried, the Metropolitan's manager, that *Azara* merited staging. Conried countered with the claim that attempts to find a contralto and bass capable of singing in English had failed. In addition, he said, the chorus could not sing in English. The opera never received a staged performance.[74]

The libretto's language is decidedly stilted. The idealized heroine, Azara, is depicted as a reserved and dignified, yet apparently shapely and sense-pleasing, woman, one capable of both highly principled thought and the strongest emotions. Her counterpart may be found in Parker's opera *Mona*, in the Boston novels of Howells, and in the paintings of local artists—like Abbott Thayer's *Caritas*, now in the Boston Museum of Fine Arts.[75] There is concern for the unimpeded flow of the music. One finds few obviously distinct set pieces (independent intermezzi, arias, and the like), although the listener easily identifies those explicitly melodic sections that stand the place of set pieces. Parts allotted to the singers are comfortable for the voice. Melodies are laid out for maximum expressive and sensuous effect. Classical restraint is pushed far into the shadows. Unquestionably, Paine employed, as needed, the more advanced melodic, harmonic, rhythmic, and instrumental devices of the late nineteenth century. The orchestra figures prominently in advancing the story, establishing the shifting atmospheres, and commenting on the characters. The flexibility in shaping dramatic forms owes a debt to Wagner. John Schmidt finds the music to have certain Wagnerian characteristics, but these are not extensive. Schmidt cites the recurring themes in *Azara*. Yet, they are not constantly modified as are the Wagnerian *Leitmotives*, except for two deviations: the motive associated with the Moors and Malek, a Saracen chief; and the motive associated with Azara, which evolves only in the orchestra.[76]

The twenty-two-measure prelude serves only as a curtain raiser. The first scene is dominated by a running sixteenth-note figure that has a similarlity to that in Chopin's Prelude No. 3, in G. Rainulf, the king of Provence and a bass, learns of his son Gontran's victory over the Saracens. He catches sight of Azara, ward of Count Aymar, and sings of his craving for her. The knights and their ladies sing a four-part victory song. Gontran, a tenor, enters to claim Azara's hand as a reward for the victory. A dramatic scene ensues in which Azara declares she loves Gontran and Rainulf becomes infuriated with his son. Gontran sings a full-fledged aria in A-flat tinged with F minor, *appassionato*, "My love is ardent as the day." (Example 4.14 begins the last part of the ternary structure.)[77] Angered by his father, Gontran frees his captive Malek, a Saracen chief. This allows Malek, a baritone, to sing an animated solo, also in ternary form, on the joys of freedom. Another dramatic scene ends the act, with Rainulf banishing Gontran from the court. Despite the awkward English and the passive role of the chorus, genuine dramatic conflict enlivens the action, and the tunes are fine ones.

The introduction to Act 2 is longer than the previous prelude and has much substance. It opens on a moving motive representative of the "poor hunted maid," Azara. The curtain rises to Aymar's account of how he and Azara have fled from Rainulf's court. A hint of Wagner comes on the words, "How shall I keep mine eye awake and watch the weary hours for her dear sake?" where the goal of the chordal progression is the A-flat triad and the voice rises from e-flat to c′. The monologue completed, Aymar falls asleep beside Azara, and a long "Orchestral Scene" in E-flat evokes clouds rolling away, moonlight, the soft lap of water on the seashore, and wood nymphs, who "appear and flit about in the moonbeams, and hover around the sleeping Azara." The scene is surprisingly impressionistic for Paine, with shimmering harmonies and a persistent sixteenth-note figure throughout. Dawn arrives. They learn that Gontran still lives. After an enthralled Azara, a soprano, sings of her "rapturous joy," she listens to the murmur of the forest and the sea and sings the lengthy, vocally demanding, and always enchanting ternary aria "Softly the balmy zephyr sighs" (Example 4.15). The calming effect of slowly changing harmonic rhythms is noticeable. Malek enters and in tempestuous tones claims Azara for himself. Gontran then appears, and this generates an excellent love duet. Rainulf also arrives on the scene. The act ends with the Saracens killing Rainulf and making off with Azara.

Act 3 takes place a year later. Gontran laments his and Azara's fate. Moorish dancing girls enter and execute three dances as a diversion. The first of the dances is made to sound the most exotic through use of the minor mode, syncopations, and numerous augmented seconds in the melody (Example 4.16). All three dances proved sufficiently attractive to warrant scheduling in many symphony concerts. Malek and Azara enter separately, both in disguise. She is in the guise of a troubadour. Invited to sing, she relates a moving tale that describes her faithful love for Gontran and escape from the Saracens. A seething Malek tries to murder her, fails, and commits suicide instead. The lovers are at last united. The opera closes on general rejoicing.

Azara contains a great deal of engaging music. Its drama and stage action are not as neglected as some critics claim. The orchestra and singers sound sad or joyous, wrathful or pensive, declamatory or lyrical as required. The artificial language of the libretto needs revision, but the vagaries of plot are no better or worse than those of most operas that have achieved popularity. One hopes that soon it will receive its first staged performance by topflight singers and an orchestra.

Paine's music continues to be valuable. In his day, his works were admired throughout America and Europe. He still has much to say to auditors free of rigidly held preconceptions. He won himself a place as America's first celebrated symphonist and encouraged others to try their hand at serious music composition. His creative goals and high standards served to guide younger composers. Music courses as part of a university's curriculum became nationally acceptable after he initiated them at Harvard. He educated some of the most distinguished composers and writers on music that came after him. Paine stands as a composer of foremost significance for American civilization.

Among the extant handwritten notes by M. A. DeWolfe Howe is one dated November 1905. It reads, "Professor Paine must bear the penalty of being an American, and also of being alive. I have already told him how he can make his works appreciated. It is simply by putting himself in the ground and putting a tombstone over himself. He does not accept the proposal with alacrity. . . . I am sure that fifty years hence musical historians will say that American classical music began with John K. Paine."[78] Many more years than fifty have gone by. Paine's works have only in the late 1980s and early 1990s begun to be appreciated anew.

NOTES

1. Vernon Louis Parrington, *Main Currents in American Thought* (New York: Harcourt, Brace, 1930), 3:14.

2. Richard Aldrich, in *Dictionary of American Biography*, s.v. "Paine, John Knowles."

3. Daniel Gregory Mason, *Music in My Time and Other Reminiscences* (New York: Macmillan, 1938), 39. Haydn was as strict with the young Beethoven; Beethoven in turn discouraged students from allowing themselves compositional freedoms.

4. Henry Morton Dunham, *The Life of a Musician* (New York: Mrs. Henry M. Dunham, 1931), 69; Clayton Jones, *Reminiscences of a Musician* (Cambridge: Washburn and Thomas, 1929), 7; Emma Eames, *Some Memories and Reflections* (New York: Appleton, 1927), 34; Walter Raymond Spalding, *Music at Harvard* (1939; reprinted, New York: Da Capo, 1977), 158; letter from Frederick Shepherd Converse to M. A. DeWolfe Howe, 11 April 1939, in the Houghton Library, Harvard University, shelf no. bMS Am 1524 (274).

5. "Music in Philadelphia," dated 26 July 1876; *Dwight's Journal of Music* 36 (1876): 280; "American Composers," *Music* 4 (1893): 257; Rupert Hughes, *Contemporary American Composers* (Boston: Page, 1900), 146; Louis C. Elson, *The History of American Music*, rev. to 1925 by Arthur Elson (New York: Macmillan, 1925), 169.

6. Karl Kreuger, album notes to recording MIA 120.

7. John Lathrop Mathews, "In Harvard University," *Music* 9 (1896): 645–46.
8. Henry T. Finck, *My Adventures in the Golden Age of Music* (New York: Funk and Wagnalls, 1926), 79.
9. M. A. DeWolfe Howe, handwritten notes on Paine, in the Houghton Library, Harvard University, shelf no. bMS Am 1826 (419).
10. Mathews, "In Harvard University," 648.
11. Aldrich, in *D. A. B.*, s.v. "Paine, John Knowles."
12. Louis C. Elson, in *Music and Drama* (3 June 1882), Supplement: 5.
13. William Treat Upton, *Art-Song in America* (Boston: Ditson, 1930), 78.
14. Hughes, *Contemporary American Composers*, 163.
15. Barbara Owen, album notes to the recording New World NW 280.
16. This and five other Paine organ compositions may be found in a modern edition: *The Complete Organ Works of John Knowles Paine*, ed. Wayne Leupold (Dayton, Ohio: McAfee, 1975).
17. Published, New York: Beer and Schirmer, copr. 1865.
18. "Music," *Atlantic Monthly* 30 (1872): 505. I have not seen the music of opus 11.
19. Published, Boston: Koppitz, Prüfer, copr. 1869.
20. John C. Schmidt, *The Life and Works of John Knowles Paine* (Ann Arbor: UMI Research Press, 1980), 261, finds this tune's beginning pentatonic. However, before two measures have gone by, the melody touches on every note of the scale except for the leading tone, and nowhere does the sound suggest the pentatonic.
21. *Four Characteristic Pieces*, in Album of Piano Pieces (Boston: Ditson, copr. 1876 held by G. D. Russell Co.).
22. Published with a copyright date of 1876 by G. D. Russell, they were reissued in the Album of Pianoforte Pieces, published by Ditson.
23. Schmidt, in *The Life and Works of John Knowles Paine*, 264, calls the tune pentatonic. The introduction of the leading tone eventually destroys any such concept.
24. Schmidt again finds the tune to be pentatonic (ibid., 265); again, it is no such thing.
25. Spalding, *Music at Harvard*, 193, describes it as a street tune entitled "Rafferty's Lost His Pig."
26. Schmidt, *The Life and Works of John Knowles Paine*, 266–67, quotes W.S.B. Mathews as stating that he had heard the piece many years earlier, played from manuscript. Schmidt finds the harmonic vocabulary conservative and indicative of Paine's youth.
27. *Boston Musical Herald* 11 (1890): 47.
28. John Fiske, *The Letters of John Fiske*, ed. Ethel F. Fisk (New York: Macmillan, 1940), 334–35.
29. Schmidt, *The Life and Works of John Knowles Paine*, 316.
30. H. E. Krehbiel, *Review of the New York Musical Season, 1887–1888* (New York: Novello, Ewer, 1888), 36.
31. John C. Schmidt, album notes to recording Northeastern NR 219–CD.
32. The two newspaper items are in the Allan A. Brown Collection, scrapbook of clippings, **M304.1, Vol. 2, in the Boston Public Library; the comment by "H. H." is among the notes of M. A. DeWolfe Howe, in the Houghton Library, Harvard University, shelf no. bMS Am 1826 (419).
33. W.S.B. Mathews, ed., *A Hundred Years of Music in America* (Chicago: Howe, 1889), 676; George Thornton Edwards, *Music and Musicians of Maine* (Portland:

Southworth, 1928), 124; Schmidt, *The Life and Works of John Knowles Paine*, 63–64, 71–72.

34. Quoted excerpts of the Mass are taken from John Knowles Paine, *Mass in D* (New York: Beer and Schirmer, copr. 1866).

35. Gunther Schuller, "Comments," in the album notes to the recording New World NW 262/63.

36. *Atlantic Monthly* 31 (1873): 506–8.

37. Ibid., 248.

38. Ibid., 249–50.

39. *Dwight's Journal of Music* 34 (1874): 246–47.

40. Hughes, *Contemporary American Composers*, 146.

41. Elson, *The History of American Music*, 166. See also Aldrich, in *D. A. B.*, s.v. "Paine, John Knowles."

42. *Atlantic Monthly* 38 (1876): 124.

43. *Atlantic Monthly* 37 (1876): 763–64.

44. Reprinted in *Dwight's Journal of Music* 25 (1876): 181.

45. See, for example, *Dwight's Journal of Music* 25 (1876): 175, where several of these observations are made; see also the reprints of the *New York Tribune* and the *New York Nation* reviews, on pages 181 and 220, respectively, of this issue of *Dwight's Journal*.

46. George Chadwick, "American Composers," in *The American History and Encyclopedia of Music* 8, *History of American Music*, ed. W. L. Hubbard (Toledo: Squire, 1908), 2.

47. Karl Kreuger, *The Musical Heritage of the United States: The Unknown Portion* (New York: Society for the Preservation of the American Musical Heritage, 1973), 98–99.

48. Examples are taken from John Knowles Paine, *Symphony No. 1 für Orchester*, Op. 23 (Leipzig: Breitkopf and Härtel, copr. 1908).

49. Several famous composers have at one time or another taken Beethoven as a model, among them Schubert, Schumann, and Brahms.

50. Allan A. Brown Collection, scrapbook of clippings, **M371.11, in the Boston Public Library.

51. *Dwight's Journal of Music* 36 (1876): 350; see also *Dwight's Journal* 37 (1877): 7 for a comment on a later presentation of the work.

52. See *Dwight's Journal of Music* 37 (1877): 128, 135.

53. Letter of John Fiske, printed in *Dwight's Journal of Music* 37 (1877): 148.

54. Allan A. Brown Collection, scrapbook of clippings, **M125.5, Vol. 5, in the Boston Public Library.

55. John Knowles Paine, Symphonic Poem: *Shakespeare's Tempest*, Op. 31 (Leipzig: Breitkopf and Härtel, copr. 1907).

56. *Dwight's Journal of Music* 38 (1878): 229–30.

57. Aldrich, in *D. A. B.*, s.v. "Paine, John Knowles."

58. *Dwight's Journal of Music* 40 (1880): 53–54.

59. Allan A. Brown Collection, scrapbooks of clippings, **M125.2, Vol. 2, and **M125.5, Vol. 3, in the Boston Public Library. Of course, the reviewers needn't have been the same ones every year.

60. Program notes for the Chicago Orchestra, conducted by Theodore Thomas, 8–9 April 1892.

61. John Knowles Paine, *Im Frühling*: Symphonie No. 2 in A für Grosses Orchester, Op. 34 (Boston: Schmidt, copr. 1880).

62. Alfred John Goodrich, *Complete Musical Analysis* (Cincinnati: Church, 1889), 285.

63. The motive has some resemblance to that of the *Adagio espressivo* slow movement of Schumann's Second Symphony.

64. Hughes, *Contemporary American Composers*, 147–48.

65. *Boston Advertiser*, 5 May 1881, reprinted in *Dwight's Journal of Music* 41 (1881): 82–83.

66. Letter to G. E. Woodbury, dated 31 January 1881, in Charles Eliot Norton, *The Letters of Charles Eliot Norton* (Boston: Houghton Mifflin, 1913), 2:114–15.

67. See the many newspaper reports in the Allan A. Brown Collection, scrapbooks of clippings, **M125.5, Vols. 1, 13, and 18, and **M304.1, Vol. 2, in the Boston Public Library. The quotations come mainly from the *Boston Transcript* for 15 Feburary 1882, 13 March 1882, 22 April 1894, and 24 April 1899.

68. Amy Fay, *More Letters of Amy Fay: The American Years, 1879–1916*, ed. S. Margaret William McCarthy (Detroit: Information Coordinators, 1986), 70.

69. The quoted examples are taken from John Knowles Paine, *Oedipus Tyrannus* of Sophocles, Op. 35, for Male Chours and Orchestra, rev. ed. (Boston: Schmidt, copr. 1895).

70. Hughes, *Contemporary American Composers*, 153–54. See also the Allan A. Brown Collection, scrapbook of clippings, **M304.1, Vols. 2 and 7, in the Boston Public Library.

71. When Paine died, in 1906, he left an incomplete orchestral work entitled *Lincoln: A Tragic Tone Poem.*

72. Daniel Gregory Mason, *The Dilemma of American Music* (New York: Macmillan, 1928), 3–4.

73. Schmidt, *The Life and Works of John Knowles Paine*, 560–61. A synopsis of the French fable may be found in *Benét's Reader's Encyclopedia*, 3rd ed. (New York: Harper and Row, 1987), s.v. "Aucassin and Nicolette."

74. Edward Ellsworth Hipsher, *American Opera and Its Composers* (Philadelphia: Presser, 1927), 306. The account of Paine's visit to New York may be found in Fay, *More Letters*, 42.

75. For further commentary on the idealized woman of the times, see Richard Guy Wilson, "The Great Civilization," in *The American Renaissance, 1876–1917* (New York: Brooklyn Museum, 1979), 46–51.

76. Schmidt, *The Life and Works of John Knowles Paine*, 563.

77. The examples are taken from John Knowles Paine, *Azara*, Opera in Three Acts (Leipzig: Breitkopf and Härtel, copr. 1901).

78. M. A. DeWolfe Howe, holograph notes on Paine in the Houghton Library, Harvard University, shelf no. bMS Am 1926 (419).

5

GEORGE WHITEFIELD CHADWICK (1854–1931)

Like Paine, George Whitefield Chadwick was obstinate in his resolve to become a composer, despite the lack of support for such a career in his community and the opposition of his family. His mother died immediately after his birth, and the small boy grew up with little direction from anybody. Thus, he was forced while young to have confidence in himself and exercise his own judgment about the future course his life would take. Eventually he left school to work for a brief period in his father's insurance office. Nevertheless, he was resolute about making music his career, however much his father objected. An older brother had given him some music lessons, and he was able to earn money as an organist. When fifteen years of age, he enrolled at the New England Conservatory as a special student, his own savings financing the move. He would never go to college.

Barely into adulthood, Chadwick went to teach music at Olivet College, in Michigan, in 1876. The appointment was a temporary one, obtained through the intervention of his friend Theodore Presser. At this early stage in his career, Chadwick showed an active concern for the propagation and teaching of music by helping to found the Music Teachers National Association. At the association's first conference, he lectured on popular music, thus revealing an interest not shared with Paine. Desiring a thorough music education, he continued his studies in Germany from 1877 to 1879. Two student works, the Second String Quartet and the overture *Rip Van Winkle*, received performances abroad in 1879. European critics judged them to be fine pieces and lauded the composer's marked talent. Wishing to experience more than a Germanic ambiance, Chadwick took time off while in Europe to meander into France with some footloose young American painters.

Chadwick was in Boston in 1880, and by 1882 he was on the faculty of the New England Conservatory, becoming its director in 1897. He also was conductor of the conservatory's choruses and orchestras, the local music clubs, and the annual festivals at Springfield and Worcester. He grew conversant with diverse musical styles after conducting works like Berlioz's *Damnation of Faust*, Franck's *Beatitudes*, Glazunov's Sixth Symphony, Saint-Saëns's *Samson and Delilah*, and Brahms's *German Requiem*. His obstinacy had paid off—he was immersed in a number of musical activities, from which he earned a living. At the same time, he had some leisure for musical composition, especially in the summers. The composer Arthur Shepherd, Chadwick's student from 1896 to 1897, describes his teacher as "an independent, virile, American spirit and a self-confident, peppery man of great charm."[1] The way he conducted his life certainly exhibited a self-reliant personality.

THE PRINCIPAL FEATURES OF CHADWICK'S MUSICAL STYLE

Most indicative of the matrix out of which his musical style emerged is the reconciliation of opposites in his thinking about music. There is a continual duality in Chadwick's creativity: in the direction of the furthering of old and the investigation of new musical techniques, the adherence to serious art and the inclusion of popular and folk music, and the security of the tried and true and the excitement of novelty. In one movement or section, his phrasing is short-breathed, his tune diatonic, and his harmony simple and consonant; in another, his phrasing is lengthy, his tune weighty with accidentals, and his harmony lush and chromatic. Possibly because of this duality, his pieces, especially the mature ones, show a great flexibility in approach. He was, moreover, a trailblazer, not only in his introduction of humor and even impudence into art music, but also in his openness to the American vernacular. Fortunately, these divergent elements in his thinking are brought into accord through the aptness and polish of the resultant style.

Chadwick's finest works, like the Second Symphony, the Fourth String Quartet, the *Symphonic Sketches*, and *Tam O'Shanter*, are superior representations of his musical sensibilities. Here he was a shrewd handicraftsman who greatly increased the worth of whatever musical ingredients he started with through his inimitable manner of developing and enriching them. The wit and the allusions to native song and dance that we find here and there, for example, are completely merged with a colorful imagination. They demonstrate that Chadwick fused imagination with a nicely honed judgment of what gestures are appropriate for sounds having artistic integrity. To portray scenes, he may apply kaleidoscopic harmonies and rhythms like the discontinuous brush strokes and thick palette-knife applications of some impressionistic painters. At the same time, the continuing solidness of structure marks him as a composer belonging to the New England group. When he permits luminous orchestrations or glaring juxtapositions of highly contrasted passages to ignite his music, he still retains a certain preciseness of tonal organization and meticulous delineation of melodic-rhythmic patterns that are characteristic of the New England composer.

John Tasker Howard comments that Chadwick was only at first influenced by the "academic-romantic tradition" taught him by German mentors. Eventually, his own particular approach to craftsmanship, his flashes of inspiration, his humor, and his genuine emotional warmth modified this influence.[2] Benjamin Lambord seconds Howard when he speaks of Chadwick's "scholarly formality" as pertinent solely to his early music. Lambord rejects Rupert Hughes's labeling of Chadwick as an academic. Instead, he finds a steady development away from rigidity in his idiom, both in the spirit and the forms of his music. The late program music, like *Adonais*, *Euterpe*, *Cleopatra*, and *Aphrodite*, is contemporary in sound and outlook. Although these appear to be programmatic, writes Lambord, they demonstrate that the composer preserved a formal control, without the "vagueries" of the French and the "polyphonic complexities" of the Germans. He found Chadwick's music at the turn of the century to have notable freedom of style, force, and mastery of orchestral color.[3]

How did another, younger contemporary not immersed in the German-academic tradition interpret Chadwick's style? Edward Burlingame Hill, who had studied music with both Paine and Chadwick, was already an eminent composer disposed toward the novel tonal inflections of French impressionism when he stated that Chadwick's main attributes were fluent and beautiful melodic inventiveness, masterful part-writing, and logical coherence of form. Although his harmonic structures were solid, Chadwick always captured impressions that were romantic, poetic, or dramatic without resort to "ultra-modern eccentricity." Hill found the instrumentation brilliant and resourceful, though Chadwick used neither an enormous orchestra nor unusual instruments. The instrumental combinations honored the natural limitations of the orchestral player's technique. His contrapuntal dexterity was remarkable; command of the sonata and symphonic forms, exceptional; and spontaneity of expression, striking. In addition, Chadwick "has shown most convincingly in the overture to 'Melpomene' that he can depart from the strict letter of the poem and justify the result." Finally, Hill states, Chadwick gives such a secure underpinning to his grander works that he can freely elaborate details as he chooses.[4]

To this listener, the assessments of Howard, Lambord, and Hill seem verified. When Chadwick's music suggests the vernacular, he usually makes reference to the melodies and dance rhythms of Yankee traditional music or to the hymnody of New England, both with Anglo-Celtic antecedents. Less often, he conjures up the sound of America's popular ballads and minstrel songs. Found least often are the intimations of cakewalk, ragtime, or novelty songs of the decades before and after the turn of the century. Frequently, the reference to a native dialect takes the shape of an epigrammatic statement that is concise, pithy, and possibly syncopated. The tune may be based on a gapped scale, especially one with the seventh omitted or half-step intervals avoided. At times, the melody sounds decidedly modal, owing in particular to the constant use of the lowered seventh. The brief, haunting French-horn solo that commences the introduction to the Second Symphony, for instance, is based on a gapped Dorian mode. The second and sixth tones are omitted; the seventh is lowered. A syncopation sounds on the second beat of each of the first three measures, which are in 4/4 time. The passage is plausibly American, whether likened to the music of African-Americans or that of Anglo-Celtic Yankees. In addition, the opening phrase permeates all of the movements of the Second Symphony, making it into a cyclical composition.

The composer completed this symphony seven years before the visit of Antonín Dvořák to the United States. It is therefore not completely true to write, as some critics have, that Dvořák showed Americans, among them Chadwick, how to incorporate native musical materials into their art music. Indeed, the opening of this symphony may well have inspired the second-movement melody of Dvořák's Symphony "From the New World," completed eight years later. In addition, the work's cyclical nature could have given Dvořák the idea to do something similar in his symphony.

Other passages in Chadwick's music capture a down-to-earth lightheartedness completely at variance with the accepted conventions of the Germanic tradition that he imbibed during his youth. One can even detect cracker-barrel humor of the sort ascribed to New England rural folk sitting around the stoves of general stores during winter. Homely Yankee wit pervaded their gossiping, joshing, and tall-tale telling. It also pervades the second movement of the Second Symphony, the third movement of the Fourth String Quartet, and "Jubilee," "Hobgoblin," and "A Vagrom Ballad" from the *Symphonic Sketches*. When an especially jocose passage breaks out, the entertained listener awaits further comicality. Yet, the movement seldom dispenses jollity from beginning to end. Chadwick astutely produces an effect also by holding back. Restraint stimulates minds to react in the particular fashion desired without surfeiting auditors' senses.

Commenting on Chadwick's Americanisms, Carl Engel hears them as New England Yankeeisms. He especially likes the blend of the simple with the touching in a melody like that of the final chorus in "Land of Our Hearts," which he describes as "both hymn and folk-song, straightforward, perfect and abiding."[5]

MUSIC FOR SOLOISTS OR CHAMBER ENSEMBLES

Like Paine, Chadwick wrote little keyboard music, and the little he wrote least indicates the composer's usual style. Some are teaching pieces; most contain pleasant music. Six Characteristic Pieces for Pianoforte, opus 7, dates back to the early 1880s, and suggests at one moment a lighthearted nothing ("Congratulations"), at another, sounds of utter insignificance ("Please Do!"). "Scherzino" smiles in a toned-down Beethoven-cum-Schumann sort of fashion; the deftly composed "Reminiscence" muses mostly upon Chopin; the "Etude" is lithesome but lacks variety. The best of the six pieces is the "Irish Melody," an attractively guileless work with some substance.

Later came Two Caprices (1888), Three Waltzes (1890), a *Chanson Orientale* (1895), and a Nocturne (1895). Five Pieces for Pianoforte, from 1905, proclaims through the titles of its separate sections that it was considered no *magnum opus*: "Prélude Joyeux," "Dans le Canot," "Le Ruisseau," "Le Crépuscule," and "Les Grenouilles." The last, a "humoresque" on the subject of frogs, has some earmarks of the later Chadwick (Example 5.1).[6] The tune suggests the jumpy rhythms and grotesque gesticulations of a comic dance. The left-hand exchanges between bass note and chord, in duple time, come out of a minstrel-ragtime milieu.

In contrast to his lack of real interest in writing piano and organ music, Chadwick's devotion to art song was strong. He wrote more than 125 songs, many having genuine merit. Most songs feature a catching tune. More often than not, a composition may have affinities to contemporary

American popular song. For Chadwick, composing a song called for the same careful effort as composing a whole opera. Here and there his songs show Chadwick exploring the possibilities of several distinct manners of expression, all of which were amalgamated into his mature style. First was the influence of his German education and the composers Schubert and Schumann. One example, "Thou Art So Like a Flower" (1885), opus 11 no. 3, has a text after Heine. It establishes that Chadwick accepted a continuity with art song's past as part of a still-active tradition. In the vein of a German *lied*, the song's smooth flow projects a disarming charm.

"A Bonny Curl" (1889), with text by Amelie Rives, acknowledges Chadwick's Anglo-Celtic ancestry with its Scotch snap and a melody stressing the tones of the submediant and mediant and avoiding the half-step progression. The vocalist rarely touches on the subdominant. Although in a major key, modal-minor cadences in the submediant are frequent and help give a Scottish seasoning to the music. Representing yet a third influence, "In Bygone Days" (1885), opus 14 no. 3, resembles the artistic and semi-artistic American ballads of sentiment. Their immense popularity during the late nineteenth century encouraged Tin Pan Alley publishers to issue hundreds of them.[7] The kinship is evidenced in the tune, harmony, and accompaniment. The lyric, by John Leslie Breck, is given an *andantino* tune that is readily sung and assimilated. It moves within a limited range and, typical of popular song, adheres mostly to one rhythmic-melodic phrase pattern. The technically undemanding accompaniment is supportive only, with no insinuation of the dance rhythms that would later invade sentimental songs. The barber-shop chromaticism in measure 10, which leads the ear back to a restatement of the opening phrase, is commonly heard in popular song of the time. Possibly because he heard connections to the music of the masses, Rupert Hughes called the song "trashy."[8] Those music lovers able to listen to it without a bias will find much to admire. Another song of this type is "Before the Dawn" (1882), opus 8 no. 3. This and "In Bygone Days" have equivalences in the widely accepted songs of Reginald DeKoven, Carrie Jacob Bond, and Ernest Ball. The comfortable contours and immediate enjoyableness of the tune's diatonic first strain easily communicate with the everyday music lover. Later, the song recapitulates the opening strain to an agitated accompaniment of eighth-note triplets stated as reiterated chords and marked *appassionato*. This is also common parlance in semi-artistic American popular songs. Moreover, it occurs in purely instrumental works of Chadwick and other composers of the New England group when intense feeling is projected. However, "Before the Dawn" interrupts its popular connection in the middle section, on the words: "In the holy repose the morning star with trembling awaits the sun." The sudden swirl of distant modulations and the suspension of tonal feeling belong to art.

A song communicating passionate desire, "Sweetheart, Thy Lips Are Touched with Flame," has the voice sing against the piano's eighth-note triplets in the right hand, again stated as a reiterated chord. Its lush harmonies, downward-plunging melody, and demands on the skills of singer and pianist place it clearly in the art category. Example 5.2 cites the beginning of the last fifteen measures of the work, where the piece mounts to its strongest climax.[9] The tempestuous musical expression of intimate emotion is Chadwick's own and is rarely found in Paine's music. "The Danza" (1885), set to a poem by Arlo Bates, on the other hand, a kind of Latin American waltz, has a decidedly catchy tune and does have correlations with popular music.

Another side of Chadwick is shown by his fascination with the Middle East. This fascination was common to many artists of his era, whether in the United States or Europe, including composers, poets, painters, novelists, sculptors, and authors of travel books. But among the New England group, Chadwick was one of the most captivated. Yet, his preoccupation, as seen in his songs, is usually limited to the subject matter of the poems he selected for musical setting. Less often does it extend to the music itself. "Song from the Persian" (1886), with words by Thomas Bailey Aldrich, does try to convey an exotic atmosphere through its music. The minor mode, frequent half steps of the tune (none from leading tone to tonic), and languorous curves of the vocalist's half-phrases convey this special aura. So also does the characteristic augmented-sixth harmony, a first inversion of a seventh chord based on the raised subdominant tone, which appears in most measures. The music is convincing; the text less so.

More usual is the "Bedouin Love Song" (1890), to a poem by Bayard Taylor. Here the words refer to an Arab lover riding over the desert sands at nighttime with the speed of desire. Yet, the music makes no bid for the exotic. A telling half-step exchange in the left hand sets forth a configuration similar to that of Chopin's Prelude in E minor, opus 28 no. 2. It produces dissonance and a sensation of nervous disturbance. The sudden switch from minor to major mode for a climax on the words "I love thee . . . with a love that cannot die" (sung *appassionato*) makes a superb impact on the listener. An equally excellent song, "Allah" (1887), to a poem by Henry Wadsworth Longfellow, also has music with no foreign accent. In fact, the diatonic melody, which avoids the leading tone and uses the submediant as a substitute dominant, could be taken as Celtic-American.

Other songs enthusiastically praised by contemporary and later critics include "The Miller's Daughter" (1881), "The Sweet Wind That Blows" (1885), "He Loves Me" (1885), "The Lily" (1887), "Sorai's Song" (1888), "Green Grows the Willow" (1888), "Love and Joy" (1892), "A Ballad of Trees and the Master" (1899), "When I Am Dead" (1910), "The Daughter of Mendoza" (1914), and the late *Three Nautical Songs* (1920). The publication or performance of a Chadwick song was almost always greeted with pleasure. If Paine was the pioneer of America's symphonic tradition, surely Chadwick deserves like status for his contributions to American art song.

The body of chamber music that Chadwick composed, as with his songs, is larger than that of Paine. It starts with one early string trio, now lost, which he completed before leaving for Germany.[10] One guesses that this first effort would have shown him gathering a cluster of different composers' musings, himself chiefly furnishing the glue to cement them together. This, however, is not true of the chamber works that are extant: five string quartets and one piano quintet. Chadwick composed them between 1877 and 1898, from young adulthood halfway into middle age. Later he added two less consequential pieces. All of these compositions have warmth and lucidity. An abundance of harmonic variety, a discreet contrapuntal grasp, a superior command or motivic development, and a pliancy of melodic lines, sometimes discursive but usually articulated in phrases more succinct than Paine's, delineate the music. Engel praises the chamber works for their bright-eyed vigor, spontaneous melody, adroitly handled instruments, sure management of the musical fabric, and evocation of a native sound with properties analogous to American folk music.[11]

The First Quartet for Strings in G minor stems from Chadwick's student days in Leipzig. He wrote to a friend in February 1878 that the quartet was "going to be pretty good; I have introduced . . . 'Shoot the pipe' [a time-honored dance piece] in the Scherzo; nothing like economy you know." In another letter to the same friend, he wrote, "I think that I have some original things in it."[12] The first movement, in sonata form, begins forcefully and a bit forebodingly. By the movement's close, Chadwick has established his credentials as a resourceful composer, comfortable in the chamber format. The slow movement sings in an engaging, romantic way. The third movement introduces "Shoot the pipe" in the midst of a ternary dance structure. The overall style is central European. Nevertheless, the student is already asserting his Americanness. More Americanisms are hinted at in the Finale, which at one moment suggests an American two-step, at another a gospel hymn. These suggestions are so diffidently made that they are easily overlooked.

No American performance of the complete quartet is known. Yet, after Chadwick returned to the United States, he arranged the slow movement as an Andante for String Orchestra. In this form, it was performed in the spring of 1882 by Louis Maas at a Philharmonic concert. The *Boston Gazette* reported that the work was richly harmonized and clearly scored and that it was "delightful throughout"; it also noted that the audience applauded warmly. The *Boston Courier* found it "in modern vein and full of tender melody."[13]

In November 1878, seven months after he wrote the First Quartet, Chadwick completed his Second Quartet for Strings in C major. In this work melody leans more toward a folk sound; harmony grows richer; rhythm is more arresting. After examining it, his teachers found him to possess "a quite extraordinary talent in composition," well above the student level. When fellow students at the Leipzig Conservatory heard the work privately performed, Chadwick says, they clapped and clapped until the director stopped them. Spring 1879 saw its public performance at a students' examination-concert, where, Chadwick says, "each movement was much applauded and in the end I was vociferously cheered."[14] In January 1881 the Beethoven Quintet Club, sponsored by the Euterpe Society, presented it in Boston. Chadwick experienced a triumph. Reviewers commented that, though he showed affinities to Mendelssohn, the composer was in no way a novice. The quartet and the *Rip Van Winkle* Overture, also composed in 1879, revealed an unequivocal melodic individuality that identified them as from the same composer.[15]

The introduction to the first movement has a faraway quality, but this mood is dispelled by the stressful fast music that follows. The second movement, *andante espressivo*, is without question lovely and acutely felt. The dynamic *Scherzo* movement was regarded as the most original of the movements. Chadwick expands with some dramatic flair on a craggy subject. The *Transcript* declared the rhythms throughout the *Scherzo* to be "strikingly odd and fascinating." The Finale, bursting with life and wit, forms a fitting close to the entire work.

The Beethoven Quintet Club performed the Third Quartet in D major on 9 March 1887, almost a year after it was completed. On the evidence of this composition, Chadwick seems to have become more himself, more liberated from whatever aesthetic bondage attended his education. Local reviewers thought this quartet equal to the best works of its class anywhere and labeled Chadwick "our junior Haydn." The New York critic H. E.

Krehbiel heard the quartet in November in New York City. He described the work as straightforward, of modest length, and with not a superfluous note.[16]

As usual, the first movement is an *allegro* in sonata form, commencing with an energetic theme and progressing to a singing secondary theme. The *adagio* movement states a spacious melody in D minor, succeeded by five variations, in turn decisive and theatrical, then wispily melodious (in the relative major), then robust (in the submediant minor), then suave (in the major mode of D), and then agitated, before fading into silence. The next movement is a lithe intermezzo of the sort that Brahms preferred to write instead of the more vigorous *Scherzo*. The Finale is a spirited caprice. The composer takes risks with novel textures, shifts in accentuation and meter, and unexpected vertical combinations.

The Quintet for Piano and Strings in E-flat was finished in October 1887. Steven Ledbetter writes that the audience was small for its premiere, when it was presented in company with the Third Quartet and a few songs, on 23 January 1888.[17] Reviewers liked the qunitet, and Schmidt published it in 1890. Writing about the quintet years after its first performance, Olin Downes said that it had deserved its popularity, owing to its melodic invention, sure craft, and the engaging and vigorous personality that was shown. On the other hand, Downes speaks condescendingly about its old-fashionedness and patronizingly asserts that, although Chadwick tried to approximate an American sound, the Americanisms were "of a younger and less sophisticated day than the present [mid-twentieth century]."[18]

The Fourth Quartet for Strings in E minor, first performed in December 1896, makes explicit what was mostly incipient in the earlier chamber music, what appears to be an American sound. Its principal musical antecedent was Chadwick's own Second Symphony in B-flat, dating from 1885, whose idiom smacks of his native soil. (It is discussed later in this chapter.) Chadwick would, of course, also have known the Americanistic music of Dvořák, in particular the Symphony No. 9 in E minor, "From the New World," opus 95, the "American" Quartet for Strings, opus 96, and the "American" Quintet for Strings, opus 97, composed during Dvořák's stay in the Untied States during the early 1890s.

In the Fourth Quartet Chadwick resorts to the melodic and rhythmic styles of traditional Anglo-Celtic American provenance, often using scales of five or six tones in the major (Mixolydian) or modal minor (Dorian). A family resemblance exists between many of the tunes. Indeed, the work is obviously cyclical. In the first movement, after a touching slow introduction and a brisk first theme, we hear a congenial pentatonic tune (Example

5.3).[19] Later in the movement a melody emerges as if from a worship service (Example 5.4). The slow movement intones a stately dance (Example 5.5), guileless and effective. The third movement starts like a fleet banjo tune out of a minstrel show that in turn had emanated in the American countryside (Example 5.6); its Trio sounds hymnlike. The ardent theme of the Finale (Example 5.7), except for a brief *lento espressivo* middle section, constitutes the basis for a set of variations before, and a fugue after, the interlude. The coda of the Finale serves as a magnificent finish to music of considerable merit. The quartet became possibly the most widely performed of Chadwick's chamber works. Most people perceived it as a modern-sounding work with a character all its own. Many thought it had an American, others a "Scotch," sound.[20]

The Fifth Quartet for Strings in D minor was premiered in February 1901 by the Adamowski Quartet. Steven Ledbetter quotes Chadwick as remarking twenty years after the event: "It was very warmly received, perhaps because the 'soil music', as Cadman calls it, that it contains makes a special appeal to our American ears."[21] The quartet, like its predecessor, breathes what seems to be an American atmosphere, but the Americanisms are less obvious. The level of creativity is high; the pleasure given, extraordinary. It was Chadwick's last large chamber work.

Conservatives of his day thought Chadwick was too modern; the genteel set found his Americanisms vulgar. A new breed of American composer, emerging out of Paris and the Nadia Boulanger classroom in the 1920s, was hostile to everything Chadwick represented. What interest Europeans had in his music soon evaporated. Chadwick was discouraged about continuing with his composing. Elson, in late 1913, found the slights given Chadwick unfair, since he had without doubt written several extraordinary compositions. Elson noted the English publication of Thomas F. Dunhill's *Chamber Music* and wondered why "German, French, and English quartets [were] cited without end, but not a word of the fact that America possesses at least one string quartet composer who takes rank with the best of the present."[22]

VOCAL MUSIC OTHER THAN SONG

Chadwick composed a great deal of music for chorus, often with keyboard accompaniment; among these pieces are anthems, original part songs, and arrangements of his solo songs. All are pleasing; few are unusual. Rupert Hughes commends *Reiterlied*, or *Trooper's Song* (1889), for its superb joyousness and *Jabberwocky* (1886), to the Lewis Carroll text, for its irresistible humor.[23] Both works are for male chorus. It took Bostonians a while to overcome their stiffness when confronted with humor in the concert hall. The Apollo Club's first performance of *Jabberwocky* was less than a success, in part because "the Apollo are wont to sing humorous music like elegies." But when they presented it again in 1895, the composition was a hit, the performance a triumph.[24]

A similar assessment can be made about Chadwick's vocal compositions with orchestra. In April 1881 the Apollo Club presented Chadwick's *Viking's Last Voyage* for baritone solo, male chorus, and orchestra. A gloomy, dramatic subject, several highly expressive melodies, heroic melancholy contrasting with untamed, tempestuous emotions—the composition was perfectly suited to the tastes of the time. Chadwick followed his success in the next year with a muscular *Song of the Viking*, for male chorus and keyboard (arranging the keyboard part for orchestra in 1914). Hughes liked *The Viking's Last Voyage* but joshed Chadwick with: "What would part-song writers do if the Vikings had never been invented? Where would they get their wild choruses for men, with a prize to the singer that makes the most noise?"[25]

Much praised in its time was the cantata *Phoenix Expirans* (1891), a setting of a Latin hymn text, for four soloists, SATB chorus, and orchestra. After the Handel and Haydn Society presented it, a writer reporting in Boston's *Home Journal* on the musical season of 1892–1893 called the performance the "marked event of the season. The eroticism of the text of the 'Phoenix' did not disturb the bulk of the congregation, as the burning lines were cooled in the obscurity of the original Latin." Today the text would strike us as sensuous rather than sensual. H. E. Krehbiel, who heard the cantata in New York City on 15 December 1892, considered it Chadwick's finest choral work up to that time.[26]

Noël, A Christmas Pastoral for four soloists, SATB chorus, and orchestra, was completed in 1908 and performed at the Norfolk Festival in 1909. It consists of a prelude and twelve vocal numbers. The prelude, entitled "The Star," opens with a hushed peacefulness evoked through prolonged harmonies of the tonic seventh, the submediant seventh, and the submediant. The first number, "This is the month," is set for *a capella* chorus singing homophonically and makes an excellent effect.

The second number, "From the eastern mountains," calls for soprano soloist and chorus. It opens with the basses alone on an impressive melody in the Dorian mode. Later the soprano begins singing on the words "Light of life that shineth ere the world began," to music that abandons all archaisms and hews to a late-romantic style, causing a stylistic clash with what has gone before. Number three, "O long and darksome was the night," for alto solo, acceptably blends the two approaches, ancient and contemporary, until the music grows animated on the words "When Thou, O Christ!" and suddenly for a short while we are in the world of late Wagner. From beginning to end the dichotomy of styles prevails. The most splendid portion of the entire composition is the ending, with the quartet of soloists singing "Hither come, ye heavy hearted," followed by the chorus singing the chorale "How lovely shines the morning star," then an elaborate choral fugue on "Wake, wake your harps to sweet songs!" If one can assimilate the two manners of procedure, there is much to enjoy. *Noël* was well liked, winning accolades for its beauty, devotion, and pastoral atmosphere. Critics deemed the writing for the vocalists to be smooth and gratifying.[27]

Given Chadwick's aptitude for the dramatic, it's lamentable that he produced so few works for the musical stage. A contributing factor was doubtless the inclination of impresarios to give preference to European stage works and to ignore native compositions, however meritorious. Already mentioned in this regard was Paine's *Azara*. Chadwick's two serious operas, *Judith* and *The Padrone*, would never receive staged performances. In 1884 and 1892, respectively, he had completed the two-act operettas *The Peer and the Pauper* and *A Quiet Lodging*, intended for private-club entertainment. Then in 1894 came the two-act *Tabasco*, a "Burlesque Opera" with a libretto by R. A. Barnet, commissioned and designed for performance by amateurs. After its initial performance, Philip Hale wrote of Chadwick in the *Musical Courier*: "He of our American composers has certain peculiar advantages in this undertaking new to him. He has not only melody, rhythm, color, facility; he has a strong sense of humor, an appreciation of values, and that quality known as horse-sense."[28] *Tabasco* won enough popular favor to persuade the Seabrooke Opera Company to take it on tour and the publisher B. F. Wood to issue the music in piano score.

Tabasco's music hilariously parodies the popular-song and operetta styles and vaudeville routines of the day. Nothing is what it's supposed to be. The locale is Tangiers; characters include the Bey, Pasha Hot-Hed-Ham, the Spanish trader Marco, the French chef Francois, the beautiful slave Fatima, and "a third-term harem favorite," Has-Been-A. The first act opens on a bustling harborside scene with the requisite opening chorus of commoners interspersed with street vendors crying their wares ("Cucumbers and fresh Tomater, Epsom salts and Cream of Tartar"; "Coffee, coffee, all male berries," etc.). The cheery music has nothing of the exotic about it. Next the grand vizier, Ben-Hid-Den, laments his destiny—"to be society's door-mat" and to botch up everything he tries to accomplish—in a recurring three-measure phrase in C minor, which gets funnier with each repetition. Later, Fatima's song "O Lovely Home" is nothing but a mock sentimental ballad. It neatly ties together into one phrase something that sounds suspiciously like "Auld lang syne" harmonized à la a sentimental ballad by Paul Dresser and given a barbershop chromatic twist at the end. The audience also hears a Spanish bolero, a French rigaudon, and a Viennese waltz, the last executed by the women in the harem.

When the French chef, Francois, sings his "Ditty," it is in an Irish brogue. His music is incongruously Irish as he longs for the "blossoms in Ireland the shamrocks between." Even more risibly discrepant is the plantation ballad, "O darkies don't yer 'member de ole Kentucky farm" (Example 5.8), complete with the four-part choral ending beloved of black faced minstrelsy.[29] Finally, the "March of the Pasha's Guard" would easily fit into one of the *Mulligan Guard* routines of Harrigan and Hart. No other composer of the New England group had such a capacity for musical jest. At the same time, Chadwick's vibrantly diverse musical numbers encourage relaxation and immediate enjoyment.

Completely opposite to *Tabasco* was the lyric biblical drama *Judith*, to a libretto by William C. Langdon, which Chadwick completed in 1900 and conducted in concert version the next year at the Worcester Festival, and later in Boston's Symphony Hall. The plot focuses on Judith, a beautiful Hebrew determined to avenge her people and her God. She enters the Assyrian encampment, where the throngs blasphemy against Jehovah; captivates Holofernes, the Assyrian leader, with her charms; and decapitates him after he has drunk himself insensible. Steven Ledbetter and Victor Yellin, in their article on Chadwick for the *American Grove*, state that some of the dramatic action and orchestral sonorities owe a debt to Saint-Saëns's *Samson et Dalila*, which Chadwick had conducted just before composing *Judith*, and some of the choral writing shows the influence of Mendelssohn. The article goes on to praise the "colorful, large-scaled opera, much of which could be acted to telling effect," and calls the Act 2 scene where Holofernes succumbs to Judith's beauty and dies by her hand, "one of the most expertly constructed and tautly lyrical passages in American dramatic music."[30] Warren Davenport, writing in *Musical America*, 2 February 1902, condemned the libretto and said the work was more an oratorio than an opera. Although he liked the orchestration and the handling of the choral numbers, he thought the opera as a whole lacked inspiration and had commonplace music.[31] One wonders whether the grisly plot, the use of leading motives and late-romantic harmony, and the demotion of classical musical principles irritated the musically orthodox Davenport.

In contrast, another of Chadwick's contemporaries, Louis C. Elson, who was by no means a modernist, relished *Judith*: "Splendid contrasts occur between the religious loftiness of the old Hebrews (chiefly broad chorales or contrapuntal choruses) and the brutal sensuality of the Assyrians, expressed in dances or in bombastic marches. A combination of these two elements, in the second part, gives a most skilful display of the composer's ability; and the simulatenous presentation of the sighs of the prisoners and the laughter of their conquerors is supported with some of the most graphic orchestration imaginable."[32]

Chadwick seems never to have settled in his own mind whether he was writing an oratorio or an out-and-out opera calling for stage action and theatrical projection of the music. The use of leading motives is cautious. Many tunes have similarities to his American style. The music for the Hebrew choruses harks back to old Yankee psalmody. One of the best numbers comes at the beginning, the dignified chorus of Israelites singing "Proud Asshur's host," in E minor, which often sounds modal. This is followed by Judith, a mezzo-soprano, singing an aria in A B C B form, starting *sostenuto ed espressivo* with the moving "O God, what bodings stir my troubled heart," in G minor (Example 5.9).[33] The music that ensues, majestic as it is, gives no sense of forward movement, and the scenes remain static. The sound affects us as noble and sorrowful but never as sentimental.

Act 2 is by far the most "operatic" of the three, with plenty of movement, contrast, exotic color, and sensuousness. Scene 2 features a forceful aria sung by Holofernes, "The King sends forth his sword," an *allegro moderato* in D minor (Example 5.10). The magnificient final scene shows a masterly hand providing perfect musical supports to depict the debauched Assyrians, Judith's struggle of conscience, and the bloody ending. Not least effective is the ironic touch of Judith fleeing with the head of Holofernes under her cloak while a sentinel sings "All's well! All's well!" Act 3, devoted to the triumphant Judith and the jubilant Israelites, is most oratorio-like, with little opportunity for suspense, dramatic shifts, and changes in mood and emotion. Nevertheless, my commentary springs from an examination of the score and playing the music at the piano. A staged production of *Judith* could well prove its operatic merits.

Chadwick's opera *The Padrone*, written in 1912 to a libretto put into final shape by David Stevens, reveals an appreciation of the stage works of Puccini and a pursuit of *verismo* in musical drama. The style, however, is more Chadwick's own and not particularly Italian. The story is a modern one, about recent Italian immigrants to the United States and the tragic domination of their lives by a criminal boss. The unidentified city setting was probably modeled after Boston's Italian section, the North End. The opera has exciting action, passion, brilliantly orchestrated music, and numerous opportunities for vocal display—everything that an opera enthusiast could desire. Yet, it has never been mounted. Apparently, the protagonists were considered of no account, too much a part of the uncomfortable American reality that existed just outside the theater, and therefore unworthy of serious consideration. Chadwick had dared too much, depicting humble people of his day, clawing their livelihood out of an inhospitable American environment, rather than heroic figures out of myth or distant history. Besides, the text was in understandable English, not in a mercifully half-understood foreign language, sung by picturesque peasants dancing tarantellas, or helping to trundle quaint donkey carts across a colorfully decorated stage, or waving wine glasses in the air and presumably singing in celebration of love of some sort. The opera remains in manuscript at the New England Conservatory of Music, neglected.

THE COMPOSITIONS FOR ORCHESTRA ALONE

Chadwick won his highest esteem as an orchestral composer. Orchestra conductors and symphony players enjoyed his idiomatic feel for instruments and considered him the outstanding American writing for brass and woodwinds.[34] The orchestral tones of Beethoven and Mendelssohn interested him, but also engrossing were the palettes of Berlioz, Wagner, Strauss, and various Russian and French composers. He tried incorporating the best they had to offer into his own music. His renderings were complex, applications multifaceted, and results urbane.

The merely derivative is absent. A singular gift for orchestral imagery infuses his scores. Earlier compositions did not transgress beyond classical limits, although he was at no time a rigid classicist. As he grew older, orchestral ideas were increasingly given form, vividness, and consequence, in order to evoke milieu, atmosphere, outward behavior, movement, or feeling. Carl Engel, a Chadwick enthusiast, states: "For 'Tam O'Shanter' chased by the host of devilish imps, for the 'Angel of Death' spreading his wings protectingly, for the impassioned worshippers of 'Aphrodite,' for pictures as varied as they are vivid, Mr. Chadwick finds an orchestral representation that is definite and telling. His orchestra can sing, it can roister. It can be droll without being grotesque. It can be graphic and yet escape being flatly imitative. Here then are paired consummate technic and real originality."[35]

Chadwick's earliest score, the *Rip Van Winkle* Overture, is a student work, written in Leipzig and performed there in March 1879. Enthusiastic audiences and satisfied critics endorsed his talent and ranked him alongside Paine. With the person of Rip, one suspects that Chadwick is already trying to comprehend the ludicrousness of the human condition, with its inevitable succession of affliction and farce. One should not seek originality in this early work, but the two dominant themes are felicitously invented and adeptly differentiated. Wisely, Chadwick abstained from giving a program, although that did not prevent writers from supplying their own: The cello in the introduction is the sleeper awakening; weird and strange sounds depict the mountain scene; the stirring coda represents the bright excitement of the village, and so forth.[36] No trace of America is found in his next work, *Beautiful Munich*, a Symphonique Waltz performed in Boston in 1881. The style is central European. The music is modest, mellifluous, and danceable.

Chadwick's Symphony No. 1 in C major received its initial performance to general acclaim in February 1882, at a Harvard Music Association concert. According to the *Sunday Herald* of 19 February 1882, this ambitious work has begun in Leipzig in 1877, and the first movement was heard in Munich early in 1880. The rest was completed in Boston. Reviewers described the symphony as beautiful, dramatic, and free of morbidity.[37]

His next composition shows Chadwick at a first stage of creative ripeness. Intended to honor the Muse of comedy, this music seems to have no programmatic connections save in an extremely general way. The *Thalia* Overture, subtitled an "overture to an imaginary comedy," had a first performance by the recently established Boston Symphony Orchestra in 1883. The audience demonstrated its pride in its second local composer worthy of international stature with a prolonged ovation. The work was strong and dignified, even if offered as comic. Unforeseen passages follow each other with some frequency. Here was some oddness in procedure, already noted in the First Symphony, which struck a few reviewers as nearing eccentricity in *Thalia*.[38] The public's emphatic endorsement of this work encouraged the Boston Symphony to look for new Chadwick compositions to perform.

The orchestra presented the Scherzo from a symphony-in-progress in March 1884. An Apollo Club concert introduced an Introduction and

Allegro from this work in April 1885. Finally, a concert of the Boston Symphony, in December 1886, premiered the entire Symphony No. 2 in B-flat major, a work worthy to stand beside the two Paine symphonies as one of the three most outstanding American works of their time in the symphonic genre. The composition was immediately welcomed as the long-awaited and unquestionably "American" symphony, in its melodies, rhythms, and overall spirit. Nevertheless, Chadwick by no means imagined himself here, nor in the Fourth Quartet, as pioneering a sharply defined "American" style. He wanted primarily to win acceptance as a composer of indisputable excellence and individuality. His aim was universality. If his personal style embraced what were considered "Americanisms," that was fine, so long as they were not deemed the be-all and end-all of his creativity. Given his nature, he could not help but introduce Americanisms into his music. Their inclusion was as much innate as calculated. The danger, as he saw it, was to have his music understood as regional and overly colloquial. That is why he enriched his native accents with all the sophisticated means available to him.

A second important observation is that before the arrival of Dvořák in the United States and his statements lauding the use of Indian, African-American, and Stephen Fosterish melodies in art music, nobody equated Chadwick's use of the vernacular in this symphony with the music of Indians or African-Americans or Foster. When the Scherzo alone was performed in 1884, reviewers spoke of its piquant individuality, its irresistible color, and its nearly Celtic humor, which, as the *Transcript* critic put it, "positively winks at you." The *Courier* review spoke of its unconventionality and the one or two moments of commonplace melody, but it judged the movement splendid.[39] When the complete symphony was heard in 1886, movements other than the Scherzo were thought to veer toward the rhapsodic, their melodies rather operatic. Original effects appeared throughout the entire piece. The symphony as a whole had such an unexpected character that to compare it with anything else was impossible for Chadwick's contemporaries. Nobody connected it with African-American music, as would be done in the next century.[40] Nobody spoke of the influence of Dvořák, as some twentieth-century writers have done, ignoring the fact that the Bohemian composer's arrival in the Untied States was still some years in the future. Indeed, one could more easily prove that Dvořák, for all his talk about tilling the native musical soil, had probably appropriated methods cultivated first by Chadwick.[41]

After a February 1891 performance, Philip Hale spoke of the symphony as smelling of the American soil, and the Scherzo as delightfully on the edge of vulgarity.[42] Finally, in 1906, we find Hale, in the *Sunday Herald*, saying that to speak of the music's Indian or Negro flavor is insufficient: "The scherzo . . . is much more American as far as 'Americanism' is concerned, for it breathes the spirit of devil-may-care independence, it snaps its fingers at judicious and conventional comments, it is good-natured, and it is cheerfully irreverent. The same composer's 'Vagrom Ballad' [from the *Symphonic Sketches*] has also an American flavor—and yet a conductor of symphony concerts might well hesitate before putting it on a programme."[43]

The scoring is for woodwinds, trumpets, and timpani by twos and four French horns, three trombones, and the strings. The first movement opens on an introduction *andante non troppo*, in 4/4 time, with the first horn sounding the principal motto for the entire symphony (Example 5.11).[44] The bucolic poetic atmosphere that is established will pervade the remainder of the movement. Note that the motto sounds modal and its scale lacks two tones. The *allegro* is in the usual sonata form. Interestingly, in the recapitulation the subordinate theme returns, played by a muted trumpet, and reminds the auditor of the sound of a New England village-band concert, presented on the village green during the summer. Incorporated in melodic phrases throughout the movement is the motto's skip first of a third and then of a fourth.

The second movement, an *allegretto scherzando* in rondo form, has a sportive main subject based on the motto and introduced by an oboe against lightly bouncing bowed staccatos in the strings (Example 5.12). The third movement, a *largo e maestoso*, opens on a variant of the motto, following which the lower strings take up a warm, rich, yet graceful melody. The middle section is much more dramatic. The highly lyrical coda features an expressive extension of the initial melody in the cellos, reminiscent of the ending to Tchaikovsky's *Romeo and Juliet* Overture. The Finale is an exuberantly festive *allegro molto animato*. As expected, the motto underlies much of the movement; less expected, themes from the other movements return and thus confirm the cyclic nature of the symphony. The work concludes with allusions both to the motto and to the main theme of the *allegro* in the first movement.

The *Melpomene* Overture, a dramatic overture devoted to the Muse of tragedy, is an obvious companion piece to the *Thalia* Overture. The Boston Symphony gave the work its first performance in December 1887. In 1870 Dvořák had completed a *Tragic (Dramatic) Overture*, originally meant to preface his opera *Alfred*. This and the Brahms *Tragic Overture*, of 1880, may possibly have roused Chadwick to write *Melpomene*. Later, in 1889,

Sir Charles Stanford produced an *Overture in the Style of Tragedy*. In 1893 another English composer, Sir Hubert Parry, composed his *Overture to an Unwritten Tragedy*. The year before, Josef Suk, Dvořák's son-in-law, had completed a *Dramatic Overture*. After the turn of the century, in 1908, Max Reger would make a contribution to the genre, *Symphonic Prologue to a Tragedy*. Composing dramatic or tragic overtures was certainly a prevalent interest among composers of the late nineteenth century and early twentieth century. In his own overture, Chadwick wished to signify an exalted universal state rather than just personal feeling. For this reason he might have felt that a detailed program would have narrowed the interpretation and that the individual musical structuring possible in a symphonic poem was less appropriate than the more ceremonious procedures of the sonata structure. The orchestra for *Melpomene* is larger than that of the Second Symphony. Chadwick adds a piccolo, English horn, tuba, bass drum, and cymbals. Like *Thalia*, its form has no connection with a program. Nor are there any Americanisms.

Throughout there is an obvious exploitation of the coloristic possibilities of the instruments. The use of appoggiaturas and the regulation of dissonance to increase and abate tension are dexterously done. The music public was completely won over. The overture quickly found its way into the repertoire of several American and a couple of European orchestras. The great majority of the critics who heard it praised its honesty, power of expression, and lack of overcharged depressive elements. Writing in the *Journal* of 15 March 1896, Philip Hale states: "Mr. Chadwick . . . did not attempt to exploit musically a strange family tree. His music is indeed tragic, nobly tragic. . . . Yet the gloom is neither peevish nor pessimistic. The mourning is a loud lamentation. There is the thought of heroic life and heroic death. His tragedy does not hint at Helen of Troy or her successors. There is no amorous parley in life; there is no sensuous regret when Death enters and dominates the scene."[45]

The premiere of *A Pastoral Prelude* took place in January 1892. Again, no program was supplied, but this time listeners detected such images as crowing cocks, gobbling turkeys, and bleating lambs in the music. An enjoyable and charming, but inconsequential, novelty—this seems to have been the opinion of most people in the audience. The Symphony No. 3 in F major was offered the public in 1894. It won a composition prize of three hundred dollars from the National Conservatory of New York. Gapped scales, modal passages, and Americanisms are much less in evidence here than they were in the previous symphony. It is apparent in this work that Chadwick was losing his interest in purely abstract compositions with intensely serious content. This would be his last symphony. The music entertains and rewards the auditor with substantive ideas, but it lacks the compelling expressiveness, the fascinating evocation of tragedy and comedy, found in the Second Symphony.

Percy Bysshe Shelley's poem *Adonais* (1821) inspired Chadwick's next orchestral work, also titled *Adonais*, "an elegiac overture, in memoriam Frank Fay Marshall (amici probe et fidelis)," which the Boston Symphony played in February 1900. In contrast to the more externalized emotion in *Melpomene*, here personal grief is to the fore. The boundaries of the sonata form are more frequently transgressed than in earlier overtures. Classical formalism has diminished. Chadwick tries to mirror in outspoken sounds Shelley's mood of perturbed pessimism and agony over bereavement. He finds room for a theme rather like one heard in Wagner's *Tristan und Isolde*. Plangency on the edge of sentimentality contrasts with passionate protest verging on the merely raucous. *Adonais* failed to win a following and was seldom performed while Chadwick lived.

From 1895 to 1904, he worked on the four compositions that together would receive the title *Symphonic Sketches*, Suite for Orchestra. The Boston Symphony performed them in February 1908. Audiences swiftly regarded the *Sketches* with special favor. In a note appearing on the title page of the score, Chadwick states: "Although these pieces are intended to be played in succession, they may be performed separately if more expedient."[46] The first and second sketches, *Jubilee* and *Noël*, were completed in 1895; the third, *Hobgoblin*, in 1904; and the fourth, *A Vagrom Ballad*, in 1896. The lugubriousness of *Adonais* has disappeared. The four pieces give off only light. The style returns to the distinctive modes of expression found in the Second Symphony and the Fourth Quartet. The underlay of central European romanticism is thinner than in all of Chadwick's previous works.

The greatest favorite of the four pieces was the first. Prefaced to the *Jubilee* score is a poem by "D. R.," which begins:

> No cool gray tones for me!
> Give me the warmest red and green,
> A cornet and a tambourine,
> To paint MY Jubilee!

The composition is an *allegro molto vivace* in the key of A major and in 6/4 time. The required orchestra is large, with a big percussion section (including timpani, bass drum, cymbals, triangle, and tambourine). The orchestra, abrim with Yankee spirits, jumps off in full voice with the first theme. Syncopations abound. Reversed dotting, stressed sixteenth to unstressed eighth note, energizes several melodic phrases. Here and there rhythms seem to have origins in the West Indies. A subsidiary idea (fourth and seventh tones missing) has the four horns appropriate the prancing steps of rustic dancers (Example 5.13). The strings answer with a smooth, diatonic, stepwise tune in popular-ballad style. Later, the headlong dash of the music is interrupted by a magical interlude *lento espressivo–assai tranquillo*, which transforms the subsidiary tune. Then a *presto* rushes the music to its vociferous conclusion.

Noël also has a verse appended to it:

> Through the soft, calm moonlight comes a sound;
> A mother lulls her babe, and all around
> The gentle snow lies glistening;
> On such a night the Virgin Mother mild
> In dreamless slumber wrapped the Holy Child,
> While angel-hosts were listening.

Conceived as a pastorale, the music is mostly a hushed meditation on the Nativity.

Shakespeare's "That shrewd and knavish sprite called Robin Good-fellow" heads the score to *Hobgoblin*, subtitled "Scherzo Capriccioso." A horn call begins the piece; a clarinet plays a syncopated melody in small skips but *legato* (Example 5.14). Other instruments work on the melody. An even more syncopated idea begins in the horns. Soon the opening horn call becomes the basis for a twenty-two-measure-long tune in the violins. The melodies would not be out of place in the overture to a staged musical or as background to a vaudeville turn. Extroverted and buoyant, the piece often turns rascally and derisive, like the Robin Good-fellow of English and New England folklore.

A Vagrom Ballad is:

> A tale of tramps and railway ties,
> Of old clay pipes and rum,
> Of broken heads and blackened eyes
> And the "thirty days" to come!

Victor Yellin states that Chadwick was thinking about a camp of homeless vagrants that he had seen as he travelled back and forth to Worcester, as well as recalling the soft-shoe vaudeville routine of the stage-hobo, a tragicomic symbol of the entirely liberated man.[47] The percussion section includes a xylophone. The piece begins in a mock-serious A minor, yet it is not without some sincere pathos. The main theme, in the bass clarinet and bassoon, is a good-natured, yet eccentrically moving, ditty, whose every phrase differs melodically and rhythmically. No information has come to us about why Chadwick saw fit to throw in a snatch of a Bach fugue. This tune lays the groundwork for the free variations that follow. Speaking about *A Vagrom Ballad*, Oscar Sonneck states: "This gem of American musical humor, worthy of a Mark Twain, was composed in 1896, though not published until 1907! If certain of our younger composers brush aside such a piece as 'old foggish,' they are welcome to this opinion as they are to their naïve preferential belief in the efficacy of French as against German measles as a musical beautifier."[48]

Other orchestral compositions came from Chadwick during these productive years. The *Euterpe* Overture, completed in 1903 and premiered in 1904, contemplates the Muse of music. It sounds fresh and lyrical. It starts gloomily but later achieves some of the exhilarating syncopated feeling found in the *Symphonic Sketches*. Alternations in feeling between melancholy and joy reveal the two aspects of the Muse.

The Sinfonietta in D major was also heard for the first time in 1904. Less demanding than a symphony, the music is instantly enjoyable. One of Chadwick's most felicitous scores, the composition continues to retain its attractiveness even after many rehearings. The first movement begins a little like Elgar, with a confidently affirmative statement. Leading tones are avoided. Continuous syncopation imparts a characteristically American swing to most measures. The subsidiary theme acquires a Middle Eastern tinge and receives canonical treatment. The second movement, a *Canzonetta*, sounds like a prolonged modal folk song. The syncopated *Scherzino* movement usually abjures the leading tone; its smooth and bucolic Trio, as with the second theme of the first movement, contains Middle Eastern nuances. The Finale, briskly marchlike, has no strong melodic profile.

Completed in 1904 and heard in 1905, *Cleopatra*, Chadwick's first symphonic poem, comes with a program based on the Cleopatra of Plutarch, not Shakespeare. It depicts her journey on the Nile, the coming of Antony, the lovers' obsession with each other, the woeful end of Antony, the lamentation and death of Cleopatra, and the entombment of the two lovers in one grave. A strangeness, sensuousness, and exoticism not normally encountered in Chadwick's instrumental music enter the melodies and harmonies. Lawrence Gilman gives a long description of the program, relating it to the music, and says that the composer sanctioned his explanation. Gilman speaks of a Cleopatra theme and an Antony theme, explains their expressive transformations, and concludes his discussion with: "The work closes with an imposing passage in which the burial of Antony and Cleopatra in the same grave is suggested by the two themes now heard for the first time simultaneously."[49]

Finished in 1909, the *Suite Symphonique* in E-flat had its premiere in 1911. Its spirit and sound have a decided connection with those of the *Symphonic Sketches*, although this suite never achieved the reputation of the earlier composition. Especially winning are the *Romanza*, in particular the haunting saxophone solo, and the *Intermezzo e Humoreske*, with its cakewalking section in 5/4 time. Three years later the Symphonic Fantasie *Aphrodite* received its first performance. Fronting the score is a verse,[50] which begins:

> In a dim vision of the long ago
> Wandering by a far-off Grecian shore
> Where streaming moonlight shone on golden sands
> And melting stars dissolved in silver seas,
> I humbly knelt at Aphrodite's shrine.

Impressionistic splashes of tonal color and a perception of linear movement combine in the music. One cannot honestly say to what extent the music interprets the poem. The overall feeling conveyed is one that attends a grave, majestic, and mysterious figure invoked in the darkness of night.

A symphonic poem, *Angel of Death*, inspired by the Daniel French sculpture, was heard in 1919. However, *Tam O'Shanter*, a Symphonic Ballade, completed and performed in 1915, was the last work of Chadwick's to make an immense impression on audiences. The composition derives from the poem of Robert Burns, written in 1790. The published score comes complete with a detailed program relating the different sections of the music to the poem.[51] A first hearing offers a lesson on how problematic it is to label any music as exemplifying a specific sort of Americanism. Here is a work illustrating an inebriated Tam O'Shanter, a Scotsman, riding through a Scottish countryside at night. We detect the gapped scales, modal progressions, psalmody, folklike balladry, and dance tunes present in other Chadwick works. Various writers have said they accentuate Chadwick's individuality or his sensitivity to things American. When one or more of these characteristics occur in other musical contexts, however, various writers have claimed them to betoken the Celts, the

English, African Americans, or American Indians. For example, in the score to *Tam O'Shanter*, just before the practice letter *L* the double reeds and a trumpet play a "hornpipe dance tune," and at the close, just before *W* the first violins execute a *crescendo molto*. Both sound not unlike parts of MacDowell's *Indian Suite*.

A tipsy Tam O'Shanter rides home through storm and darkness. He is delineated by "a jocund, roistering chorus in the style of a Scottish folk-tune, given to the horns and trombones [Example 5.15], sometimes in different keys simultaneously." Shortly, an insistent eighth-note figure in the lower strings indicates the horse's canter; above occur fragments of Tam's tune. Later he nears Kirk Alloway, and part of an old Scottish tune, "Martyrs," materializes. To his amazement Tam glimpses an orgy taking place in the church, "described in a series of dances very much in the Scottish style." One dance is the hornpipe tune already mentioned (Example 5.16). Bagpipes squeal in the oboe and bassoon; bones rattle in the xylophone; "unearthly shrieks" come from the clarinets and muted horns; the trombones groan. The dance gets faster and faster, developing into a wild and "furious reel." Two threatening booms of a gong unleash screaming witches, who dash after Tam. The furious pursuit ends with Tam hurtling over a bridge to his home and safety. The prolonged coda is meditative, with quiet, sustained melody and simple harmonizations. Reminiscent phrases from previously heard tunes return, and the composition dies out on Tam's own theme.

Tam O'Shanter is certainly one of the most colorful scores by any American up until that time. Pomposity and sham are absent. Chadwick manifests an acute faculty for instrumental combinations and music appropriate to the poem. After the Chicago Symphony presented the composition in January 1916, a correspondent to the *Boston Transcript* praised its "sense of the sardonic," finding the music "quizzically humorous," "imaginative," "at once wry and picturesque." Chadwick, the writer said, had a sure sense of the Scottish, especially in the rhythms and in "a quirk of cadence." Yet, the reviewer found the Scottish tunes "closely akin to prevalent 'Americanisms' of music."[52]

Beginning in the twenties, Chadwick's music went out of fashion. In the latter part of the century, however, musicians began to rediscover the musical riches that had gone unnoticed for decades. Chadwick's compositions, along with those of other members of the New England group, received a few performances. Several were recorded. How long this will continue is hazardous to guess. We are reminded how uncertain, transient, and treacherous the vogue for an American composer is. Chadwick's persistence in seeking performances, his position as a prominent educator, and the support of powerful patrons sustained his music for the decades of his lifetime. With his death and the disappearance of his patrons, however, whatever vogue existed for his music departed. Now the interest in Chadwick may never become strong enough to become permanent. Nevertheless, he deserves to escape the fate of almost all other American composers no longer living, who are as much beyond the reach of the music public as though secreted away in Neolithic graves.

Chadwick's compositions are too fine to remain engulfed by silence. His orchestral writing glows. The melodies cheer the heart. Accompaniments add to the music's expressiveness. The introduction of counterpoint is always fitting. Harmonies progress logically. Yet, when Chadwick desires to summon a special mood or paint a sound picture, the music is as evocative as one might wish. He sees the value of glee as well as anguish. Chadwick remains an artist of sturdy integrity and splendid individuality.

NOTES

1. Richard Loucks, *Arthur Shepherd, American Composer* (Provo, Utah: Brigham Young University Press, 1980), 6.

2. John Tasker Howard, in *Dictionary of American Biography*, s.v. "Chadwick, George Whitefield"; also in John Tasker Howard, with the assistance of Arthur Mendel, *Our Contemporary Composers* (New York: Crowell, 1941), 11.

3. Arthur Farwell and W. Dermot Darby, eds., *Music in America, The Art of Music* 4 (New York: National Society of Music, 1915), 337.

4. *Grove's Dictionary of Music and Musicians*, 2nd ed., Vol. 6: The American Supplement, ed. Waldo Selden Pratt (Philadelphia: Presser, 1926), 158.

5. Carl Engel, "George W. Chadwick," *Musical Quarterly* 10 (1924): 440.

6. The example comes from George W. Chadwick, *Five Pieces for Pianoforte* (New York: Schirmer, copr. 1905).

7. I have discussed at length the musical characteristics of the artistic and semi-artistic songs that achieved popularity in this period in Chapter 9 of my book *The Way to Tin Pan Alley* (New York: Schirmer, 1990).

8. Rupert Hughes, *Contemporary American Composers* (Boston: Page, 1900), 214.

9. "Sweetheart, thy lips are touched with flame," No. 1 of *Lyrics from "Told in the Gate"* by Arlo Bates, set to music by George W. Chadwick (Boston: Schmidt, copr. 1897). The music is transposed for low voice.

10. Victor Yellin, "The Life and Operatic Works of George Whitefield Chadwick" (Ph.D. diss., Harvard University, 1957), 46.

11. Carl Engel, "Chadwick, George Whitefield," in *Cobbett's Cyclopedic Survey of Chamber Music*, 2nd ed., ed. Walter Willson Cobbett (London: Oxford Universtiy Press, 1963), 1:237.

12. Steven Ledbetter, album notes to recording Northeastern NR 236-CD.

13. Allan A. Brown Collection, scrapbook of clippings, **M371.11, in the Boston Public Library.

14. Ibid.

15. Ibid., **M371.4.

16. Ibid.; H. E. Krehbiel, *Review of the New York Musical Season, 1887–1888* (New York: Novello, Ewer, 1888), 36.

17. Steven Ledbetter, album notes to recording Northeastern NR 235-CD.

18. Olin Downes, "American Chamber Music," in *Cobbett's Cyclopedic Survey of Chamber Music*, 2nd ed., ed. Walter Willson Cobbett (London: Oxford University Press, 1963), 1:12.

19. All examples of the quartet are taken from the first-violin part, of George W. Chadwick, *String Quartet* No. 4, in E minor, parts only (Boston: Schmidt, copr. 1902).

20. These and other commentaries on the Chadwick Fourth Quartet are found in the Allan A. Brown Collection, scrapbook of clippings, **M. Cab. 1.38, in the Boston Public Library.

21. Steven Ledbetter, album notes to recording Northeastern 234-CD.

22. I first heard about Chadwick's discouragement around 1939, from someone who had known him and with whom I was studying musical theory while still a teenager, Walter Starbuck, of Waltham, Massachusetts. The Elson comment, from the *Advertiser*, is reprinted in the *New England Conservatory Magazine and Alumni Review* 4 (1913): 48.

23. Hughes, *Contemporary American Composers*, 212.

24. See especially the report in the *Courier*, available in the Allan A. Brown Collection, scrapbook of clippings, **M304.1, Vol. 5, in the Boston Public Library.

25. Hughes, *Contemporary American Composers*, 213; see also the Allan A. Brown Collection, scrapbook of clippings, **M304.1, Vol. 2, for reviews of its first performance.

26. Allan A. Brown Collection, scrapbook of clippings, *M122.5 and **M165.8, Vol. 2, in the Boston Public Library.

27. *New England Conservatory Magazine-Review* 7 (1917): 84.

28. Engel, "George W. Chadwick," 448.

29. George W. Chadwick, *Tabasco*, Burlesque Opera (Boston: Wood, copr. 1894).

30. Steven Ledbetter and Victor Fell Yellin, in H. Wiley Hitchcock and Stanley Sadie, eds., *The New Grove Dictionary of American Music* (London: Macmillan, 1986), s.v. "Chadwick, George Whitefield."

31. Allan A. Brown Collection, scrapbook of clippings, **M433.5, in the Boston Public Library.

32. Louis C. Elson, *The History of American Music*, rev. to 1925 by Arthur Elson (New York: Macmillan, 1925), 175.

33. The examples are from George W. Chadwick, *Judith*, Lyric Drama (New York: Schirmer, copr. 1901).

34. Allan Lincoln Langley, "Chadwick and the New England Conservatory of Music," *Musical Quarterly* 21 (1935): 51.

35. Engel, "George W. Chadwick," 452.

36. "Music in Boston," *Dwight's Journal of Music* 29 (1879): 205.

37. Allan A. Brown Collection, scrapbook of clippings, M125.2, Vol. 2, in the Boston Public Library.

38. See especially the reviews in the Gazette and the Advertiser (ibid., **M125.5, Vol. 2).

39. Ibid., Vol. 3.
40. Ibid., Vol. 6.
41. A few years ago I studied the Chadwick Second Symphony and the two piano concertos of MacDowell in relation to the Dvořák Ninth Symphony, "From the New World," which was composed later, comparing themes, rhythms, phrase patterns, harmonic progressions, and orchestrations. What had spurred me on was my noticing that several passages in the Chadwick composition especially, but also in those of MacDowell, sounded similar to some pages of the Dvořák work. Furthermore, I found out, the Bohemian composer might have attended performances of these American compositions while he was in the United States and giving shape to his own work. Some day in the future, an article will present my conclusions.
42. Allan A. Brown Collection, scrapbook of clippings, **M125.5, Vol. 10, in the Boston Public Library.
43. Ibid., **M165.9, Vol. 6.
44. Examples are from George W. Chadwick, *Symphony No. 2*, in B flat (Boston: Schmidt, copr. 1888).
45. Allan A. Brown Collection, scrapbook of clippings, **M125.5, Vol. 15, in the Boston Public Library. For other reviews, see Vols. 7, 8, and 18.
46. George W. Chadwick, *Symphonic Sketches*, Suite for Orchestra (New York: Kalmus, n.d.).
47. Victor Fell Yellin, "Chadwick, American Musical Realist," *Musical Quarterly* 61 (1975): 91.
48. Oscar G. Sonneck, *Suum Cuique: Essays in Music* (1916; reprinted, Freeport, N.Y.: Books for Libraries, 1969), 33.
49. Lawrence Gilman, *Stories of Symphonic Music* (New York: Harper and Brothers, 1908), 54–55.
50. George W. Chadwick, *Aphrodite*, Symphonic Fantasie (Boston: Schmidt, copr. 1912).
51. George W. Chadwick, *Tam O'Shanter*, Symphonic Ballade (Boston: Boston Music, copr. 1917).
52. Reprinted in the *New England Conservatory Magazine Review* 6 (1916): 76–77.

6

EDWARD MACDOWELL (1860–1908)

Edward MacDowell, beginning with his earliest compositions, was a composer with a stronger devotion to the principles of romanticism and a weaker allegiance to classical tradition than Paine and Chadwick had. He allowed free rein to his creative imagination. Personal feeling was translated into as full a musical expression as possible. Careful invention of subject matter suited to a logical and balanced structure was not a priority. Delineating mood or emotion was a prime consideration.

During boyhood, MacDowell studied piano with Latin American teachers, among them the Venezuelan virtuoso Teresa Carreño. They encouraged the cultivation of imagination and feelings in the aid of musical expression. Later, his instructor in composition was the composer Joseph Joachim Raff, a friend and admirer of Franz Liszt and identified as belonging to the new Romantic school of Liszt, which had cast off most classical inhibitions. Not surprisingly, MacDowell came to admire the music of Raff, Liszt, and Wagner. Grieg and Tchaikovsky also excited him. On the other hand, the more classically oriented Brahms usually left him indifferent,[1] and French music held no attraction for him. Old music classics "drained his strength," so he avoided listening to them. He found "new and other modern works more interesting, and their scoring more important."[2]

Every now and again in MacDowell's music (for example, in the first movement of the First Piano Concerto), one hears a musical theme similar to one of Grieg. Yet, as John Tasker Howard correctly points out, MacDowell's music is significantly different from that of Grieg. Despite his fondness for brief characteristic pieces for the piano, MacDowell built more spacious structures into his ambitious compositions, especially the piano sonatas. More often than Grieg, he sought to make large, heroic statements. Unlike Grieg, he avoided what he considered an invidious attachment to one's country and had no desire to be a nationalist composer.[3] He read omnivorously; what he read fired his creativity. He relished poetry, mythology, medieval tales, and the writings of Mark Twain and Joel Chandler Harris.[4] Paintings, sculptures, and the outdoors also enkindled his inventiveness.

He left Germany after failing to find a permanent position abroad and went to live in Boston in September 1888. Piano and composition students flocked to him, among them Henry Gilbert and Ethelbert Nevin. His concerts were well attended and his own works enthusiastically endorsed. MacDowell's piano performances featuring his own compositions became important musical events for Bostonians. This favorable reception encouraged him to produce fantasy pieces, idylls, poems, nocturnes, mood pictures, virtuosic studies, and sonatas for solo piano. Moreover, the Boston Symphony performed his orchestral works regularly: suites, symphonic poems, and concertos with the composer at the keyboard. He was thus stimulated to write several pieces for orchestra.

Leaving Boston in 1896 for a teaching post at Columbia University was a tragic mistake. Visits to Boston and the purchase of a much-loved summer home in Peterborough, New Hampshire, could not relieve the mental strain brought on by overwork and the battles with administration over financing the music department and recognizing the academic worthiness of musical studies. John Erskine, one of MacDowell's students at Columbia, states that the atmosphere for anyone in music was "heart-chilling." When Erskine told Dean Van Amringe of his interest in taking music courses, the dean tried to dissuade him from doing so: "The idea had not yet penetrated the academic skull that music is a house-broken subject, deserving polite toleration if not hospitality. For most of the cultural high priests, music was still something you 'took up' on the side, a mental discipline less rigorous and possibly less rewarding than poker."[5] MacDowell resigned in 1904, succumbed to acute nervous prostration, and died in 1908.

On a subsequent page, Erskine sheds light on MacDowell's attitude toward introducing sounds identifiably American into a music piece. MacDowell once told his composition students that their pieces might pass as European; however, neither the themes nor rhythms suggested that they lived in New York. He added that he set no value on conscious nationalism, "but an artist must accept himself for better or for worse." According to

Erskine, MacDowell told his students that "what we whistled, sang or played in moments of relaxation more often than not was ragtime. Well, if syncopated rhythms were natural to us, why not try to make them something important? 'I would do it myself,' he went on, 'if I had not lived so long in Europe. Ragtime is not instinctive with me as it is with you—though I did make an attempt at it in the scherzo of my *Second Concerto.*' "[6]

Jo Shipley Watson amplifies Erskine's statements about MacDowell in an article entitled "MacDowell as a Teacher," which appeared in the *Boston Transcript* of 14 September 1907: " 'Harmony,' Professor MacDowell used to say, 'gives atmosphere for the melody; it is the tone background for melody; it enforces the melodic trend; but the main thing is the melodic trend. . . . Nationalism must be based upon the spirit of the people, not upon the clothes they wear. . . . Out of our idealism, our music will grow.' "[7]

MacDowell's music is usually serious, emotional, and shaped by an introspective contemplation of remembered experiences. He considered himself a poet-singer and invariably wrote around a poetic idea. He wished to compose music that captured an aspect of nature, the essence of myth and fairyland, or the spirit of romance, chivalry, and heroism. Although he might provide an evocative title, he rarely supplied a detailed program to accompany a work. A broad suggestion of its character sufficed. Each work set forth a primary ambiance and sustained it to the end. Marian MacDowell explained that her husband held that a poetic title aided a performer's interpretation without limiting imagination. MacDowell's "writing was never descriptive in a realistic sense; it was the expression of a mood which might be awakened by a scene, a poem, an idea, or an experience." His music was seldom "pictorial or imitative. It presents the spirit of a picture rather than the picture itself."[8]

Most melodies receive particular contours and figurations that are peculiarly his own. They seem unlabored, pliant, and directly appealing. More than with Paine or Chadwick, MacDowell's harmony is notably individual in construction and deployment. Textures tend to be more solid and full. Harmonic and nonharmonic dissonance has increased for coloristic or expressive purposes. Chromaticism, frequent modulation, and appealing or forceful contrasts abound. The entire paraphernalia of rhythmic devices exploited by the late Romantics and some rhythms unique to America were at his command.

His piano miniatures display an assortment of charms. His piano sonatas alternate passages of dramatic power with others of great tenderness.

MacDowell stated that he intended his structures to give "poignant expression" to his poetic thought. He arranged sounds "so that they constituted the most telling presentation of a musical idea." The miniatures were normally cast in a simple A B A ternary form because that was how they best showed themselves off. The sonatas employed freely elaborated, though traditionally derived, structures, like the sonata-allegro, rondo, and sonata-rondo forms. Symphonic poems were given unique designs. No form was a matter of periods, sections, and main and subsidiary themes. It had to be the "most telling presentation of a musical idea." Form was "nothing more than a synonym for *coherence*."[9]

MacDowell was not interested in experimental concepts and techniques for their own sake. For the most part, he accepted the sound-world as defined by Raff, Liszt, and Wagner. He worked within clearly marked confines with a continual return of certain interrelationships of sound and with a circumscribed range of expression. Nevertheless, he managed to impress a number of musicians from his own time. An English admirer of MacDowell quotes the French composer Jules Massenet in the *Musical Times* of London (1904): "Que j'aime les ouvres de ce jeune compositeur Américain MacDowell! Quel musicien! Il est sincére et personnel—quel poète—quelles exquises harmonies!"[10] The New York *Evening Post* (1906) cites the Viennese musician Bruno Weigl as saying of MacDowell's late works: "His music becomes passionately agitated, with gradations and climaxes of overwhelming power and grandeur; then again, there are melancholy, serious, profound strains that contrast marvelously and strikingly with his impassioned style. As for his harmonies, they share the inclination of the most modern masters to the feint [*sic*] closes, the motley 'Chromatik,' and 'Enharmonik,' and the multiplicity in the thematic elaboration. At the same time there is astounding technical skill in the formation of the most varied suspension harmonies such as we find in a few only of our modern masters."[11]

THE SONGS

MacDowell composed forty-six songs for voice and piano. The melody is of fundamental consequence in all of them. In several songs, it shows a kinship to American folk song of Anglo-Celtic origin in its simplicity and somewhat formulaic traits. Above all, MacDowell tried to create a smooth, emotionally convincing, and rhythmically attractive tune to evoke the main expressive thrust of the poem. The unforced evolvement of the vocal line had priority of importance over accurate declamation. Music engendered its own inflections, and MacDowell believed it was an error for a composer to comply subserviently with those of the verse. Harmony had to enhance the potency of expression, thus adding to the music's *élan vital*. He opted for flexibility and a chordal approach in the accompaniment, showing only slight interest in any characteristic figuration that continues for any length of time in the piano part. Few American composers had MacDowell's facility for capturing the implicit attributes, the psychological intent, of a poem. He selected poetry for setting that suited his temperament and special gifts, or he wrote his own.

Henry Finck says that MacDowell's own characteristic song style appears with his opus 26, *From an Old Garden*, a set of six songs composed in 1886 and 1887. A fine mellifluousness pervades the vocal line, especially in the best song, "The Mignonette," lyrics by M. Deland. The *Three Songs*, opus 33, and *Two Songs*, opus 34 (1887–88), reveal growing sensitivity to the harmonic background. Finck finds that the variegated harmonic colorings in "Idyll," verse by Goethe, are particularly interesting; "Menie," verse by Burns, breathes an "exquisite melancholy."[12] These were the last songs MacDowell produced while he lived abroad.

In 1890, and now in Boston, MacDowell composed *Six Love Songs*, opus 40, to poems by W. H. Gardner. The public found number 3 of this set, "Thy Beaming Eyes," the most pleasing of all the songs that he wrote during his lifetime. As in most poems that the composer chose to set, the subject is love. A nicely thought out tune having few complications and an accompaniment of slowly changing chords that are easily executed account for much of its popularity. The song lacks a prelude and closes with a perfunctory postlude. Hardly any melodic interest is found in the piano part. The piece is to be sung "with sentiment, passionately." The song has that elusive capability of making a listener believe it addresses him or her alone.

Number 5 of opus 40, "O Lovely Rose," is also attractive. In this strophic song, to be sung "slowly, with great simplicity," the composer introduces hardly any dissonance. The accompaniment is light; the tonality swings between home key and submediant.

Eight Songs, opus 47, finished in 1893, was set to three poems by MacDowell, three by Howells, and two by Goethe. All are likable examples of his mature style. Number 1, "The Robin Sings in the Appletree," with words by the composer, has music given a fragile, yearning quality meant to delineate love that has died and having the lilt of a grave dance. Number 2, "Midsummer Lullaby," has melodic allure, graceful movement, and polished penetration of the subject. Number 3, the slow-moving, pathetic "Folksong" to Howells's verse, is not really folklike, its use of the Scotch snap (accented sixteenth to unaccented eighth note) and opening in the submediant modal minor notwithstanding. All seven tones of the C-minor home key are utilized. Leading tones are always present. Harmonic structures and progressions reveal a great deal of sophistication.

Each of the songs that follow—"Confidence," "The West-wind Croons in the Cedar-trees," "In the Woods"—has its attractions. Then comes possibly MacDowell's finest song, number 7, to Howell's poem "The Sea." MacDowell wishes this song to be sung "broadly, with rhythmic swing." The subject concerns a lonely woman standing on the seashore and awaiting the return of her lover, not knowing that his ship has sunk and he has drowned. The composer provides neither prelude nor postlude, preferring to allow the singer to tell the story from the start, while the pianist underlies the vocal line with tones that heighten the perception of calamity. The piece sounds at first like a guileless sea chantey, but at the fifth measure art replaces artlessness in order to summon up the strange, ominous atmosphere surrounding the sinking ship (Example 6.1).

The last song of opus 47, "Through the Meadow," has been criticized in a recent book on American song as having a "cloyingly sentimental" text (by Howells) and an undistinguished melody.[13] This listener disagrees. The piece is deliberately kept easy to perform and appreciate. If sung "Not too slow, piquantly," the tune sounds not unlike several from the world of American popular song. Howells's light satire on a coquette acting to attract admiration does not aim for profundity, nor does the music. The constant use of *staccato*, the scarcity of half steps in the melody, the admonitions to perform the music "lightly" and "in time," and the six artificial slackenings in tempo to emphasize the flirtatiousness dilute the sweetness.

MacDowell later wrote at least three other sets of songs worthy of attention: *Four Songs*, opus 56 (1898); *Three Songs*, opus 58 (1899); and *Three Songs*, opus 60 (1901). The fine song "Constancy (New England A.D. 1899)," opus 58, number 1, discourses on a deserted house and garden in order to bring out the theme of neglect, decay, and mortality. The verse, by MacDowell, ends on the lines "For house and ye shall pass away, / Yea! even as my song." Considering the decades of misunderstanding and neglect that followed his death, these words could stand as an epitaph for MacDowell and his music.

MUSIC FOR ORCHESTRA

The Piano Concerto No. 1, in A minor, of 1882, was MacDowell's first large work requiring an orchestra. Written and premiered in Europe, this bold and ear-catching composition was heard and praised by Franz Liszt, who urged the young musician to devote himself to musical composition. The first movement begins with a solemn solo-piano introduction that anticipates the main theme of the *Allegro*, where solemnity changes to conflict and confrontation between piano and orchestra. The subordinate theme supplies a welcome lyrical relief to the strife. The second movement presents a serene, discreetly orchestrated melody, and the Finale is fittingly exuberant.

MacDowell's only other piano concerto, number 2 in D minor, was also composed in Germany, between 1884 and 1886, and had its American premiere in New York City on 5 March 1889, with Theodore Thomas conducting and the composer at the keyboard. Most critics who heard it then and over the next two decades described it as skillfully written, dazzlingly virtuosic, fanciful, and accoutered with outstanding musical ideas. A few found it too modern for their tastes, too prodigal in ideas, or too diffuse in structure.[14] An enthusiastic review came from H. E. Krehbiel, in the *New York Tribune*, March 1889, who wrote that the work was original, poetic, and possibly the finest concerto "produced by either a native or adopted son of America."[15]

The first movement, no matter what the tempo markings, strikes the listener as essentially slow moving. A disarmingly elegiac melody in muted strings leads to an impassioned declamatory statement in the piano, then back to the elegy, now played by the flute. The speed increases somewhat as the piano enters with the tempestuous principal theme. The subordinate theme, based on the melody of the opening, is in the relative major key. After a fiery development, the recapitulation metamorphoses the materials already introduced. The conclusion seems rather abbreviated. Because a follow-up of this first movement with something slow may have seemed redundant, MacDowell instead wrote a scherzo *presto giocoso*. The bulk of the movement is given over to the fleeting-note passages and syncopations of the piano. The Finale recycles the themes of the first movement, heard in a variety of transformations, both in the *largo* introduction and in the ensuing *molto allegro*. The music comes across resplendently, yet with elements of regret and heartache.

The two piano concertos called forth the best in the composer. The several symphonic poems that MacDowell wrote do not portray him at his best, at least to this listener. The first, *Hamlet and Ophelia*, subtitled "two poems for large orchestra," dates from 1884–85. A London performance of Shakespeare's *Hamlet* in 1884, while the newlywed composer was on vacation in England with his bride, prompted its creation. The premiere of the complete work took place in Boston on 28 January 1893. The composer never supplied a program. It exists as two movements: the first, entitled "Hamlet," in D minor; the second, "Ophelia," in F major. Both share the same musical material. Although the work is warmly romantic and richly scored, its attempts at drama and tragedy seem overdone. Episodes are loosely connected. Only in the highly lyrical theme, first presented in "Hamlet" and, one assumes, meant to depict Ophelia, does a really attractive melody emerge. The instrumentation employed here and in most of MacDowell's orchestral compositions represents the usual enlarged orchestra of his time.

The second symphonic poem, *Lancelot and Elaine*, inspired by the poem of Alfred, Lord Tennyson, dates from 1886. The Boston Symphony Orchestra gave its American premiere on 10 January 1890. Again, the composer failed to supply a program. Presumably, the music depicts Lancelot's chivalric nature and Elaine's love for him. For those in need of a program, Lawrence Gilman has invented a lengthy one, in *Stories of Symphonic Music*.[16] The composition seems an improvement over the first tone poem. Musical ideas are stronger. However, despite its attractive moments, the work is even more episodic and lacks a compelling vision of the whole.

A poem by John Keats lies behind MacDowell's third symphonic poem, *Lamia* (1887). A preface to the score, published by Schmidt in 1908, gives the program. The serpent-enchantress Lamia loves Lycius, and in the form of a beautiful young moman she gets him to marry her in her enchanted palace. Soon, the magician Apollonius comes on the scene and exposes the sorcery. Lamia reverts to serpenthood, the palace vanishes, and Lycius dies. The piece starts off well, with a sad theme in cellos, then violins, that represents the yearning Lamia, followed by the chromatic slithering about of the lower strings and bassoons. Later, a flute plays a recast version of the opening. This is followed by three horns on a staunch new theme *allegro con fuoco*, pleasing in itself, but whose connection to the program is unconvincing. Nor is the depiction of the rest of the drama particularly persuasive. The structure remains wobbly.

MacDowell's last attempt at symphonic poetry was *The Saracens and the Beautiful Alda*, two fragments after the *Song of Roland*, first performed in 1891. Two excerpts from the *Song of Roland* head the score, published by Breitkopf and Härtel in 1891. The music is more solid than that of the previous tone poems and its working-out more convincing, but the two movements are over almost before they begin. One wishes that more had been made of them.

Perhaps by 1891 MacDowell had wearied of all the seriousness, Germanic *ängst*, and flustering need to integrate into his music Romantic *eros* and *agape*, physical and idealized love, virility and softness. At any rate, he ceased writing symphonic poems and composed a less weighty but delightful First Suite for Orchestra, opus 42, in four movements. Another movement, "In October," was added two years later.[17] Creation of mood and evocation of atmosphere supplant the programmatic story-telling, implied or stated, of the symphonic poems. The composition as it now stands has five movements: "In a Haunted Forest," "Summer Idyll," "In October," "The Shepherdess Song," and "Forest Spirits." The Boston Symphony played the original, four-movement suite in September 1891, and the complete suite in October 1895. The titles come straight out of German Romanticism; much in the music does not. A style characteristic of MacDowell and having some affinity with that of Chadwick prevails in most movements. Lawrence Gilman, who admired all of MacDowell's program music for orchestra except for *Lamia*, felt let down. He admired the suite's moods, freshness, buoyancy, and exquisite scoring but found it lacked "persuasion [and] . . . inspiration."[18] Perhaps Gilman erred in his assessment.

The A-minor first movement, "In a Haunted Forest," is the most Germanic of the lot. Its opening subject, slow, quiet, and mysterious, resembles the start of Schumann's Fourth Symphony in D minor. Yet, the idea is handled quite differently. After thirty-four measures, the music bounds into a tumultuous *allegro* that nicely delineates the night-obscured commotion of forest sprites. The "Summer Idyll" in A major, is a captivatingly graceful dance in 6/8 time. A buoyant tune prances about mostly in the violins against a deftly colored accompaniment. "In October" begins with a French-horn motive that instantly conjures up an autumnal forest scene. This motive dominates the movement. The next movement, "The Shepherdess song," is based on a version of an oboe melody heard in the previous movement. It no sooner begins than it is over. It seems to function as a buffer between the prior movement and the final one. The most American-sounding of all the movements is "Forest Spirits," in A minor. A blithely syncopated tune, played *staccato*, sounds off. In the middle, the composer introduces a syncopated tune heard in the violins and violas that seems to stem from American minstrelsy (Example 6.2).

Between 1891 and 1895, MacDowell worked on one of his most important compositions, the Second ("Indian") Suite for Large Orchestra, opus 48. H. E. Krehbiel maintains that the composer had fully sketched the piece before Dvořák had written his "New World" Symphony. On the other hand, T. P. Currier insists that he heard MacDowell mention a connection with the Dvořák work, although he is uncertain what that connection was.[19] The Boston Symphony introduced the suite in New York and Boston in January 1896. The Boston audience, in particular, approved it, recalling the composer a dozen times, according to his wife Marian. She adds: "It is a symbol of his love for Boston that of all the many trophies he received throughout his life, the great laurel wreath that was given him on this occasion was the only one he cared to preserve."[20] One or two Boston reviewers disliked the composition. The *Boston Transcript* critic found it tedious and hideously adorned with "barbarous folk-tunes." The *Herald* writer found masterly instrumentation and original effects but little real music. In the *Advertiser*, the reviewer spoke of the composer's high skills, but he also disliked his music. He said that no national music could be based on aboriginal themes. However, Philip Hale, in the *Journal*, stated that composers are not Indians and cannot build a national school on Indian or African-American music; nor did he think that MacDowell attempted to do so. He praised MacDowell's sincerity, original use of instruments, and avoidance of conventional procedures. The work had rare beauty for him and deserved the designation of masterpiece.[21]

Like the First Suite, this work has five movements: "Legend," "Love Song," "In War-time," "Dirge," and "Village Festival." A prefatory remark by the composer states that the thematic material was suggested by melodies of the North American Indians, which occasionally show similarities to northern European themes.[22] He freely embroiders these melodies and adds several of his own. All of them bear a likeness to one another, thus helping to unify the several movements. The listener finds that, because of the inventive ways MacDowell handles his material, fascination rather than boredom predominates. The composer grabs one's attention from the beginning and holds it to the end.

MacDowell had no intention of composing a national piece; he did have in mind the emotions arising out of a poetic contemplation of Indian life. The tunes had come to him secondhand, probably from Theodore Baker's *Über die Musik der nordamerikanischen Wilden* (Leipzig: Breitkopf and Härtel, 1882), and he used them as he saw fit. They became completely his own through the way he treated them. Indianisms are absent. Subjective feeling is to the fore. Charles Wakefield Cadman, a composer deeply interested in Indian music, found the Second Suite fascinating and "not a mere ethnological report set to music." He heard a happy balance of musical values, "of atmosphere obtained, of triumph, of dignity, even of melancholy, wedded to finely conceived contrasts and dynamics."[23]

The "Legend" introduces Iroquois and Chippewa melodies. No story is told. It begins with an evocative horn call. The movement soon doubles its speed, and clarinets and bassoons present a resolute principal theme *staccato*, which is eventually metamorphosed to reflect a variety of moods. The second movement, "Love Song," to be played "tenderly," uses a melody of the Iowas. Later, a second tune, which has obvious affiliations with the principal theme of the first movement, sounds.

The third movement, "In War-time," borrows themes of the Atlantic Coast Indians, which are to be played "with rough vigor, almost savagely." An Iroquois war song, in modal D minor and 2/4 time, starts up in the flutes. When the violins take up the idea, twenty-nine measures later, the sprightly melody resembles the sort of English folk tune that Ralph Vaughan Williams and Gustav Holst liked to introduce into some of their compositions. A development ensues. Then suddenly activity ceases. A soft *pizzicato* string chord brings in a clarinet in the low chalumeau range, playing an anguished wail, characterized by a half-step and an augmented-fourth descent, played *legato*. A feeling of desolation prevails. Then the war dance returns.

MacDowell requests the orchestra to perform the "Dirge" slowly and mournfully. The theme, heard throughout the movement, is the bleak one that had appeared briefly in the middle of the previous movement. Based on a Kiowa melody, it begins in G minor and 4/4 time, played by the low violins against a constantly sounding tone G given to a piccolo, flutes, and two muted horns, one of them in the orchestra and the other behind the scene (Example 6.3). The poignant dissonance of f′ descending to e′, against the several tones G spread over three octaves, generates the desired expression with a masterly economy of means. The theme is pursued through a number of modulations. The movement ends with a hushed trumpet behind the scene murmuring a final lamentation. Gilman recorded MacDowell's own comment on the "Dirge": "In 1903 . . . he expressed a preference for the 'Dirge'. . . above anything that he had composed. 'Of all my music,' he confessed at this time, 'the "Dirge" in the "Indian" suite pleases me most. It affects me deeply and did when I was writing it. In it an Indian woman laments the death of her son; but to me, as I wrote it, it seemed to express a world-sorrow rather than a particularized grief.' "[24]

The last movement is the fast and light "Village Festival." Although the material is said to be of Iroquois derivation, one notices that the initial melody is a mutation of the lamentation theme and also has a link to the secondary theme of the first movement. A brisk, dancy tune implies revelry, but MacDowell leaves everything to suggestion; no pictoralism is attempted. A slower variant on the theme occurs in the middle. A final return to the brisk tune forms a swift conclusion to the entire composition.

In his notes for the Boston Symphony program booklet, Philip Hale spoke of the Second Suite's force and tenderness. He thought it unnecessary to wonder if the composition consisted of distinctively American music, "for the best pages of the suite are not parochial—they are not national. They are universal in their appeal to sensitive hearers of any land."[25] Quite a few listeners have concurred with this opinion.

THE PIANO MINIATURES

MacDowell produced a far greater quantity of works for the piano than did Paine or Chadwick. MacDowell himself once confessed that he preferred to write for piano rather than for orchestra, because getting an orchestra to perform a work was a headache, and usually he would hear such a work played perhaps once every two or three years. On the other hand, he himself could play any of his piano compositions whenever he wished.[26]

Whether miniatures or lengthy sonatas, his piano music had tremendous success with the men and women of his time. His finest keyboard works struck several contemporary experts in music as supreme artistic achievements. Discriminating music lovers were moved by a romantic ardor and contagious lyricism rarely heard in the piano compositions of other Americans. Quite a few listeners prized his piano music because it allayed their concerns about a viable American body of piano composition that was subjectively romantic in a manner analogous to the piano works of Chopin, Schumann, and Liszt. The music furnished by Paine and Chadwick, to whom they could not avoid comparing MacDowell, had a deliberateness and an overly objective control that lacked appeal for those wishing a less inhibited play of fancy. They proved responsive to the way MacDowell's piano compositions embodied the feelings awakened in him by external things or happenings. They also savored MacDowell's playing of his own works, which was definitely impressionistic, according to Currier. The music could sound as if "floating in space. Pieces clearly written and 'splendid for practice,' became streams of murmuring or rushing tone. Delicate chord-groups, like his melodies, floated in air; while those in *fortissimi* resembled nothing so much as full orchestral bursts."[27]

Fine as his most mature pieces may be, however, they can now and again strike the ear of a later listener as close to becoming too alike in the types of mood projected and the way the music realizes a mood. A better appreciation arises when one listens to one piece at a time or to batches of two or three pieces. The moods heard in most of the miniatures of MacDowell's maturity are restricted mostly to three: the tender song-without-words with the tune in the upper part, melodious, *legato*, and the fingers of both hands occupied with a chordal accompaniment; the majestic statement, somewhat declamatory in nature, sonorous, thickly textured, the most significant part set forth in octaves, and the deep bass utilized; and the high-spirited, playful bagatelle, such as the pieces depicting autumnal scenes or "Uncle Remus" or "Bre'r Rabbit," where patterns of sound are less chordal and dense, syncopations are often introduced, and sixteenth notes are likely to dart about in a whimsical manner. Real contrapuntal activity is rare. Thin textures are normally not for him. Foreign to his style is a plain single-note tune in one hand, accompanied by some sort of broken-chord figuration, also set forth in single notes, in the other. Interestingly, a majority of the miniatures, even many of the études, pose no great technical difficulties. Their challenge lies in the interpretation of the poetic expression required by the composer.

He loves to muse upon things outside himself—lovers, sunset, a flower, an abandoned building, an ocean scene, the New England of Pilgrim and Puritan times—and tell in music how they affected him. Titles, at times a line or a brief poem, indicate the direction of his thought. Otherwise, he leaves it to his listeners to fill in the details from their own imaginations.

The compositions written during MacDowell's sojourn in Germany cannot, of course, compare with the consummate works of his later years. The young musician modeled his music after the examples of his European mentors and Raff in particular. Piece after piece shows the artist eager to prove his command of his craft, yet reluctant to strike out on his own. One should not look for boldness and individuality. Nevertheless, several of the early compositions are satisfying in their own right, especially when heard in their revised versions. Indeed, the older MacDowell had an inveterate tendency to amend almost all of his earlier music, normally for the better. When a year is cited for the compositions that follow, it represents the original date that a work was completed, not the date for any revision. The titles given are those of the later, usually revised,

American editions. The early works were first published in Leipzig or Breslau; the revisions, usually in Boston.

The First and Second Modern Suites (1881, 1882) persuaded masters like Liszt to take notice of the aspiring composer. Breitkopf and Härtel of Leipzig published the suites at Liszt's urging. The unassuming *Serenade*, opus 16 (1882), has a fetchingly subdued melody to a guitar-like accompaniment heard before and after a succinct but bright middle segment. The "Witches' Dance" from *Two Fantastic Pieces*, opus 17 (1883), proved popular in its time, although the composer later scorned it. Even if unoriginal, it has a facile charm more appropriate for the parlor than for the recital hall.

The four pieces in *Forest Idyls*, opus 19 (1884), suggest that the composer is beginning to find his own voice through a poetic rendition of a mythological outdoor scene. The pieces are titled "Forest Stillness," "Play of the Nymphs," "Revery," and "Dryads' Dance." Reality supplants myth as the starting point for his mood-pictures in *Six Idyls after Goethe*, opus 28, and *Six Poems after Heine*, opus 31 (both finished in 1887). The poems refer to real objects, people, and settings. His skill in distinguishing subjective states of mind has grown. Commenting on "Scotch Poem," opus 31 no. 2, Marian MacDowell observes: "In so much of his music one feels the strong influence of his Scotch-Irish (Keltic) blood." Throughout all of his compositions one senses a "Northern atmosphere," so distinctive "that he would never be mistaken as having been, for instance, of Latin birth."[28]

Four Little Poems, opus 31 (1887), contains two particularly fine pieces: number 1, "The Eagle"; and number 4, "Winter." The former sounds with fitting grandeur as full chords high in the piano commence an interpretation of Tennyson's poem on the eagle who "clasps the crag with crooked hands." Later, a wide void between the two hands perfectly symbolizes the void between an eagle's aerie and the earth below. The latter piece, on a poem by Shelley, captures the stillness of the frigid landscape, starting with the quiet arpeggiated opening to a birdlike twitter on a″, and later in the ruminative tune in the piano's mid-range that starts on measure 17.

Marionettes, opus 38, was originally published in 1888. MacDowell later completed a much-improved, revised edition, which Schmidt of Boston issued in 1901, with two new items, a "Prologue" and an "Epilogue." The composer conceives of these puppet figures as in part mechanically moving comic absurdities, and in part oddly human in their capacity to feel. Caprice, humor, sardonicism, and a queer kind of sadness mingle in these little pieces. The men and women of the audience may perhaps perceive themselves in the music, but MacDowell is sufficiently canny that they could easily miss seeing their caricatures. The "Prologue" is very much in the style of an American stage musical à la Victor Herbert, and it is a fitting curtain raiser for what follows. The music of the "Prologue" mirrors the two sides of drama: the serious, in the mid-range *legato* tune, to be played "pleadingly"; and the comic, in the higher-pitched detached eighth notes, performed "mockingly," that abruptly cuts off the seriousness.

"Soubrette" becomes a manipulated doll dancing without suppleness. Yet, in the middle of the piece, the music slows and a smooth tune gives her a measure of humanity. "Lover" exhibits the same duality. The dynamics always remain subdued, as if too much feeling would overwhelm the piece. "Witch" and "Clown" display rigid *staccato* motion throughout. The figures are entirely artificial. The witch never threatens; the clown never cries. All is pleasant make-believe. "Villain" sports music to accompany stage action. Obviously, MacDowell's "with sinister emphasis" was set down tongue in cheek. For a couple of minutes, in the winsome "Sweetheart," the marionettes are allowed to appear very human. The lover sings "simply" and "sweetly" about the charms of his beloved. The brief "Epilogue" discloses the feelings of the composer as he reminates for a last moment on his characters. The suite concludes, as it began, in F major and 3/4 time but without the earlier amiability. Instead, the curtain closes with a final compassionate glance at the marionettes. Allusions to the mediant and the submediant minor key elicit pity for them. The sound remains subdued throughout.

MacDowell published two sets of studies, twelve in 1890 (opus 39) and twelve more in 1894 (opus 46). Each étude is prefaced with a title. For example, in opus 39, the first is a "Hunting Song"; the fifth, "In the Forest"; and the last, "Hungarian." In opus 46, the first is "Novelette"; the seventh, "Burlesque"; and the last, "Polonaise." All twenty-four numbers are enjoyable. Possibly the freely communicative and subjective "Novelette" is the most outstanding of them all. "Burlesque" puckishly entertains; the conventional "Polonaise" is agreeably rousing.

The finest of MacDowell's short characteristic pieces are collected in four suites: *Woodland Sketches*, opus 51 (1896); *Sea Pieces*, opus 55 (1898); *Fireside Tales*, opus 61 (1902); and *New England Idyls*, opus 62 (1902). Each work is clearly structured and compact. Each is an individual tonal painting executed by a sure hand certain of what it wants to achieve and how to achieve it. One may be a modest diatonic ditty supported by consonant triads; another, a complex chromatic melody heard above altered seventh and ninth chords. Most conform to the three stylistic approaches mentioned earlier. Ternary form prevails.

Lawrence Gilman, a MacDowell enthusiast, wrote of the ten *Woodland Sketches* as follows: "The method is the method of Shelley in the 'Sensitive Plant,' of Wordsworth in 'The Daffodils,' as it is the method of Raff rather than of Wagner—although Raff could never have written with precisely that order of delicate eloquence. . . . Always he is the admirable poet, intent upon realizing through the medium of tones rather than of words, a deep and intimate vision of the natural world."[29] The natural world was that surrounding his Peterborough summer home, purchased in 1895, which he envisioned in most of the pieces. And it was in Peterborough that he wrote all of them. Whether the recurrence of a few melodic-rhythmic motives and chord constructions in several works is deliberate, one cannot say.

MacDowell's wife Marian explained how "To a Wild Rose" became number one of the set. Every morning her husband wrote a short melody—which he later threw away—because he wished to keep up the technique of composition. Hearing one tune, Mrs. MacDowell told her husband that its charm reminded her of the wild roses growing close to his log cabin in Peterborough. He retrieved the tune and made it into a composition.[30] It is the epitome of his tender song-without-words style, novel in expression, comely in sound, and illusory in its artlessness. "To a Wild Rose" soon became one of MacDowell's most popular compositions.

Number 2, "Will o' the Wisp," provides an example of his swiftly propelled and seemingly effortless bagatelle style. The indication "fancifully" shows that its interpretation must exhibit impulsive caprice. Number 3, "At an Old Trysting-Place," according to Mrs. MacDowell, reveals her husband's interest in the men and women of Peterborough who had travelled to the west in search of more fertile farmland. Many of them, pining after their birthplace, had returned to take up again the harsh life around Peterborough. The title refers to them, not to lovers: "He was trying to express the wistful homesickness, one might call it, that had enveloped these people."[31] The composition remains gentle and warm from beginning to end and comprises a single likable melody given a ternary shape.

The next number, "In Autumn," vibrates with the cheer of brisk harvest days after the summer's languors. "From an Indian Lodge" opens in MacDowell's majestic, declamatory style. The austere octaves, followed by the low tremolos of the first five measures in 3/2 time, have a blunt, raw strength to them. Deep, sonorous chords replace the octaves for four measures. Then one hears the main body of the work, a touching yet dignified slow dance. Never does the music enter the piano's higher reaches.

"To a Water-Lily," in ternary form, has "a dreamy, swaying rhythm" in its choice A section and a gradually accelerating and crescendoing B section, performed "questioningly." The puzzle in the second expressive indication is explained by Marian MacDowell, who says that her husband first smelled the scent and then caught sight of a water lily alongside an old deserted road. It was the first time he had seen one growing out of a coal-black pool. His comment was: "I have been thinking of the resemblance between that pool and the tenements I found when I went to look for my birthplace. Suddenly I realized that the slums are a great deal like that black pool. Some of our finest citizens have come out of that environment, just as the water-lilies force their stems to the surface to flower in great beauty."[32]

Number 7, "From Uncle Remus," is a marvelous tribute to Joel Chandler Harris and his folktales, ostensibly told by an old black Uncle Remus. This jolly and assuredly American-sounding movement is filled out with eccentrically jumping figures gathered in off-balanced five-measure phrases. Next come the withdrawn and forlorn tones of "A Deserted Farm," the eighth number. To MacDowell, such a place symbolized something important in New England's history. He found the empty homestead as interesting and romantic as the ruins of an old castle. It called to mind the families that had left the homes they loved, often meaning to return but seldom doing so.[33] The music to number 9, "By a Meadow Brook," never babbles. It does, however, radiate a certain blitheness. The last number, "Told at Sunset," resembles an epilogue, with its title and musical references to themes from "A Deserted Farm" and "From an Indian Lodge."

Sea Pieces, opus 55 (1898), contains eight numbers, all superb, all prefaced not with just a title but also with a line or a short stanza of verse. MacDowell's presentations are as concise and intuitive as ever. Each number introduces a moving and striking concept of great distinction. The composer's affinity for the oceanscape and wonder at the mystery and might of the vast waters are unmistakable in the music. However beholden to late-Romantic musical practices, he expresses his poetic conceits in original ways. Sounds not found in the works of other composers come from the piano. The full-textured, sonorous, regal class of composition is well represented in number 1, "To the Sea"; number 2, "From a Wandering Iceberg"; number 3, "A.D. MDCXX"; number 6, "From the Depths"; and number 8, "In Mid-Ocean." The delicate, tender type is heard in number 4, "Starlight"; number 5, "Song"; and number 7, "Nautilus." None of the high-spirited bagatelle type is included.

Fireside Tales, opus 61 (1901–2), composed about the same time as the Fourth Sonata ("Keltic") for Piano, has a flavoring of Celtic melody, especially in number 1, "An Old Love Story," and number 2, "Of Br'er Rabbit." The melody of the first piece begins like the old Irish air that Fred E. Weatherly would later adapt for use in his well-known song "Danny Boy" (Example 6.4).[34] The melody of the second, in its first four measures, avoids the fourth tone altogether and employs the leading tone once in passing. "Of Br'er Rabbit" also has the humor, syncopations, and brusque gesturings that one associates with minstrel-show dance. In several numbers (1, 3, 5, and 6), one sometimes detects a curious distancing of the composer from reality, a privacy in his musing, and a gentle, serious fancifulness. The tender song-without-words pieces are number 1, "An Old Love Story"; number 3, "From a German Forest"; and number 6, "By Smouldering Embers." The fast-moving, highly spirited types are number 2, "Of Br'er Rabbit" (another tribute to Joel Chandler Harris), and number 4, "Of Salamanders." The sonorous type is found in number 5, "A Haunted House," whose directions include "mysteriously," "very dark and sombre," and "somewhat vague" (Example 6.5).

The ten numbers of the *New England Idyls*, opus 62 (1901–2), are entitled "An Old Garden," "Mid-Summer," "Mid-Winter," "With Sweet Lavender," "In Deep Woods," "Indian Idyl," "To an Old White Pine," "From Puritan Days," "From a Log Cabin," and "The Joy of Autumn." The nature of their contents is, to be sure, indicated by their titles. Only the last adheres to the fast, buoyant type. "Mid-Winter," "In Deep Woods," "To an Old White Pine," and "From Puritan Days" are magnificent examples of the majestic, thick-textured kind of composition. The remainder record dreamlike fantasies, mostly of a tender nature. All are impeccably rendered miniatures.

THE PIANO SONATAS

MacDowell's four piano sonatas are surely the most aspiring and weighty creative statements to come from his years of maturity. A complete understanding of MacDowell's vital contributions to musical literature is impossible without them. Nobility is the first word that came to writers' minds when trying to characterize them.[35] All four sonatas resonate with the bardic tones of one who took pride in an ancestry that embraced the

Celtic poet-singers. Like them, he tried to capture epic thoughts and sing of heroism, courage, love, and suffering.

The sonatas explore meaningful areas of expression little touched upon in his other works. Without doubt, certain of his thoughts were so grandly conceived that it was necessary to deal with them in a three- or four-sectioned sonata rather than in another format. In these compositions, contrasts within and between movements are conspicuous and frequent, thus stimulating interest. Specific melodic, rhythmic, and harmonic patterns are shared by all sections of a movement and by all movements of a sonata, thus giving structural coherence and helping to alleviate the threat of sectional sprawl. Striking rhetorical command, intricacies of feeling, dramatic drive, and variety of means for attaining creative ends distinguish each work. So much do all available pianistic resources come into play that at times MacDowell seems impatient with the fetters on the imagination imposed by the keyboard's limitations. Sometimes one feels the orchestra would have been a more suitable vehicle for his music.

The first sonata, his opus 45, the *Sonata Tragica* in G minor,[36] was completed in 1892, although its slow movement was begun shortly after the death of Raff, in 1882, and was composed in his memory. Bostonians heard the slow movement alone in March 1892 and the entire sonata in March 1893. The sonata proved deeply moving and like nothing composed by an American up until that time. The contemporary writer on music James Huneker, carried away by its beauties, declared it "the most marked contribution to solo sonata literature since Brahms' F-minor piano sonata."[37]

Loud, portentous chords intone a solemn three-note motive over and over again, and a clamorous downward plunge of octaves in each hand effectively sets the scene for a tragedy. The principal theme of the ensuing *allegro risoluto* has a definite connection with the music of the first two measures of the introduction. As the music evolves, the listener has an immediate perception of adversity that the composer has intensely experienced and wishes to communicate as lucidly as possible.

The fast second movement lacks joyousness. In fact, it has a granitic quality and at times a sternness that are not unlike the attributes of Johannes Brahms's Scherzo in E-flat Minor for Piano, opus 4, and of the Scherzo movement from his Piano Sonata in F Minor, opus 5. Thus, the movement affixes another dimension to the portrayal of tragedy. MacDowell's aim is apparently not to let up on the drama but to add to it. The main subject is a recasting of the material from the first two measures of the first movement's introduction.

The center of gravity for the entire work is the very slow third movement. Its lamentation is an exalted outpouring from beginning to end. The music, submerged in sorrow and despondency, reaches a peak of intensity in the three-octave run, going from *pp* to *ff* in less than a measure, that is heard four times in measures 60 to 63. The movement was a favorite of the composer and requires a flair for drama to perform it properly, according to Percy Scholes.[38]

The last movement's opening theme derives from the first two measures of the introduction to the first movement. Valiant struggle invests the music. The coda consists of a reinterpretation of the material from that introduction, and thus the sonata ends, not with heroism triumphant but with heroism questioned or, as Lawrence Gilman suggests, with heroism shattered and "catastrophe in the hour of triumph."[39]

The second sonata, opus 50, the *Sonata Eroica* in G minor,[40] was finished in 1895 and displays the motto *Flos regum Arthurus*. The Arthurian legend was very much on MacDowell's mind when he composed it, although he also insisted that the sonata was not descriptive program music in the usual sense. According to the composer, the first movement contemplated the coming of Arthur; the second, a scherzo, was suggested by a Doré picture of a knight surrounded by elves; the third was an interpretation of Guinevere; and the last was a commentary on the passing of Arthur.[41]

The sonata begins with an introduction played "slow, with nobility." The thematic material presented in this opening is superb in its own right and germinal, since it will permeate every theme in all four of the sonata's movements. The movement proper opens "fast" and "passionately," the main theme twice going from extreme softness to extreme loudness in the first fifteen measures. At measure 55, the unpretentious and affecting subsidiary melody enters, which in the third movement MacDowell transforms into the Guinevere theme. The contrast between the two themes is constantly exploited. When the recapitulation of the main theme begins, with a background of pounding tonic-minor chords, the effect is dramatic in the extreme. Equally dramatic is the coda, which consists of one extended scalar race upward of five octaves, completed in three measures, and crescendoing from *ppp* to an overpowering *fff*.

The ternary second movement is meant to sound "elf-like" and "as light and swift as possible." The lack of connection with the Arthurian legend notwithstanding, this deft and resourceful movement serves as a welcome cushion between the intensely serious first and third movements.

The third movement, from first to last measure, contains music that lingers in the consciousness of the listener. Surely it was one of

MacDowell's most inspired creations. The composer felt that its themes and their treatment had to bring out the tenderness, longing, and ardor that constituted the nature of Guinevere. In E-flat major, the main subject refers back principally to the subsidiary theme of the first movement and secondarily to the first movement's introduction. The middle section grows tonally unstable and more fervid. At the end, the main theme returns.

The last movement dashes along at a furious and exhausting pace. The first subject is that of the last four measures of the first-movement introduction but varied. A dignified melody in whole and half notes brings some relief to the listener. Then the fury returns and builds to an immense climax. A reprise of the main subject ends up on a surprising legato passage, marked *pppp*, directly followed by the coda that denotes the passing of Arthur. This last, which contains one final recall of the Guinevere melody, breathes tranquility and gravity.

The composer's love for north European myth and his rapport with Edvard Grieg found expression in the third sonata, opus 57 (called the *Norse*), in D minor,[42] which MacDowell completed in 1899 and dedicated to Grieg. He wrote three movements only. One does not find an interior fast movement. Heading the score are these lines of verse:

> Night had fallen on a day of deeds.
> The great rafters in the red-ribbed hall
> Flashed crimson in the fitful flame
> Of smouldring logs.
> And from the stealthy shadows
> That crept 'round Harald's throne,
> Rang out a Skald's strong voice,
> With tales of battles won;
> Of Gudrun's love
> And Sigurd, Siegmund's son.

Nevertheless, nothing unequivocally Nordic sounds in the music.

The composition has an unusual potency, a uniqueness of approach, and highly personal shifts in meaning. All of the music the composer sets down is integral to the total emotional picture he tries to paint in tones. Every musical idea shares the same basic material with every other musical idea in all three movements of the composition. This is apparent not only in the themes, but also in the harmonies, harmonic progressions, and even in the rhythms. Not that excessive repetition occurs. Each new representation of the basic material appears as a metamorphosis of both the music and the expression.

The first movement, in common time, begins with the slow, mournful tolling of bells (octave A's in the right hand) against a lugubrious melody sounding in octaves deep in the bass. After the music accelerates and increases in volume, a faster, second theme enters very loud. The first two notes of this theme, in the rhythm of a Scotch snap, grab one's attention. The music continues in a robust and impetuous manner. It strikes the fancy as the imperious, cavalier gait of a heroic figure.

MacDowell describes the slow middle movement as mournful yet tender. The tune commences simply and diatonically and on the fifth measure grows chromatic. Elements from both themes of the first movement find their way into the treble line. For thirty-nine measures, the music has unfolded more or less quietly. Then, on measure 40, a mighty *fff* restatement of the tune, handled chordally, catches the listener by surprise. At the last, the initial tune returns high in the keyboard. The earlier intensity recedes, though not entirely.

The last movement, as expected, recycles the material introduced in the two themes of the first movement. The initial theme abounds in "character and fire." The movement grows increasingly perturbed, the composer allowing no technical resting place for the pianist and no mental respite for the audience. The composer freely fantasizes on motives from his theme, which move with speed and nervous vigor. The theme itself returns briefly for ten measures. We hear it plainly stated, albeit doleful in its quietness and unstable in its tonality. Clearly, the composer is recalling the enjoyable tune laced with woe of the middle movement. The rapid movement resumes until the initial theme returns *fff*, in D major. Abruptly, the fast pace ceases, and the slow, mournful tolling of bells (octave B-flats in both hands) heard at the beginning of the composition recurs. A dirgelike reminiscence on the slow-movement melody follows. In the last four measures, the first theme of the first movement reappears to end the work as it began—in gloom.

In 1900 MacDowell completed his fourth and last sonata, opus 59 (called the *Keltic*), in E minor. This was, like the Third Sonata, a work dedicated to Grieg, in three movements, and without a slow introduction to the first movement. As in the previous sonatas, the essential musical ideas are stated from the first and find their way into the themes of all three movements. Here and there, MacDowell introduces a moment of gentleness, but the ambiance is primarily epic, with an atmosphere of imposing grandeur set from the beginning. Again his love for myth finds expression. The stimulus to creativity came from Irish legend, the Cycle of the Red

Branch, and the Gaelic tales of Fiona MacLeod (pseudonym of William Sharp).[43] The first movement involves the feats of the hero-warrior Cú Chulainn. The middle movement depicts Deirdre, the most beautiful woman in all Ireland, whose great love for Naisi leads to their tragic deaths. The last movement concerns the death of Cú Chulainn, who falls a victim of magic during single-handed battle against an army.

Heading the score are the following four lines:

> Who minds now Keltic tales of yore,
> Dark Druid rhymes that thrall,
> Deirdre's song and wizard lore
> Of great Cuchullin's fall.[44]

To Gilman, MacDowell said, "The music is more a commentary on the subject than an actual depiction of it." To Mr. N. J. Corey, he wrote: "Like the third, this fourth sonata is more of a 'bardic' rhapsody on the subject than an attempt at actual presentation of it, although I have made use of all the suggestion of tone-painting in my power,—just as the bard would have reinforced *his* speech with gesture and facial expression."[45] The first movement does start with a majestic theme mostly in stepwise motion, moderate in tempo, and having "great power and dignity" (Example 6.6). Eventually it progresses to an immense culmination of extreme loudness at measures 21 and 22. The music quickens during the transition to the subsidiary theme. Upward runs of eighth notes and, later, sixteenth notes culminate in crashing chords. A Scotch snap is heard twice. The secondary theme begins moderately fast. Texture thins; tension lessens; the tone brightens. The commencement of every phrase commands the listener's attention. Each phrase starts loudly, with upward leaps. Immediately after the end of most phrases appears a quiet and unforgettable treble response of a downward skip of a minor third. The development of the material from the exposition, as is usual for MacDowell, is not so much a manipulation of ideas for musical purposes as a contemplation of different aspects of the heroic state, using the main theme as a point of departure. The recapitulation is brief and contains some surprises.

The directions for the slow second movement call for an expression of "naive tenderness." Yet, only in the first twenty-five and last seventeen measures is tenderness of any sort found and a connection with Deirdre readily recognizable. During the middle fifty-four measures, the mood is more passionately heroic or melancholically bardic, the music more beholden to the main theme (Cú Chulainn) of the first movement. Interestingly, the only music in the entire sonata that is identifiably Celtic in idiom occurs in the Deirdre melody at measures 1 and 2 and 17 to 24.

The Finale requires "swift and fierce" performance. Magnificently muscular, dynamically strong, and decisive in gesture, the movement is undoubtedly one of the most impassioned composed by any American up until that time. The E-minor main theme, mostly in detached eighth notes, has a spectacular urgency and forward propulsion to it (Example 6.7). A lyric and *piano* secondary theme offers some relief. However, the main theme and its relentlessly driving energy return, first in a free-fantasy elaboration, then in a recapitulation that gradually increases "in violence and intensity" (the composer's direction). Without forewarning, the Cú Chulainn theme of the first movement comes back, now tragic and emotionally wrought. References to the Deirdre movement are made. The movement closes quietly, with the piano intoning a treble skip of a fourth four times as a signal of farewell, followed by an abrupt upward dash of octaves, *fff*, to the final E-minor chord.

MacDowell liked the Fourth Sonata best of all the sonatas; his next favorite was the Second Sonata. In addition, he loved the slow movement of the First Sonata. He felt that not a measure of the *Keltic* needed revision. Gilman explains that "he had scarcely ever written anything so rounded, so complete, in which the joining was so invisible. He played it *con amore*, and it grew to be part of himself as on other of his works ever did."[46] The four sonatas are among the most notable musical compositions written by any American up until the turn of the century. They confirm what was also evident in the *Indian Suite* and the piano miniatures of MacDowell's adult years—that he had an easily identifiable individual style, an imagination requiring music for its explication, and sufficient command of large structures to render his poetic concepts convincingly to auditors of his own era. Unlike Paine and Chadwick, he wrote no operas, no oratorios or symphonies, and very little choral music. His symphonic poems are beautiful in spots, but less interesting in the aggregate. His expertise lay principally in solo-piano music. He cultivated this special area assiduously, and the resultant compositions obviously surpass the piano works by Paine and Chadwick. The flame of personal emotion kindled the ideas he invented for piano and made of him the definitive exemplar of the pure Romantic among American composers.

NOTES

1. Lawrence Gilman, *Edward MacDowell* (New York: Lane, 1909), 72, 75.

2. T. P. Currier, "Edward MacDowell As I Knew Him," *Musical Quarterly* 1 (1915): 42.

3. John Tasker Howard, *Our American Music*, 4th ed. (New York: Crowell, 1965), 325.

4. Gilman, *Edward MacDowell*, 61–62.

5. John Erskine, *The Memory of Certain Persons* (Philadelphia: Lippincott, 1947), 72–73.

6. Ibid., 76–77.

7. Allan A. Brown Collection, scrapbook of clippings, *M165.8, Vol. 8, in the Boston Public Library.

8. Marian MacDowell, *Random Notes on Edward MacDowell and His Music* (Boston: Schmidt, 1950), v, 34.

9. Gilman, *Edward MacDowell*, 80–81.

10. Karl Kreuger, album notes to recording MIA 119.

11. Reprinted in the *Boston Herald*, 1 April 1906. See Allan A. Brown Collection, scrapbook of clippings, *M165.8, Vol. 7, in the Boston Public Library.

12. Henry T. Finck, *Songs and Song Writers* (New York: Scribner's Sons, 1900), 242.

13. Ruth C. Friedberg, *American Art Song and American Poetry* (Metuchen, N.J.: Scarecrow, 1981), 1:242.

14. See the newspaper reviews in the Allan A. Brown Collection, scrapbook of clippings, **M125.5, Vols. 8 and 18; Richard Aldrich, *Concert Life in New York, 1902–1923* (New York: Putnam's Sons, 1941), 136–37.

15. Quoted in David Ewen, *American Composers* (New York: Putnam's Sons, 1982), s.v. "MacDowell, Edward Alexander."

16. Lawrence Gilman, *Stories of Symphonic Music* (New York: Harper and Brothers, 1908), 191–94.

17. Edward MacDowell, Suite for Large Orchestra, Op. 42 (Boston: Schmidt, copr. 1891). *In October*, Supplement to the First Suite for Large Orchestra, to be placed between the second and third movement (Boston: Schmidt, copr. 1893).

18. Gilman, *Edward MacDowell*, 129.

19. H. E. Krehbiel, in *Grove's Dictionary of Music and Musicians*, 2nd ed. (Philadelphia: Presser, 1926), s.v. "MacDowell, Edward"; Currier, "Edward MacDowell As I Knew Him," 37.

20. Abbie Farwell Brown, *The Boyhood of Edward MacDowell* (New York: Stokes, 1924), 191.

21. Allan A. Brown Collection, scrapbook of clippings, **M125.5, Vol. 15, in the Boston Public Library.

22. Edward MacDowell, Second ("Indian") Suite for Large Orchestra, Op. 48 (Leipzig: Breitkopf and Härtel, copr. 1897).

23. Charles Wakefield Cadman, "The 'Idealization' of Indian Music," *Musical Quarterly* 1 (1915): 390.

24. Gilman, *Edward MacDowell*, 70–71.

25. Philip Hale, *Philip Hale's Boston Symphony Programme Notes*, ed. John N. Burk (Garden City, N.Y.: Doubleday, Doran, 1935), 186.

26. Currier, "Edward MacDowell As I Knew Him," 43.

27. Ibid., 30.

28. Marian MacDowell, *Random Notes*, 8.

29. Lawrence Gilman, *Phases of Modern Music* (New York: Harper and Brothers, 1904), 34.

30. Marian MacDowell, *Random Notes*, 10–11. John Porte, in *Edward MacDowell* (New York: Dutton, 1922), 118, claims the melody was based on a tune of the Brotherton Indians.

31. Marian MacDowell, *Random Notes*, 11.

32. Ibid., 12–13.

33. Ibid., 14.

34. "Danny Boy," words by Fred E. Weatherly, music adapted from an old Irish Air (London: Boosey and Co., copr. 1913). Examples 6.4 and 6.5 are taken from Edward MacDowell, *Fireside Tales* (Boston: Schmidt, copr. 1902).

35. See, for example, Gilman, *Edward MacDowell*, 152; Howard, *Our American Music*, 328; and Percy A. Scholes, *Everyman and His Music* (1917; reprinted, Freeport, N.Y.: Books for Libraries, 1969), 166.

36. Edward MacDowell, *Sonata Tragica* in G Minor, Op. 45, for the Piano (New York: Schirmer, copr. 1922).

37. Gilman, *Edward MacDowell*, 149.

38. Scholes, *Everyman and His Music*, 166.

39. Gilman, *Edward MacDowell*, 149.

40. Edward MacDowell, *Sonata Eroica* in G Minor, Op. 50, for Pianoforte (New York: Schirmer, copr. 1924).

41. Gilman, *Edward MacDowell*, 151.

42. Edward MacDowell, Third Sonata for Piano, Op. 57 (Boston: Schmidt, copr. 1900). The designation "Norse" does not appear on the title page.

43. Marian MacDowell, *Random Notes*, 20; Gilman, *Edward MacDowell*, 159.

44. Edward MacDowell, Fourth Sonata (*Keltic*) for Piano, Op. 59 (Boston: Schmidt, copr. 1901).

45. Gilman, *Edward MacDowell*, 156, 158.

46. Ibid., 71.

7

THREE COMPOSERS: PARKER, FOOTE, AND BEACH

Contemporary music lovers had considered Horatio Parker (1863–1919), Arthur Foote (1853–1937), and Amy Beach (1867–1944) to be splendid composers. However, none of these three musicians, on balance, was as vital to the establishment of a viable American musical literature as were Paine, Chadwick, and MacDowell. Yet, the three made important contributions to American cultural life, as music educators or performers, and each created several musical works of first rank, such as Parker's oratorio *Hora Novissima* and opera *Mona*; Foote's Suite for Strings in E Major, *Four Character Pieces after the Rubáiyát of Omar Khayyám* for orchestra, and *A Night Piece* for flute and strings; and Beach's Browning songs and "Gaelic" Symphony.

HORATIO PARKER

Parker's devotion to music began with adolescence. So compelling was music's call, when it came, that he wished to engage in no other activity, neither in any sort of nonmusical education nor in outdoor diversion.[1] His father was a prominent Boston architect; his mother, a keyboard player, music teacher, and poet. She was also adept in Latin and Greek. Inevitably, his mother encouraged his musical pursuits from the moment he showed his first interest. She later translated Latin passages into English for his ambitious *Hora Novissima* and wrote the texts for his *Holy Child* and *St. Christopher*. Chadwick, who instructed the budding composer, writes that the eighteen- year-old Parker already had exceptional skill in the management of harmony and modulation and a gift for lyric melody. The successful works of other American composers, like the symphonies of Paine, stimulated Parker's early creative efforts.[2] Before he was twenty, he had composed songs and keyboard, chamber, and orchestral pieces. Like the composers already discussed, he completed his musical education abroad, studying in Munich from 1882 to 1885, with Rheinberger as his instructor in composition. In his day, Rheinberger was an eminent organist, teacher, and composer, noted for works of some gravity, including operas, masses, motets, keyboard concertos, organ sonatas, and chamber works.

On returning to the United States, Parker located in New York City, where he was active as a teacher, organist, and choir director. In 1893 he moved to Boston to direct music at Trinity Church. The next year he added a professorship at Yale University to his responsibilities, commuting between Boston and New Haven until 1902. He then gave up the Boston position to take up similar duties at New York City's Church of St. Nicholas.

Throughout the years of studentship and maturity, Parker turned out many compositions for solo voice or chorus—art songs, anthems, sacred services, cantatas, oratorios. He put less effort into writing symphonic, instrumental chamber, and keyboard works. After the turn of the century, he attempted compositions for the stage, the most ambitious being his two operas, *Mona* and *Fairyland.* Little about his musical style, early or late, seems daring or individual. Charles Ives, Parker's best-known student, found him a strict and praiseworthy teacher and admired much of his music, finding dignity and depth in the choral works especially. On the whole, Parker's works, Ives said, revealed a fine intellect, high ideals, and technical mastery. However, no spirit of adventure showed through.[3]

For his counterpoint and for some forms, Parker looked back to Handel and Bach; for melody, Mendelssohn was an influence; for harmony, he noted the rich tonal blends and diverse harmonic progressions favored by Liszt, Wagner, and Strauss. Further, he savored compositions as assorted as those by Brahms, Franck, Gounod, d'Indy, Elgar, and Dvořák.[4] During 1892 and 1893, he taught at New York's National Conservatory of Music, where Dvořák was director. Parker's music contains nothing especially American, except for scattered passages in his choral works that hint at a Puritan psalmodic heritage. This legacy may also help explain why critics of his time described his music as sometimes forbiddingly severe, overly intellectual, or lacking charisma.

An urge to create in sound and a perception of a talent in himself that he believed it was his duty to explore drove him to compose music. Indeed, a sense of duty figures large in his makeup. Whatever his capabilities, he felt an obligation enjoined by conscience to exploit them to the highest degree. It meant, first, an exacting commitment to his vocation and, second, the entire devotion of his being to purposive and significant works. In this engrossment lies the key to understanding his artistic conscientiousness. A New York *Musical Courier* article (5 April 1893), possibly by Krehbiel, describes him making "copious notes" and having "quantities of books laden with rhythmic morsels. Some he uses later, some rejects, some recalls without reference." The writer continues: "His greatest difficulty lies in determining upon the value of ideas. . . . The final chorus of 'Hora Novissima' troubled him extremely, varying in its impression upon him each time it was examined, and finally receiving his unqualified approval as a fit ending to his big work. He wishes there might be a standard for this 'worth of an idea'; but that would restrict taste and limit invention."[5]

Although a masterful orchestrator capable of writing subtle instrumental shadings when he desired, Parker rarely exploited the orchestra's coloristic possibilities, satisfied instead to orchestrate as if transliterating organ passages. Nor did his use of harmony, skillful as it was, call attention to itself or venture beyond the parameters established by his contemporaries. Here and there it sounds formulaic, rarely daring, despite the increasingly elusive tonalities and dissonance of the late works. His strength is in melody: usually clear, symmetrical, and lyric. From the 1890s on, his tunes lengthened and turned more chromatic and supple, more determined by harmony. In one or two later works, like the grand opera *Mona*, strains occur that skip about a great deal and appear stiff rather than smooth. Yet, in several works, including *Mona*, other strains may reveal a lyrical intensity like that of Italian arias. In the *Musical Courier* article just quoted, the author says Parker believed melody should catch the ear. This it does in works representative of his best efforts, like *Hora Novissima* and the Concerto for Organ and Orchestra.

Concerning his solo keyboard and chamber compositions, little need be said. Rupert Hughes calls them "the incidental byplays and recreations of a fancy chiefly turned to sacred music of the large forms."[6] They are mostly short characteristic pieces identifiably of the Romantic era and well put together. (The String Quartet [1885]), String Quintet [1894], and Organ Sonata [1908] are exceptions, both in their length and in their blend of the classical with the Romantic.) These pieces fall agreeably on the ear, then fade in memory. Almost all of them derive too plainly from other composers' music, Mendelssohn's and Schumann's primarily and Beethoven's sometimes. For example, in Four Sketches for piano (1890), the engaging "Romanza" is indebted to Mendelssohn, while the brisk, trenchant "Scherzino" more than hints at Schumann. Similar things can be said of the organ compositions, for example of opus 17, 20, 32, and 36, composed from 1890 to 1893. In the main, they charm. When most serious, as in the "Fugue" in C minor, opus 36 no. 3, the music impresses us, as Barbara Owen says, with the skillful counterpoint, the easy motion of the parts, and the technical reasoning.[7] Yet, the piece is soon forgotten. As for chamber music, the Suite for Piano, Violin and Violoncello, of 1893, certainly illustrates the characteristic-piece (brief and lyric) approach and Parker's affinity to Mendelssohn. The four movements are a Prelude in A major, Menuet in D minor, Romance in B-flat major, and Finale in A major.[8] A prominent melodic line plus an unobtrusive homophonic accompaniment describes the usual musical treatment. Nothing of fundamental importance transpires.

His songs are a different story. Melody is stronger; rhythm, more varied; accompaniment, more imaginative. Harmony often serves expression. After adolescence, Parker composed more than seventy secular songs. Several represent him at his best. He established preeminence in the genre as early as 1886, with his Three Love Songs, opus 10. Number 2, "Night Piece to Julia" (words by Robert Heinck),[9] captures an intimate ambiance of stars and moonlight as the proper setting for newfound passion. Fervor rules the music. The end-climax is intense. Accompaniments vary to accommodate changes in sentiment. In the last strain, the singer explodes with an impassioned plea for Julia's love. Here, the vocal melody rings out loudly and mostly in a high range, supported by full chords in the piano left hand and a duplicate of the tune in octaves in the right (a frequent Parker procedure for the climax of a song). The song is altogether successful.

At the opposite extreme, and also effective, are the fine Six Old English Songs (1899), deliberately simple in technique, direct in expression, and restrained in emotion. Number 1, "Love Is a Sickness Full of Woes," is especially winning. It unfolds like a touching but stately minuet in two strophes, the second a modification of the first. Number 6, "The Lark Now Leaves His Watery Nest," was once fairly popular. Other admirable songs are "Pack, Clouds Away" (1891), "O Ask Me Not" (1891), "I Know a Little Rose" (1893), "Love in May" (1901), "Serenade" (1904), "Good Bye" (1904), and "Only a Little While" (1910).

Parker's orchestral compositions are few. The Overture *Count Robert of Paris* (1890) first gave him stature as a composer but seems scarcely more than a competently composed work typical of its time. When Thomas and the Chicago Orchestra performed it in 1893, Parker wrote a laconic program note linking his views with those of Paine and Chadwick: "Count Robert of Paris is a symphonic picture of the trials and triumphs of Count Robert, as told in Sir Walter Scott's romance of the same title. The connection between the romance and the overture is rather one of sentiment than of accurate detail. The second theme is in strong contrast to the first, and indicates the womanly element on the story. The work is not intended as program music strictly."[10]

Chadwick writes that Parker usually needed words to stimulate him, thus the few purely instrumental works. Chadwick considered the tone poem *A Northern Ballad* (1899) praiseworthy and Parker's most important orchestral work.[11] Ironically, nobody saw fit to publish the score. The New Haven Symphony premiered it in April 1899, and in the next few months it was performed in Boston, Chicago, Cincinnati, and New York City. Parker never explained why the work was "Northern." A moderately fast piece in sonata form, it derives most themes from the introduction. Once in a while an intimation of pentatonicism enters. Possibly, the melody of the introduction is folklike, as claimed in the Chicago Symphony program notes for 10 February 1900. The work's one bow toward boldness is the tonality, which starts in E minor and closes in D-flat. When heard in Boston, in December 1899, it received not entirely enthusiastic reviews, mainly because some passages too obviously implied the music of others. However, reviewers credited the composer with naturalness, consistency, and poetic imagination. Most critics thought the composition suggested the moods and music of Dvořák and Tchaikovsky. They found the harmony lush, the melodies convicing though not unusual, and the scoring effective, despite the mostly "cloudy grey colors," to quote W.F.A. of the *Boston Transcript*. References to other composers notwithstanding, the *Ballad* struck its reviewers as a worthwhile addition to the growing body of native orchestral literature.[12] American music would be poorer without it.

Three years later, Parker completed his Concerto for Organ and Orchestra (premiered by the Boston Symphony on 29 December 1902), which is qualitatively equal if not superior to the *Ballad*. William Kearns, in his study of Parker and his music, declares it the best of Parker's instrumental works, praising the unusual structure, the quality of ideas and their inventive development, and the idiomatic writing for organ and orchestra.[13] After hearing the concerto at a concert in Boston's Trinity Church, given on 3 March 1989, I came away convinced that Kearns's assessment was correct. Unlike those in *A Northern Ballad*, the ideas in the concerto belong to Parker and to no one else. The work is basically lyric and about twenty-four minutes in length. Its abundant and mellow tunes openly communicate what seem to be the composer's personal emotions. The organ is not a contender with the orchestra, nor usually heroic, except in the Finale. The orchestra itself consists of strings, brass, harp, and drums.[14] Woodwinds are absent, perhaps because they might have obscured the organ colors.[15] The first movement, *allegro moderato*, begins with an imposing diatonic melody, forty-two measures in length. Eventually, a syncopated tune based on motives from the initial melody sounds. From then on, tonality continues to shift, as a fantasy-like series of free variations unfolds. Especially lovely is the *andante* section, where first a solo violin and next a French horn perform a gentle duet with the organ. The close is tranquil. The second movement is a delicate scherzo in ternary form. The outer sections make much use of a dotted eighth note–sixteenth note–eighth note rhythm set against brief, alternatingly staccato and legato phrases in the treble. The middle section contains smooth, graceful melodic phrases. The Finale supplies an unexpectedly dramatic ending to the concerto. For the most part, the movement is monothematic, its substance treated fugally but with homophonic episodes. Toward the end, the organ executes an impressive cadenza just before the full ensemble storms forward to the final measure.

One other orchestral work requires mention, the tone poem *Vathek*, completed in 1903. Concerning this work, Brooks Shephard, Jr., Yale music librarian, wrote to Karl Kreuger: "The inspiration was William Beckford's picaresque romance by the same title, and Parker himself oddly suppressed the title in his list of works submitted to *Grove's Dictionary*. We have been unable to find that it was ever performed, even by the New Haven Symphony."[16] (Beckford, an Englishman, lived from 1760 to 1844.) The work calls for a large orchestra and makes considerable use of percussion. However, it does not approximate the quality of the concerto or *A Northern Ballad*. A few measures owe something to Strauss or to Debussy, but the major portion of the piece owes an even greater debt to the d'Indy of the *Istar Variations* (1897).

The genre to which Parker devoted most of his energy was choral music, from the modest to the complex. Long after his death, states Leonard Ellinwood, many people still considered his to be the best musical setting of the Episcopal Hymnal. William Kearns observes that, of the more than twenty-five anthems written by Parker, "Bow Down Thine Ear," "The Lord Is My Light," "Give Unto the Lord," and "I Will Set His Dominion in the Sea" were popular in Parker's time and remain in the church repertoire.[17] This highly singable and serviceable music grew out of English and American roots and the Protestant church music composed over the previous 125 years. Parker wished to address the common congregational ear, so these pieces lack "sternness," have an "ingratiating . . . New England buoyancy," and are never lackluster.[18]

During his student days and until the writing of *Hora Novissima*, Parker produced six secular cantatas calling for various soloists and choruses with orchestral accompaniment: *Ballad of a Knight and His Daughter* (1884), *King Trojan* (1885), *Idylle* (1886), *The Norsemen's Raid* (1888), *The Kobolds* (1890), and *The Dream King and His Love* (1891). He was eager to take advantage of the strong choral-society movement in the United States and knew that any cantatas he wrote would have a ready reception. Moreover, such works were more apt to receive repeated performances than orchestral pieces. These last had to chase after the few symphony orchestras then in existence and win over mostly German instrumentalists and music directors more inclined to look across the Atlantic for their new repertoire.

Parker's texts were authored by central Europeans, with one exception, *The Kobolds*, written by Boston's Arlo Bates. All of them have subjects suited to nineteenth-century American tastes, which had been shaped by German romanticism. We discover knights, elves, fairies, warriors, and lovely maidens; depictions of duels, battles, wild nocturnal rides, and love consummated and unconsummated; and settings in forests, on the sea, or within castles. Melodies allotted to the soloists are persuasive. Flawless workmanship distinguishes the choral writing. Harmony sounds rich. Chromaticisms are handled judiciously. Homophony prevails. In most cantatas, his music attempts to balance the lyrical and the dramatic. All things considered, he evidences more imagination and ingenuity in his musical realization of words than in the creation of purely instrumental compositions. The orchestra is more sensitively handled and its myriad colors more aptly exploited for mood, heightened emotion, or scenic description. Curiously, even with this said, there is not always great diversity in mood or striking contrast within or between works. Although the music is not easily identifiable as deriving from another composer, nothing is arrestingly individual either.

Unquestionably one of Parker's finest works and a valuable contribution to music literature, the oratorio *Hora Novissima* was written for the Church Choral Society of New York and received its first performance on 3 May 1893. It quickly won fame and performances even in England, the

Three Choirs Festival of Worcester being the locale for the most important of the English performances. The oratorio also led to Parker's receiving an honorary musical doctorate from Cambridge University. Trying to explain its meaning for his time, Chadwick cites its "solid musical worth," its "skillful and impressive choral writing," the "poetic beauty of the solos," and its "varied and colorful instrumentation," which "endear it to musicians, while its lofty spiritual atmosphere, its fervent religious expression, although tinged with a romantic mysticism, make a strong appeal to the general musical public."[19]

Parker first mentions Hora in a diary entry for 13 April 1891: "Wrote a little on 'Hora Novissima.' " A year later, he records: "Scored 'Hora Novissima.' " Constant anguish had assailed the composer during the months of its creation. He experienced the deaths of his father, sister Mary, and infant son.[20] Possibly his emotional and psychological ordeal caused him to treat the oratorio's pessimistic subject with considerable empathy. His mother translated the original Latin poem, by a twelfth-century monk of Cluny, into English. The score's title page reads "*Hora Novissima: The Rhythm of Bernard De Morlaix on the Celestial Country*, English translation by Isabella G. Parker."[21]

The text contrasts the evils of earthly existence with visions of the longed-for "Golden Jerusalem," attainable only through death. Divided into eleven sections, *Hora* includes numbers for soprano, alto, tenor, and bass soloists, for solo quartet, and for chorus. Everything about the work is finely conceived. Everywhere in the score is evidence of a master able to put his strongest feelings into music that was entirely within the bounds he had set for himself. Passage after passage is rich in significance. Parker enlarges on his ideas with proficiency and emotional acuteness. A clarity and a vividness are evidenced that underscore how completely he realized what he set out to accomplish. Expression is direct and genuine. Ideas stripped to essentials communicate candidly with the listener.

Musically related phrases pour forth smoothly and naturally. The redeployment of a few melodic and rhythmic motives is an obvious integrative device. (His rationale is not entirely that behind Wagner's *leitmotif* manipulations.) Many phrases have symmetrical correspondences in length and shape. Chromatic alterations are tactfully introduced. While the gravity of utterance remains, the austerity that characterized much of his other writing is less in evidence. At times a lyricism akin to that in the Italian operatic aria reveals itself.

Rhythms are steady and rarely subject to violent change. Owing to their firmness, they add forcefully to the total expression. Chord constructions and harmonic progressions observe the conventions and the limits defined by Strauss and Wagner. However, they always abet the mood or sentiment to be encompassed. An increased recourse to counterpoint enters, especially into big choral statements. Polyphony occurs within a secure and logical harmonic frame. It invariably heightens the listener's thoughtfulness about the work as a whole. *Hora*'s orchestration commands interest because of its ear-catching assortment of textures and instrumental combinations, and because of its appropriateness in epitomizing the text's meanings.

The first number, an instrumental Introduction and the choral "Hora Novissima," warns of earth's last hour and the judgment to come. Over a timpani pedal, a melody in the low strings (measures 11–15) descends modally through a series of fourths. Woodwinds repeat it. This theme will undergo extensive use in its original form, in inversion, in retrograde, and in retrograde inversion. One cannot help but discover a resemblance between it and the theme of the opening of Mahler's First Symphony, whose premiere took place in Budapest in November 1889, and whose first American performance was in New York City in December 1909. The similarity is fortuitous. At the opening of the Introduction and within the theme appears a significant rhythmic pattern of a dotted quarter-eighth-quarter note. The pattern will recur in most numbers of the oratorio. (Example 7.1 reproduces the first nineteen measures of the Introduction.) The chorus enters grandly and homophonically. Later, homophony and polyphony receive equal weight. The music twice moves away from and returns to the home key. Melodic and rhythmic patterns go through constant elaboration until the movement's satisfying conclusion.

The second number, "Hic breve vivitur," for solo quartet, contrasts the brevity of life on earth (in the minor) with the eternity to come (in the major). The third number is the highly successful bass aria "Spe modo vivitur." Number four, "Pars mea, Rex meus," a prelude and double fugue for chorus, sounds singularly imposing, especially in the last eighteen measures, marked *maestoso*, when the chorus in unison and octaves thunders out the words "Pars mea, Rex mea." The fifth number, "O bona patria," an aria in ternary form for soprano solo, beautifully conjures a vision of the bliss to come. Part 1 of the oratorio concludes with "Tu sine littore," for solo quartet and chorus, whose prelude is obviously descended from the Introduction of the first movement. The vocal parts reutilize material from the first movement and touch on ideas from movements two through five, though never in obvious fashion. The movement proceeds in a stately, mostly homophonic manner.

Part 2 equals Part 1 in interest. It opens with the tenor solo "Urbs Syon aurea," followed by the double chorus on "Stant Syon atria" and the alto aria "Gens duce splendida." Number ten has an *a capella* chorus sing "Urbs Syon unica." Quartet and chorus sound a final paean to the heavenly city, "Urbs Syon inclyta." Text and music are laden with world-weariness and personal contrition, as the singers cry out, "Burdened with guiltiness, / Weary and comfortless, / Help, I implore Thee," then plead for God's "light to shine / In this dark soul of mine."

Philip Hale was loud in his praise of *Hora Novissima*. "Pars mea," he called "a masterpiece, true music of the church"; "Urbs Syon unica" is so individual that "no one in the country or in England . . . could by nature and by student's sweat have written those eleven pages." He continues: "I have spoken of Mr. Parker's quasi-operatic tendency. Now he is a modern. He has shown in this very work his appreciation and his mastery of antique religious musical art. But as a modern he is compelled to feel the force of the dramatic in religious music."[22]

Other works for voice or voices and orchestra followed. All of them display the same expressive and somewhat dramatic impulses as *Hora*. Most of them are worth rehearing, but none is as successful from beginning to end as *Hora* is in completely realizing the composer's intentions. They include *Cáhal Mór of the Wine Red Hand* (1893), a rhapsody for baritone; *The Legend of St. Christopher* (1897), an eloquent and dramatic oratorio; *A Wanderer's Psalm* (1900), a cantat for chorus; *A Star Song* (1901), a rhapsody for chorus; *King Gorm the Grim* (1907), a ballad for chorus; and *Morven and the Grail* (1915), a final oratorio. Near the end of Parker's life, two more compositions were completed: *The Dream of Mary*, a morality for adult and children's chorus and congregation; and the cantat *A.D. 1919*.

Earlier, I had depicted Parker's mature style as sounding somewhat dramatic. It failed, however, to develop into an idiom capable of taking forceful possession of an audience's attention and emotions, which is so essential for the stage. Possibly he was too erudite and academic to introduce swift flexibility into his music, too elevated in his thinking to portray the seamier side of life, or too fearful of overpersonalized feeling. He had twice tried his hand at incidental music for staged plays, with *The Eternal Feminine* (1904) and the *Price of India* (1906). Then, in 1910 he completed the grand opera *Mona*, which won him contemporary but not lasting fame. Parker, who had thought opera a "beautiful mess" of drama and music, also felt a growing desire to compose one. Undoubtedly he had in mind the Metropolitan's offer of a ten-thousand-dollar prize for the best opera with libretto and music by Americans, which he hoped to win, and the fully staged New York performance that went with the prize. He asked Brian Hooker for a libretto, received one, and commenced setting it in July 1909. Completed the next year, *Mona* won the prize. A delighted Parker noted that the Metropolitan had the resources needed to produce the work, "so that if the work does not appeal to the public, I think it will be our fault." The first performance took place on 14 March 1912. Nine days later, at a dinner given by the Metropolitan's directors, the composer stated: "The result of our labors is not Italian opera or French opera or German opera. I believe it is American opera, for it certainly is nothing else, and whether one likes it or not is a matter of taste concerning which others may dispute."[23]

The plot centers on the self-destructive fanaticism of Mona, a British princess in revolt against Roman rule around A.D. 100. She also loves Gwynn, disguised son of the Roman governor. Within her, patriotic fervor and womanly ardor for her lover compete for ascendancy. When, in the third and final act, Gwynn reveals his identity, Mona slays him; she is then captured by the Romans and led away to her death. The ending is rather inconclusive, even unsatisfying, as Mona expresses some regret over Gwynn's death yet also recalls her former vision of victory. Hooker's libretto in verse is literary, stilted, and sometimes hard to understand. The nine principals talk too much about religious and political matters. The actual stage action is slow, though the audience hears about actions already, or about to be, taken.

Parker's score does contain a great deal of outstanding music, all of it sincere, most of it gloomy and severe.[24] Leading motives abound that identify characters and clarify beliefs and feelings. The composer heeds the normal accentuations and pitch variations of the words, but characters tend to declaim on the same tone and in skips, with stepwise movement in abeyance. Sensuous lyricism and tender sentiment scarcely exist. Melodies to take the fancy of a general audience are scarce and short-breathed. Tonality changes constantly, modulations are sudden, and cadences rarely appear. Chadwick, assuredly a champion of Parker's music, had to conclude: "He had little sympathy for the conventions and the artificialities of the stage, and perhaps he was lacking in what the Germans call *theatre blut*. This, combined with inexperience in composing for the stage and plots which made little appeal to the average theatre-goer, militated against the popular success of these works [*Mona* and a later opera, *Fairyland*], but they proved his complete mastery of modern harmony and modern orchestration."[25] Musicians can admire the excellence of the details, the occasional suppleness with which the music adapts itself to the activities on the stage, and even the inspiration that fired the composer. However like an oratorio rather than an opera *Mona* strikes us, it is a creative work of moment and deserves respect.

One of the more successful scenes is Mona's Act 1 narration, in a dramatic monologue, of a dream she had. The angular vocal line comprises many repeated tones and skips. At the end of Act 1 another fine scene occurs, when Gwynn objects to the planned British uprising and a furious Mona rejects him. Act 2 has a choice first scene, in which Nial, a changeling, dances with his shadow before a forest altar. He talks with birds and innocently ponders the unsubstantial quality of the human psyche. No big tune emerges, although the rhythms prove elastic and traces of melody dart in and out of the narration. When he states that he lacks a soul, an eighth-note passage in open fifths (lacking the third) follows, after which is heard a four-note figure in thirds that recurs throughout the scene (Example 7.2). Effective also is the prelude to Act 3. Two loud chords sound. Then comes a sudden hush. Texture becomes much thinner; a four-note melodic figure is heard. Then slowly the texture thickens, while the music remains quiet. A mood of foreboding and unreality prevails.

On the other hand, the ends of both Acts 2 and 3 sound unsatisfactory. In the former, a ceremonial handing out of swords to bards and druids takes place. All sorts of strong and savage colors could have been evoked. Instead, a lifelessly bland homophonic chorus drains the scene of tension. In the last act, Mona murders Gwynn after he reveals he is the Roman governor's son. Roman soldiers capture her. She then laments Gwynn's death, though no great remorse is evident in her words or in the music. Also, she continues to dwell on the victory she had hoped to win. One wishes a more decisive finish to the opera. Dramatic gestures do occur in the music; few of them ring true.

In 1914 Parker completed a second opera, *Fairyland*, the libretto again by Hooker, which won the ten-thousand-dollar prize of the National Federation of Music Clubs. It saw six performances in Los Angeles. Regrettably, the libretto lacks force; the characters, believability. Despite the praise of composers like Chadwick, Cadman, and Beach, the opera failed. As Parker's daughter admitted, it was "not generally considered so unified, vigorous or important a work as 'Mona.' "[26]

Starting about the time that he was composing *Mona*, Parker found himself less and less applauded for his vocal music. He was now seen as one who adhered to a high standard that allowed few concessions to entertainment and popular appeal. *Hora Novissima* continued to be his most highly rated large work for voices. This oratorio, plus several songs, *A Northern Ballad*, and the Organ Concerto, must be numbered among the select works that the New England group of composers bequeathed to posterity.

ARTHUR FOOTE

Foote was the first composer of note to receive his musical education entirely in the United States. He was born in Salem, Massachusetts, where his father edited the *Salem Gazette*. His mother died when he was a child, and his upbringing was left to an older sister, Mary Wilder Tiletson. He began piano lessons with a local teacher at the age of fourteen. While an adolescent, he discovered the piano music of Schumann. Soon he began the study of theory with Stephen Emery and keyboard with Benjamin Lang. Later, several German musicians resident in Boston influenced his thinking. In 1870 he enrolled at Harvard, where Paine was his teacher. He eventually earned the degree of Master of Arts in music from Harvard, the first such degree granted by an American university. A respect for Wagner's operas began with a visit to Bayreuth in 1876, although this esteem did not carry over as a strong influence on Foote's own style. He states that later, in the eighties, "it seemed natural to have all . . . [the Beethoven] symphonies in one season of the symphony concerts."[27] From the evidence of his music, Foote also cherished Brahm's compositions. Although acquainted with the startling innovations of the twentieth century, he felt the tonal elusiveness, ceaseless discord, and savage rhythms in this new music to be foreign to his own open and nonassertive temperament.

Foote earned a living by teaching keyboard and theory, playing the organ and directing choirs in Boston churches, and performing on the piano in chamber-music concerts. The Allan A. Brown Collection of the Boston Public Library includes three volumes of clippings that Foote himself gathered and which contain programs and newspaper notices of concerts in which Foote was a participant.[28] He was also a cofounder of the American Guild of Organists and its president for four years.

For his entire life, he remained a modest man, diffident about his keyboard and creative abilities. After reading his autobiography and his *Musical Quarterly* article "A Bostonian Remembers,"[29] one must believe that the diffidence grew out of deep-seated humility and a profoundly reverent regard for music. Underlying it was a feeling that notes should be set down cautiously. Writing what you desired to express, he hints, was often infeasible, sometimes hazardous. The reader recognizes a composer devoted to those masterpieces of the past that had endowed his own works with their noble language. He was troubled that he might not deserve to follow in the footsteps of the masters he admired. This deference toward music, this modesty mingling with apprehension, breathes from every paragraph he wrote and every work he composed. When he died, Redfern Mason's obituary for him, printed in the *Boston Transcript* of 17 April 1937, read: "Arthur Foote had a trait which, in the eyes of the world, is a fault. He never blew his own trumpet; he was utterly unskilled in the art of crying up his own wares. Chadwick would try to stir him up. 'When I want a work produced I go to Chicago and get Stock to do it,' he would say. But Foote would shake his head. . . . The art of self-advertisement was something he was ashamed to learn."[30]

One must praise Foote the composer. He speaks to the listener face-to-face, plainly, and without resorting to elaborate artifice. His music can sound poignantly beautiful or circumspectly refined, but never maudlin or spectacular. Romantic melody predominates, for his talents lay in lyricism, not in overly rhetorical, theatrical, or pretentious gestures. He understood his limits and never moved beyond them. His mature works exemplify a New England cultural development at a highly discriminating stage. Frederick Jacobi writes that his refinement never turned precious and his music never lacked humorous and ingratiating traits. Originality could be found in the turn of a phrase, in subtle harmonic change rather than in something striking. The practice of restraint was a New England tradition and one applicable to his art. Auditors came to admire his music for itself and not for its Americanisms or modernity.[31]

Foote composed about one hundred songs several of them achieving renown—among them the "Irish Folk-Song" and "I'm Wearing Awa' to the Land o' the Leal."[32] A fetching tune and a tailor-made accompaniment are common to most of them. The strophic "It Was a Lover and His Lass" (1885), the poem by Shakespeare, is an ingratiating composition that demonstrates Foote's talent for inventing a memorable vocal line, a sympathetic piano background, and harmonies verging on the modal. The third of *Three Songs* issued as opus 10,[33] "The Milkmaid's Song," the text from Tennyson, shows him both witty and charming. A genial G-major melody permeated with mild syncopations successfully captures the sentiments of a coquetting girl teasing a youth who is trying to kiss her. "I'm Wearing Awa' to the Land o' the Leal," poem by Lady Nairn (1887), is simplicity itself. The words reveal a person wearied of life and awaiting welcome death. In D-flat major, the song begins with a laconic one-measure prelude, an unadorned arpeggio on the tonic triad, and lacks a postlude.[34] The harmony's frequent references to the key of the subdominant minor add to the melancholic mood. The song addresses the listener personally and relates to his or her most private concerns. The sad "A Roumanian Song," poem by "The Bard of the Dimbovitza" (1899), [35] is in A B A form. The A section sounds in C-sharp minor, although the melody itself is in the Dorian mode. Measures 10 through 15 of the A section are singularly attractive as the voice sings the word "Ah!" on long tones, while the piano takes over the melody in a commentary that conveys the muted anguish behind the sigh (Example 7.3).

Foote composed around fifty part songs and thirty-five anthems. The anthems "God is our refuge," "And there were shepherds," and "Awake, thou that sleepest" were particularly praised in their time.[36] His three major compositions for chorus and orchestra employ secular texts by Longfellow: *The Farewell of Hiawatha* (1885), *The Wreck of the Hesperus* (1888), and *The Skeleton in Armor* (1891). All three are dignified, expressive in some parts and monotonous in others. One longs for soloists to relieve the constant choral singing. The music often fails to capture the moments of high drama. None satisfies from beginning to end as the songs do.

In general, the solo works for piano and organ are workmanlike and fluent. Few sound truly spontaneous. They do exhibit Romantic sentiment in the manner of Mendelssohn, but rarely the intensity of a Schumann, Chopin, or Brahms. Foote exploits the full resources of the keyboard only occasionally and never surprises us with a singular pianistic stroke. His entire output comprised brief characteristic pieces. His best-known piano composition, *Five Poems after Omar Khayyám*, opus 41 (1898), did not achieve its complete realization until he revised and orchestrated four of the five pieces, reissued as *Four Character Pieces after the Rubáiyát of Omar Khayyám*, opus 48 (1900), with the third of the five pieces omitted. His best organ works are the Suite in D Minor, opus 54, and Seven Pieces, opus 71.[37] Opus 54 represents a contemporary reinterpretation of a Baroque suite. Opus 71 begins with a *Cantilena in G*, an expressive *andante* that begs for performance by a string orchestra. Its most haunting number is the *Canzonetta*, whose treble melody is one of Foote's most exquisite creations.

Foote left behind a splendid collection of chamber music. As expected, his style is highly finished and a combination of diverse elements, mainly Germanic. Foote states that the Kneisel Quartet performed most of his chamber music and that he "learned much from [Franz] Kneisel through his suggestions as to practical points in composition."[38] He still prefers creating discernible tunes against a homophonic background. The classical principle of tonal and thematic contrast prevails. However, church modes from the Middle Ages and structures from the Baroque may make an appearance. Full harmonies and varying rhythms enrich the extensive melodies he writes. Self-possessed meditation seems the prevalent mood. Nevertheless, strong emotion lies beneath the surface and, not infrequently, manages to break through.

The Three Pieces, opus 1, for cello and piano, and the Three Character Pieces for violin and piano, opus 9, date from the early eighties. Ternary structures and prominent lyric lines given to the string instruments identify them. The First Piano Trio in C minor, opus 5, was heard in April 1882. Limber melody predominates; strongly contrasted sections are lacking. The First String Quartet in G minor, opus 4, was performed in Boston in 1883, and again in 1887. The collective opinion of the critics found the third movement, the *Andante*, to be the most irresistible. The listener hears little real thematic development and few contrapuntal textures. Yet, greater coherency prevails when the music is compared with that of the Trio in C minor.[39] Foote introduced more vigor, contrast, harmonic variety, contrapuntal activity, and emotional scope into the chamber works he wrote in the late eighties and nineties: the Violin Sonata in G minor, opus 20 (1889); the Piano Quartet in C major, opus 23 (1890); and the Second String Quartet in E major, opus 32 (1893). All three are notable compositions and reward the listener who seeks them out.

Possibly his finest chamber work is the Piano Quintet in A minor, opus 38 (1897).[40] In the first movement (an *Allegro qiusto: appassionato*), all members of the quintet share important thematic material. Shifts in mood, mostly melancholic, happen frequently. At the end, the music acquires a brightness hitherto missing in the movement. The second movement, a moderately paced *Intermezzo*, begets a dreamy mood. The next movement, a vivacious *Scherzo*, thrives on a rhythm similar to that in the second movement of Beethoven's first Rasoumovsky string quartet. Nevertheless, Foote manages it differently from Beethoven. The Finale in A major is a rondo. A lively, dancelike first theme has an intimation of the gypsy about it. The first contrasting section features a running sixteenth-note figure in the piano; the second contrasting section has the broody lyricism usually associated with Brahms. All in all it is a winning work.

Three marvelous compositions worthy of high praise followed: the Second Piano Trio in B-flat, opus 65 (1908); the Third String Quartet in D major, opus 70 (1911); and the Cello Sonata, opus 78 (ca. 1913). Contemporary audiences found the music endearing—clear and strong in structure, astute in its detail, noble to blithesome in expression, and deserving of undivided attention from beginning to end. In 1918 he completed his Nocturne and Scherzo for flute and string quartet. When Pierre Monteux later suggested arranging the Nocturne for string orchestra, it became one of Foote's most loved compositions, *A Night Piece*.

Foote's first important orchestral piece was the Overture *In the Mountains*, opus 14 (1886).[41] When the Boston Symphony premiered it in February 1887, it was hailed more for its urbane, wholesome, and contemplative sound; less for its originality, for which auditors were glad he did not strive. No connection appears between title and music.[42] The Boston Symphony premiered a Suite for Strings, opus 12, in May 1886, and a Suite for Strings, opus 21, in November 1889. Both works glance back to the Baroque. The first suite is in three movements: *Allegro Commodo*, *Andante*, and *Gavotte*. The second suite contains a *Prelude*, *Minuetto*, *Air*, and *Gavotte*; the melody of the first movement returns in the last. Foote resorts to Baroque practices not as an antiquarian but to evoke certain distinctive sound characteristics. The results are anything but academic and imitate neither Bach nor Handel. Romantic lyricism and an expanded harmonic palette invest the measures. The Serenade for Strings in E major, opus 25, is an 1891 reworking of movements from both the previous suites.

The next work, the symphonic prologue *Francesca da Rimini*, opus 24, dates from 1890. If influence must be found, Brahms, not Tchaikovsky and his work of the same title, can occasionally be detected in the music. In a free sonata-allegro form, the composition is solidly written and eminently likable; it captures qualities in the Dante original not encompassed by Tchaikovsky's treatment. For much of its length, the piece reveals the composer reflecting on the lover's inner feelings rather than trying to capture pictorial gestures of dramatic conflict and passion. However, intense feeling remains manifest throughout. The second theme, Foote says, describes the two lovers.[43] The recapitulation, shorter than the exposition, reaches a strong climax, at which point a recitative indicates "the catastrophe of the story" (Foote's words). This turning point occurs just before the final return of the lovers' theme. Softly the piece ends with muted sounds to depict "*Nessun maggior dolore / Che ricordarsi del tempo felice / Nella miseria*." Writing in the *Boston Musical Herald* of March 1891, George H. Wilson praised the work's solid structure, vital ideas, and compact discourse: "It is a concise and telling composition, a little freer in form than an overture. . . . It tells us how near we are in this country to forming a school, and recalls with pleasurable excitement the fact that right here among us is the nucleus of this school!"[44]

A Cello Concerto, which Foote began in 1887 and finished in 1893, is one of his least-known major works. The one or two contemporary musicians familiar with it claim it is a fine composition worthy of resurrecting.[45]

The composer completed the Suite for Orchestra in D minor, opus 36, in 1895. Its premiere by the Boston Symphony came the next year. Some years later, Foote said: "It was only fairly successful, but with two really good movements. . . . Its fortune has been the usual one of American compositions of its sort. It had a few performances by orchestras here (and one in England by Henry J. Wood) and afterwards little chance. The movement in variation form really satisfied me."[46]

Syncopations abound in most of its themes. The first movement, *Allegro energico, con brio*, begins dazzlingly with a bold, forward-thrusting theme. This theme in turn is superseded by two quiet subsidiary ideas. Development centers on the principal theme. One has the impression of a distinctly lyrical basis for all the material of the movement. The deeply searching second movement is headed *Expressivo, non troppo Adagio*. Its first section is given over to a long legato melody in the first violins, the second half of which is enhanced with a throbbing rhythm. An episode heard in the brasses forms a colorful and effective contrast to this tune and to the middle section. A fresh, graceful, and syncopated melody inhabits the second section. Especially dramatic is the recapitulation of the episode material supported by abrupt rhythms, now heard in the full orchestra. The third movement consists of a calm theme sporting mild rhythmic displacements, then a chain of resourceful variations. The buoyant Finale brings Dvořák to mind. Persistent dance rhythms give a festive character to the opening. The next theme, when it is eventually heard against a descending French-horn phrase, sounds as if Chadwick might have written it. The Suite will reward the curious listener.

The *Four Character Pieces after the Rubáiyát of Omar Khayyám*, opus 48, arranged from his piano music, opus 41, came out in 1900 and proved instantly popular. A friend, the pianist Helen Hopekirk, had urged him to recast the original. Evidently, when composing the piano pieces, Foote had relished the evocation of a variety of moods and distinct contrasts called for by his subject, realizing also that he had to modify his usual style. The transfer of the music to the orchestra was a logical consequence of this inclination. The composition reveals an individual character that easily distinguishes it from the rest of Foote's output. The shifting harmonic nuances and diverse orchestral colors suggest musical Impressionism. The first piece, *andante comodo*, is prefaced by the following verse:

Iram indeed is gone with all his Rose,
And Jamshyd's Sev'n-ring'd Cup where no one knows;
But still a Ruby kindles in the Vine,
And many a Garden by the Water blows.

A nocturnal atmosphere prevails, in which a long, languorous clarinet solo and delicate modal references obliquely (never directly) intimate a setting in a Persian garden. The music is not readily forgotten.

The second piece, *allegro deciso*, has the following verse:

They say the Lion and the Lizard keep
The Courts where Jamshyd gloried and drank deep:
And Bahram, that great Hunter—the Wild Ass
Stamps o'er his Head, but cannot break his sleep.

Later, when the tempo changes to *più moderato*, the verse reads:

Yet, ah, that Spring should vanish with the Rose!
That Youth's sweet-scented manuscript should close!
The Nightingale that in the branches sang,
Ah, whence, and whether flown again, who knows!

The first section has an assertive, driving theme in the full orchestra, with the brasses to the fore. Suddenly the mood changes to one quiet and pensive; clarinet and flute solos are featured. For the conclusion, one hears a return to the opening material, boldly and vigorously stated.

The third piece, *comodo*, interprets the following:

A Book of Verses underneath the Bough,
A Jug of Wine, a Loaf of Bread—and Thou
Beside me singing in the Wilderness—
Oh, Wilderness were Paradise enow!

The movement conveys the ambiance of a pastorale. A mellifluous theme steadily expands in the strings, mounts to an eloquent climax, and then returns to tranquility.

The last piece begins *andantino ben marcato*, interpreting the following verse:

> Yon rising Moon that looks for us again—
> How oft hereafter will she wax and wane;
> How oft hereafter rising look for us
> Through this same Garden—and for one in vain!

Then tempo shifts to *molto allegro*:

> Waste not your Hour, nor in the vain pursuit
> Of This and That endeavor and dispute;
> Better be jocund with the fruitful Grape
> Than sadden after none, or bitter, Fruit.

For this final movement, Foote has a solemn tune open on a low pitch. Gradually he clothes it in a richer and richer texture, as more and more instruments contribute to the interpretation, sounding at once fatalistic and saturated with yearning. The tempo picks up. Strings playing *tremoloso* produce a scurrying effect. A new melody enters that refers back to the theme of the first piece and goes from loud to very soft before ushering back the solemn tune of the movement's beginning. Melancholy sounds then end the composition.

The immensely successful Suite for Strings in E major, opus 63, was completed in 1908. Throughout his tenure with the Boston Symphony, Serge Koussevitzky sponsored and Boston audiences enjoyed it. The work consists of three movements: a *Praeludium*, *Pizzicato* and *Adagietto*, and *Fugue*.[47] The composition gives the impression of effortless musical flow, restrained grace, and stately beauty. The music's virtues include simplicity and laconism. A few ideas are thriftily elaborated. When counterpoint occurs, it is generated by the harmonic progressions. The style of Bach and Handel is the point of departure, but a connection with the music of Brahms and Tchaikovsky cannot be denied. Nevertheless, the expression is totally Foote's own.

The first movement, *allegro comodo*, is based on a two-measure motive that expands, for the most part quietly and lyrically (Example 7.4). The second movement is captioned *capriccioso* and *allegretto*. Its two themes are distantly related to the motive of the first movement. A brisk and airy pizzicato first section gives way to an expressive adagietto played by muted strings using their bows. The beginning is repeated for the movement's finish. The last movement is a fugue, *allegro giusto*. The subject, its recurrences, and the intervening episodes are marvelously handled and always fresh sounding. Rhythmic energy and textural lucidity continue throughout. The close comprises a grand peroration to the entire composition.

One last composition requires mention, *A Night Piece* for flute and strings with optional bass (1922),[48] a restatement of the first movement of the Nocturne and Scherzo for flute and string quartet. Pierre Monteux and the Boston Symphony gave it a first performance in 1923. Like the Suite, it won wide appreciation. Few compositions by other American composers equal its absolute musical loveliness, brought about by a combination of transparent harmonies, gently patterned harmonic rhythms, sensitively placed dynamic inflections, and above all an ethereal melody for the flute. The heading *Andantino languido* gives an indication of its character. As the flute renders its solo, the strings engage in harmonically activated contrapuntal phrases that dovetail frictionlessly with the tune (Example 7.5).

A closer acquaintance with *A Night Piece* and the Suite for Strings in E compels the conclusion that if a composer like Foote writes when absorbed in calm reflection he does succeed in transmitting his individual essence, however unassuming the musical discourse may appear. From these two compositions one gains a profound and touching perception of Foote's nature. In what manner and place the music communicates this nature, it is difficult to determine. As in so many of his other compositions, the music is governed by a fragile type of self-effacement, thus making a firm determination impossible. His writing is extraordinary for its lack of clichés and its refusal to imitate other composers' styles. Although content with traditional practices and averse to experimentation, the composer creates sounds at once vivid, sincere, and in their own way original.

Waldo Selden Pratt summed Foote up in the "American Supplement" to *Grove's Dictionary*, as follows: "Few American composers [up to 1920] have won such high esteem. The uniformly high quality of his work in diverse forms has been coupled with a surprising uniformity of success. His orchestral works are played by leading orchestras, his chamber-music has been a staple in American programs, his organ-music is everywhere popular, and his songs are prized by singers, accompanists, and audiences. . . . On Thanksgiving Day in 1914, organists throughout the country, by concerted arrangement, played his Festival March in F as an expression of gratitude for his recovery from a serious illness—a tribute seldom paid to any musician."[49]

AMY BEACH

Musical precociousness, a well-disciplined mind, and an active furthering of her compositions distinguished a young Amy Cheney determined to make her mark as a composer. She was only a year old when she began to surprise her family with her musical feats. She had absolute pitch, a facility for memorizing innumerable melodies, and an ability to sing an accompaniment to any given tune. By the age of four, she was exploring the piano keyboard; shortly she was trying to compose brief pieces.[50]

Her mother, a singer and pianist, nurtured her gift. Born in Henniker, New Hampshire, Amy was about four years of age when she moved with her parents to the Boston area. Further musical instruction came from Ernst Perabo, Junius Hill, and Carl Baermann. At sixteen, she made her debut as a pianist, performing a Moscheles concerto and a Chopin rondo. In composition, Amy claimed she was mostly self-educated, translating and studying the musical treatises of Berlioz and Gevaert and living with the scores of the finest composers. She married Henry Beach, a prominent Boston physician, in 1885.

She had to combat the contemporary prejudice against art composers in general and women composers in particular. Her first appearances as a pianist and composer took place even as the Chicago writer on music George Upton, in *Woman in Music*, was declaring that a scrutiny of musical history showed that music compositions by women failed to remain in the repertoire, despite the fact that several women, including Fanny Hensel and Clara Schumann, had equal advantages with men. The explanation, he claimed, lay in women's emotional natures, which prevented them from projecting their inner natures. According to Upton, women were better fitted to absorb, not create, music. The greater success of male composers was attributable to emotional control, which facilitated the outward expression of inner feeling. Furthermore, Upton said, women were unable to withstand discouragement, privation, apathy, and the spitefulness of other musicians.[51]

Five years later, Boston's Arthur Elson was saying that women did have a right to compose music if they wished. Most of them, however, studied it merely as an accomplishment, to give pleasure to family and friends. Few were serious about their studies. Compositions by women, he believed, would always contain more delicacy and refinement than those by men and would to some degree shun strong feeling. He added: "In our country, Mrs. Beach holds the foremost position at present, with Miss [Margaret] Lang a good second."[52] A few years later, the New York critic Richard Aldrich credited Amy Beach with an excellent command of compositional technique and consequential works that commanded respect. Nevertheless, he downgraded her abilities because he heard striking reminiscences of other composers and no marked originality or true distinction in her music. He said her Violin Sonata, opus 34, had warmth and brilliance but owed much to Wagner; her Piano Quintet, opus 67, was eloquent but too obviously so; and her Prelude and Fugue for piano, opus 81, derived from Rachmaninov.[53]

Luckily for Amy Beach, she lived in a musical city where, more than elsewhere, women were free to pursue intellectual and artistic interests. Also of infinite value was her husband's prominence in Harvard's academic and Boston's social circles. She had the endowment, the means, and the determination to prove the Uptons, Elsons, and Aldriches of this world wrong. Closed-minded male critics might aim carping attacks at her, but they could neither ignore her nor treat her with the usual condescension they reserved for women.

The last years of the nineteenth century registered the advent of a number of American women extremely proficient in painting, writing, and the performance and composition of art music. What is more, they won recognition not only from family and friends but also from the general public. Among them were the poet Emily Dickinson, the painter Mary Cassatt, the novelist Edith Wharton, and the composers Mary Carr Moore, Margaret Lang, and Amy Beach. The composers wrote not only songs and salon pieces, the genres cultivated by women in the past, but more ambitious compositions—overtures, symphonies, concertos, string quartets, piano quintets, cantatas, sacred masses, and operas. Mary Carr Moore (1873–1957), who was born in Tennessee but lived on the West Coast, composed mainly operas. Margaret Lang (1867–1972), daughter of Benjamin Lang, composed works for orchestra alone or for voices and orchestra. Yet, her total output was small, and she apparently ceased writing music after 1917. Amy Beach alone became noted for her major compositions in several genres. Her reputation eventually spread to Europe. Her musical knowledge and the quality of her compositions were such that she could maintain her position as an equal to Parker and Foote. What is more, she persisted as a virtuosic performer and composer throughout her life. In addition, she was a force in the Music Teachers National Association and cofounder, in 1926, and first president of the Association of American Women Composers.[54]

Her compositions normally exhibit melodies of expansive, wide-ranging length. A few sound innocently lovely, especially when she uses folk tunes (Gaelic, Afro-American, Indian, Eskimo, Balkan) or their equivalent; most others are quite complex. Her harmony brims with chromatically altered chords of every description. Textures tend to opulence. Frequent pedal points notwithstanding, tonalities may be obscured by incessant secondary-key references and enharmonic twists. Now and again, muscular rhythms occur. She specializes in fervid climaxes, which are often maintained at length. The larger structures are those of classicism employed flexibly. Regrettably, she was not as self-critical as she should have been. Musical statements may sound too diffuse or overwrought.

The influence of Brahms, Liszt, Wagner, Franck, and MacDowell is detectable. In some later compositions, French Impressionism has sway. Whatever the sources for her style, forthright emotional expression remains her goal. In turn, her works can appear strongly passionate, even verging on frenzy, or delicately refined, on occasion laden with excessive sentiment. Certainly her music is more intensely emotional than that of any other composer belonging to the New England group.

Beach wrote more than 120 art songs. They proved popular and saw frequent performance in her lifetime. Celebrated songs include "Ecstasy" from opus 19 (1893) and "The Year's at the Spring" and "Ah, Love, but a Day!" from opus 44 (1900). In a majority of the songs, idiomatic vocal melodies move appealingly above variegated accompaniments that communicate the ambiences of the poems. No passage overstays its welcome. Expression is clear-cut, concise, and distinctive. Her first songs appeared in 1885. By the turn of the century, when her three Browning songs, opus 44, came out, critics deemed her one of America's foremost song composers. One reviewer remarked about a recital given in 1903 that featured her songs, some still in manuscript: "Covering as these pieces do, a period of years, it was interesting to mark the progress toward liberty which they indicate. The earlier are elegant, well studied, nicely balanced between voice and instrument. . . . But the later ones, while losing nothing of thoughtful studiousness, yet have the spring, the warmth and the independence which one describes in the common phrase, 'letting go.' They have a ring of their own."[55] "The Blackbird" (1889), composed to a poem by William Ernest Henley,[56] is one of her most insouciant efforts. This delightful piece confirms her instinctive bent for the genre. It surveys the caroling of nightingale, lark, and blackbird—the last loved best of all because it is about "the joy of life"—and captures the emotions of two listening lovers. Cheer and affection are projected. The four-measure prelude is analogous to the vamp-until-ready introduction to many contemporary popular songs. A light, jaunty staccato accompaniment of eighth notes, punctuated at phrase endings by a charming flourish of four sixteenth notes, supports a tune laid out in two strains. The piano part, curiously enough, suggests the style of the Serge Prokofiev still in the future.

In contrast, "Dark Is the Night" (1890), again on a poem by Henley,[57] exposes the restless thoughts of the singer, comparing them to turbulent seas, driven clouds, and wild winds. The song, in three agitated strains and rapid tempo, is through-composed and has a prolonged end-climax where the voice skyrockets to b′′. A slower middle strain reflects on past happiness. As in most of the "Blackbird" tune, that of "Dark Is the Night" uses not one accidental, however much the accompaniment cites other keys. This contrast between (diatonic) singer and (chromatic) piano has a great deal to do with the effect produced by the song, that of a blameless victim assailed by forces beyond his control.

"The Year's at the Spring" (1900), the first of the Browning songs, makes one statement twenty-nine measures long. A new plasticity in the interpretation of the subject matter manifests itself. The music's 3/4 meter twice changes to 4/4 at climactic moments. Skillfully managed harmonic progressions coordinate tightly with the melodic phrases, thus conveying total expressive logic. Again, the vocal melody is completely diatonic. The next Browning song, "Ah, Love, but a Day!" concerns the impermanence of love. Beach's unaffected rendition exposes a depth of emotion (Example 7.6). Poignant melody and accompaniment allow chromaticisms in keeping with the song's intense nature.

When around forty years of age, Amy Beach could still wonderfully and sincerely capture a childlike innocence in "The Candy Lion," poem by Abbie Farwell Brown.[58] Especially delicious is the way she makes the candy lion "roar" on a highly dissonant supertonic seventh chord, with third raised and fifty lowered. In the same year, 1914, "The Lotus Isles," poem by Tennyson, was published.[59] Here she creates a musical fantasy land by means of a style borrowing from French Impressionism.

Her sacred and secular works for chorus were well received during her lifetime. Although pleasant to hear, and once favored by church choirs and secular choruses, none of them achieves the distinction of her best songs.[60] Her most ambitious vocal work, the Mass in E-flat major for chorus, vocal quartet, and orchestra, was completed in 1890, when she was in her early twenties.[61] Although a remarkable achievement for one so young and almost entirely self-taught in composition, the Mass lacks the necessary specialness to designate it as a truly choice work. When it was premiered in 1892, it brought Amy Beach favorable criticism but negligible popular success. She tends to linger too long on an idea, preferring repetition to development. Moreover, the Boston audience's notion of what was proper to sacred music excluded solo passages that veered toward the operatic, harmonies made sensuous by the insertion of chromatics, and an orchestra employing the colors of late Romanticism.

The tripartite "Kyrie" makes too much use of the chorus singing in unison and octaves and too little use of contrapuntal variety. The "Gloria" has so many short-breathed phrases that one longs for broader lines. Despite the loud passages, no impression of real power and brilliance results. The "Laudamus te" opens with soprano-alto-tenor soloists, followed by a fine ternary aria alto, on the words "Gratias agimus." The slow, flexibility rocking lyricism of the alto line unfolds mostly in four-measure phrases. This movement and the "Qui tollis" that follows heighten listeners' interest because of the longer lines and convincing lyricism. The "Quoniam tu solus" at last joins vigorous tempi to dynamic polyphonic textures and makes prominent use of brass and percussion, which add to the sensation of splendor and power. The "Credo" often resembles a stately dance of impressive dignity. It is another strong movement with telling utilization of the orchestra. Other highlights include the beautiful English-horn solo against pizzicato strings that opens the "Sanctus" and the cello-harp preluding of the "Agnus Dei." Furthermore, the sections for both the soloists and the chorus in the "Agnus Dei" display some of the finest vocal writing of the entire composition. Indeed, the Mass's effect is cumulative, with the devout "Agnus Dei" and its final plea of "Dona nobis pacem" examples of Beach's music at its most ecstatic.

Amy Beach's pieces for solo piano baffle characterization. The earlier ones normally are brief compositions, agreeable ephemeralities that are quickly consumed, easily digested, and forgettable. One easily traces their descent from Chopin's and Liszt's piano compositions. Later works seem more Lisztian. A few borrow the techniques of Debussy and Ravel; others are leaner in texture or bolder in their dissonance. The Ballad (1894) is one of the more outstanding early pieces, with Beach enlarging passionately on a lyric theme. The Variations on Balkan Themes, of 1904, shows her style more beholden to Liszt and MacDowell than to Chopin; *Eskimos*, four characteristic pieces based on Eskimo themes (1907), shows her employing a leaner style. Works like *Les Rêves de Colombine* (1907), *By the Still Waters* (1925), and Three Pianoforte Pieces (1932) show her looking toward French masters; Five Improvisations (1938) shows her more dissonant than usual.

The highly effective Balkan variations, opus 60, involve one main Balkan theme, "O Maiko Moya," and three subordinate Balkan themes, provided her by the Reverend William W. Sleeper, who had been a missionary in that region. She states: "In the first five variations and the seventh [the main] theme is the only one employed. As a prelude to the sixth variation, 'Stara Planina,' an ancient hymn to the mountains, is introduced; and as a Coda the dance-tune, 'Nasadil e Dado' (Grandpa has planted a little garden). The eighth variation is preceded by a Macedonian appeal for help, made centuries ago to a neighboring country."[62]

Throughout the composition, the diversity of expression and resourceful treatment of the keyboard grab the listener's attention. The slow, woeful yet seductive theme fills out twenty measures. The calm first variation goes a bit faster and comprises a canon at the octave. The more chromatic second variation features thirty-second-note flourishes and powerful dramatic gestures. The fast third variation emphasizes light staccato sixteenth notes. The fourth variation is a gracefully swaying barcarole. The slow fifth variation seems fantasy-like. The sixth variation starts with languorous preluding, then changes into a brisk Hungarian gypsy dance, with something of Rachmaninov showing through. The seventh variation is a waltz. Most of the eighth variation consists of a lugubrious funeral march. The coda first replicates the dramatic expression of the second variation but eventually returns to close on the original tune, simply and chordally stated.

Among the chamber works are a Violin Sonata in A minor (1896), a Piano Quintet in F-sharp minor (1907), a Theme and Variations for flute and string quartet (1920), a String Quartet in one movement (1929), and a Piano Trio (1938). The four-movement Violin Sonata is well crafted, warmhearted, and vitally inventive. Brahms seems to have looked on when she composed it. Writing about the sonata in *Cobbett's Cyclopedic Survey of Chamber Music*, the composer Arthur Shephard says it was once enthusiastically received in America and Europe. Auditors liked its "genuine creative power" and "glowing fancy."[63] The composition is certainly one of Beach's finest efforts.

The first movement, an *allegro moderato*, begins with an engaging diatonic first theme in the piano. From measure 6 on, the violin plays a high countermelody. After a short-lived but potent climax, the violin sounds a serene subordinate theme. The development is more a rhapsodic outpouring than a true working-out of ideas. After the expected recapitulation, the coda provides a sedate conclusion to the movement. Rhetorical gestures are convincing because, however passionate and rhapsodic, they are not exaggerated and are inserted into carefully regulated sections that are tonally secure and structurally lucid. One finds balance, imagination, disciplined sentiment, and a fascinating assortment of ideas. Absent are the fuzzy, fussy chromatics constantly on display in, say, her Quintet; absent are the undisciplined gushes of feeling that mar some of her later compositions.

The second movement is a sprightly Scherzo, with a slower, more melodious Trio. The elegiac third movement is in ternary form. The two instruments achieve a pinnacle of emotion just before the restatement of the main melody. The last movement has a fast and impetuous first theme, a choice subordinate theme that resembles the Wagner of the *Siegfried Idyll*, and a close brilliant in effect and ardent in feeling.

Compared to the Violin Sonata, the Quintet seems more overwrought, more given to emotive passages loaded with chromaticisms, complicated harmonies, and blurred tonalities.[64] Unresolved dissonances discourage relaxation. When the composer is not dispensing restless energy, she tends toward the sugary, as in the slow movement. The listener is not always convinced that the parts are integrated into the structure as a whole. The movements are freer in form and jumbled in their collective effect. Yet, Beach is attempting a musical discourse more powerful and persuasive than that of the Sonata. "Rhapsodic" is the term critics frequently use to describe the Quintet's character. Assuredly, it adheres to the ecstatic and effusive. At the same time, Beach meticulously elaborates her motivic elements and tries for overall coherence by having the mournful music in the preamble to the first movement return in the middle of the final movement and in the *presto* conclusion to the entire work. The rapid first movement is distinguished by melodic phrases that often descend from the F-sharp tone, a tone that persists throughout the movement, whatever the key area. Nevertheless, the movement never moves into a distinct secondary key for any length of time. The *adagio espressivo* middle movement has an initial legato passage for strings alone, followed by the passage's restatement in the piano, which is captivating. The opulent textures of the Finale, analogous to those in César Franck's music, magnify the impact of the chromatic lines. The Quintet's protracted melodies, lush harmonies, and heated sentiment did appeal to contemporary audiences. It offers rewarding moments to latter-day audiences.

Late chamber compositions, like the Theme and Variations for flute and strings and the String Quartet, turn down the Romantic heat and favor sparer patterns of sound. The former work lightens the usual seriousness of her music with a playfulness novel for Beach; the latter work concentrates on the exploitation of a limited number of motives backed by austere spread-out harmonies and an increased dissonant presence.

Two of her most ambitious compositions remain to be discussed, the "Gaelic" Symphony in E minor (1894) and the Piano Concerto in C-sharp minor (1899). The Symphony, the first composed by an American woman to be performed by an American orchestera, the Boston Symphony, is notable for its gravity, dynamism, and innate power. When it was premiered in October 1896 and performed again in February 1898, reviewers, all of them male, were not sure how to take it. Hale, in the *Journal*, praised Beach's indisputable talent and declared the work superior to her Mass. He criticized her, however, for feeling she had to be virile at any cost, and he found the slow movement weak and too long. Elson, in the *Advertiser*, named her America's foremost woman composer, but he chided Beach for her "meaningless chromaticism," "heavy scoring," and "determination to sound powerful." The consensus was that she excelled in the lighter second movement and resorted to excessive repetition in the slow third movement. Nobody questioned the sincerity of the composer.[65]

The attractive first movement is cast into a sprawling sonata structure, mostly grand and impassioned. Nothing Gaelic appears (the sound is more that of Franck and Wagner) until the oboe and flute present a new melody of decided Celtic flavor, based on a gapped scale with fourth and seventh tones missing. The ternary second movement proceeds *alla siciliana*, except for an *allegro* middle section. This is the most winning part of the symphony, eschewing excessive passion, chromatics, and big orchestral effects. The bucolic *siciliana* melody heard in French horn and oboe is like a Celtic song without words, and the middle *allegro* presents a spirited dance of like origin. Again, in the slow movement (the third), Amy Beach exposes a Celtic-like melody. Here her manner is unassuming; complex configurations are few. A violin cadenza leads at once to a disarming tune played by a solo cello, later extended by the oboe and flute. Next a loud, theatrical modulatory *più mosso* section unfolds, until a return to the main theme is effected, this time with a pleasant countermelody added. The last movement seems the least Celtic of all the movements. As in the other movements, musical ideas are clear-cut and lucidly elaborated, congested passages in abeyance. The Symphony represents the composer at her best.

The Piano Concerto was premiered in April 1900, with the composer as soloist. Although regarded as a magnificent contribution to concerto literature, the work was found less attractive than the Symphony. Critics complained about noisiness, muddy orchestration, overabundant ideas, not all of them strong, excessive ornamentation, and passionate discourse that did not always lead anywhere.[66] The first movement, alternately lyric and impassioned, is very long.[67] The Scherzo, *perpetuum mobile*, introduces tantalizingly brief ideas against the constant sixteenth-note motion of the piano. It strikes the ear as music waiting for something to happen. The Largo, an affecting deploration that is linked to the Finale, relieves the usual ardor with moments of meltingly tender lyricism.

Four instrumental works—the Violin Sonata, Piano Quintet, "Gaelic" Symphony, and Piano Concerto—were the principal reasons why the music world took Amy Beach seriously as a composer. Songs and characteristic piano pieces would not have been enough to establish her reputation. She herself concertized in America and Europe, playing her concerto with orchestras and presenting her songs and piano compositions in recitals. In addition, the Sonata and Quintet were avidly taken up by other musicians, at least for a few years. Then, changes in musical styles and tastes made her music sound dated to a younger generation. Her eclipse began to end in the 1980s, however, owing in part to the women's movement and to the revaluation of Romanticism.

NOTES

1. H. E. Krehbiel, in *Grove's Dictionary of Music and Musicians*, 2nd ed., ed. J. A. Fuller Maitland, (London: Macmillan, 1907), s.v. "Parker, Horatio William."
2. George W. Chadwick, *Horatio Parker* (New Haven: Yale University Press, 1921), 7.
3. Henry Cowell and Sidney Cowell, *Charles Ives and His Music* (New York: Oxford University Press, 1969), 33–34.
4. William Kay Kearns, "Horatio Parker" (Ph.D. diss., University of Illinois, 1965), 16, 476.
5. Allan A. Brown Collection, scrapbook of clippings, **M165.8, Vol. 3, in the Boston Public Library.
6. Rupert Hughes, *Contemporary American Composers* (Boston: Page, 1900), 176. Hughes includes the songs in this assessment. One must keep in mind that he was writing before the appearance of Parker's operas.
7. Barbara Owen, album notes to *Fugues, Fantasia & Variations*, New World Records NW 280.
8. The Suite was published in New York, by Schirmer, in 1904.
9. "Night Piece to Julia," words by Robert Heinck, music by Horatio W. Parker (Boston: Schmidt, copr. 1886).
10. Allan A. Brown Collection, scrapbook of clippings, **M371.9, in the Boston Public Library.
11. Chadwick, *Horatio Parker*, 22–23.
12. Several reviews of the Boston concert may be found in the Allan A. Brown Collection, scrapbook of clippings, *M125.5, Vol. 19, in the Boston Public Library.
13. Kearns, "Horatio Parker," 681.

14. The score that I have seen is the reduced one published by Novello in London, copr. 1903.
15. This is the conclusion of Louis C. Elson, in *The History of American Music*, rev. to 1925 by Arthur Elson (New York: Macmillan, 1925), 181.
16. Karl Kreuger, record-album notes to MIA 138, on which Director Kreuger has recorded the composition.
17. Leonard Ellinwood, *The History of American Church Music* (New York: Morehouse-Gorham, 1953), 155; Kearns, "Horatio Parker," 583.
18. I quote Chadwick; see Isabel Parker Semler, in collaboration with Pierson Underwood, *Horatio Parker* (New York: Putnam's Sons, 1942), 72–73.
19. Chadwick, *Horatio Parker*, 12.
20. Semler, *Horatio Parker*, 77–79.
21. Published in London, by Novello, in 1900.
22. Quoted in Hughes, *Contemporary American Composers*, 186.
23. Semler, *Horatio Parker*, 224, 227; the first quotation is from p. 237, the second from p. 244.
24. *Mona*, "an opera in three acts, the poem by Brian Hooker, the music by Horatio Parker" (New York: Schirmer, copr. 1911).
25. Chadwick, *Horatio Parker*, 18.
26. Semler, *Horatio Parker*, 245.
27. Arthur Foote, *An Autobiography*, with an introduction and notes by Wilma Reid Cipolla (New York: Da Capo, 1979), 22–23. The original edition of this reprint came out in 1927.
28. Shelf number **ML46.F65, Vols. 1–3.
29. Arthur Foote, "A Bostonian Remembers," *Musical Quarterly* 23 (1937): 37–44.
30. Allan A. Brown Collection, scrapbook of clippings, **ML46.B6F6, in the Boston Public Library.
31. Frederick Jacobi, "Homage to Arthur Foote," *Modern Music*, Vol. 14 (May–June 1937): 198–99.
32. Other songs praised for their excellence are "It Was a Lover and His Lass," "The Night Has a Thousand Eyes," "When You Become a Nun, Dear," "A Ditty," "The Road to Kew," "I Know a Little Garden Patch," "In Picardie," "In a Bower," "Ho, Pretty Page," "Constancy," "A Twilight Fear," "A Roumanian Song," "The Hawthorn Wins the Damask Rose," "The Red Rose Whispers of Passion," "Sweet is True Love," "Tranquility," "How Many Times Do I Love Thee," and "Ashes of Roses." See Henry T. Finck, *Songs and Song Writers* (New York: Scribner's Sons, 1900), 232–33; Benjamin Lambord, in *Music in America* 4, *The Art of Music*, ed. Arthur Farwell and W. Dermot Darby (New York: National Society of Music, 1915), 339–40; William Treat Upton, *Art-Song in America* (Boston: Ditson, 1930), 113–16; and David Ewen, *American Composers* (New York: Putnam's Sons, 1982), s.v. "Foote, Arthur William."
33. From Arthur Foote, *Three Songs*, Op. 10 (Boston: Schmidt, copr. 1885).
34. Arthur Foote, "I'm Wearing Awa' to the Land o' the Leal," Op. 13 no. 2 (Boston: Schmidt, copr. 1887).
35. Arthur Foote, "A Roumanian Song," Op. 43 no. 2, "The Poem from 'The Bard of the Dimbovitza,' " trans. Carmen Sylva and Alma Strettell (Boston: Schmidt, copr. 1899).
36. Ellinwood, *The History of American Church Music*, 212.

37. Both were published by Schmidt in Boston, and copyrighted in 1904 and 1912, respectively.

38. Foote, *An Autobiography*, 45.

39. Allan A. Brown Collection, scrapbook of clippings, **ML46.B6F6 and **M371.4, in the Boston Public Library.

40. Arthur Foote, Quintet in A minor for Piano and Strings, Op. 38 (Boston: Schmidt, copr. 1898). On the title page of the copy of the score that I have seen at Harvard University is the handwritten inscription "To John K. Paine. This as well as the quartet. Arthur Foote, March '99."

41. Foote revised the work in 1910.

42. Allan A. Brown Collection, scrapbook of clippings, **M125.5, Vol. 6, in the Boston Public Library.

43. George H. Wilson, program notes for the Boston Symphony Orchestra Concert, 23–24 January 1891, with a sketch prepared by Foote.

44. George H. Wilson, "Music in Boston," *Boston Musical Herald* (March 1891): 46.

45. Its principal champion has been the cellist Douglas Moore, of Williams College, who has prepared a performing version of the work.

46. Karl Kreuger, album notes to the recording MIA 122.

47. Arthur Foote, Suite in E major for String Orchestra, Op. 63 (Boston: Schmidt, copr. 1909).

48. Arthur Foote, *A Night Piece* (Boston: Schmidt, copr. 1934).

49. "American Supplement," ed. Waldo Selden Pratt, to *Grove's Dictionary of Music and Musicians*, 2d. ed. (London: Macmillan, 1920), s.v. "Foote, Arthur William."

50. Arthur Elson, *Woman's Work in Music* (Boston: Page, 1904), 196.

51. George P. Upton, *Woman in Music*, 6th ed. (Chicago: McClurg, 1899), 22–24.

52. Elson, *Woman's Work in Music*, 234–35, 237, 239.

53. Richard Aldrich, *Concert Life in New York, 1902–1923* (New York: Putnam's Sons, 1941), 464–75.

54. Adrienne Fried Block, in H. Wiley Hitchcock and Stanley Sadie, eds., *The New Grove Dictionary of American Music* (London: Macmillan, 1986), s.v. "Beach, Amy Marcy (Cheney)." For an excellent discussion of the changing role of women in music, see Judith Tick, "Passed Away Is the Piano Girl: Changes in American Musical Life, 1870–1900," in *Women Making Music*, ed. Jane Bowers and Judith Tick (Urbana: University of Illinois Press, 1986). 325–48.

55. Neither writer nor publication is identified in the clipping, dated 19 March 1903. It may be found in the Allan A. Brown Collection, scrapbook of clippings, **M165.9, Vol. 3, in the Boston Public Library.

56. Published by Schmidt in Boston.

57. Published by Schmidt in Boston.

58. Published by G. Schirmer, in New York, in 1914.

59. Published by G. Schirmer in New York.

60. The two Browning songs that I have discussed and "The Candy Lion" were arranged for four-part women's chorus. They are not nearly as effective as their art-song setting.

61. It was published in 1890 by Arthur P. Schmidt of Boston.

62. All of this information comes from the preface to the score, first published in Boston, by Schmidt, in 1906.

63. Walter Willson Cobbett, ed., *Cobbett's Cyclopedic Survey of Chamber Music*, 2nd ed. (London: Oxford University Press, 1963), 1: 770.

64. Mrs. H.H.A. Beach, Quintet in F-sharp minor for piano and strings, Op. 67 (Boston: Schmidt, copr. 1909).

65. Allan A. Brown Collection, scrapbook of clippings, **M125.5, Vols. 16 and 17, in the Boston Public Library.

66. Ibid., Vol. 19.

67. Mrs. H.H.A. Beach, Concerto in C-sharp minor, for Piano and Orchestra, Op. 45 (Boston: Schmidt, copr. 1900).

8

EVALUATING THE SIX COMPOSERS AND THEIR MUSIC

The inquiry into late-nineteenth-century musical America relies on written, pictorial, and oral records. It also draws from the evidence in music scores and, where available, sound recordings. Several twentieth-century chroniclers have already advanced interpretations of the composers and compositions discussed in this study that they say are founded on such documentation. Unfortunately, many gaps exist in our recorded information. Historians should concede that interpretations involving conjecture do enter into their thinking about this cultural era, and they should identify opinions as such and allow for other points of view where opinion is involved. In bridging lacunae, writers should keep a leash on personal predilections and the biases of their own time period. The reality is that for our six composers this has rarely occurred.[1]

Because so many widely accepted estimates of these musicians and their compositions were disapproving in the extreme, and because these estimates stemmed largely from private opinion, I have found it essential to reevaluate both and see how they stand up to a more sympathetic critical scrutiny. I recognize that the formation of judgments about the quality of the music literature we have inherited from late-nineteenth-century Americans is notoriously troublesome. Such judgments rely on taste; taste is mostly subjective and governed by changes in fashion; and vast changes in taste have occurred in the past hundred years. New preferences in music and ideologies on music's meaning have resulted in generally negative appraisals of the New England group. The requisite circumspection has been shunted aside. Historians with perceptions unlike those of the six composers, or with political or cultural views that affect their objectivity, have issued opinionated appraisals of these artists and their works. Moreover, some twentieth-century writers have also disagreed fundamentally with the composers' way of life, with the way their society thought, felt, and behaved, and with what it held dear. Such negative reactions are understandable, though not condonable, in a modern composer who employs one of various posttriadic practices, since his sense of worth is tied to his difference from an earlier generation. They require cautionary insertion into scholarly judgments.

When Gilbert Chase first published his influential *America's Music* in 1955, he described the six composers as mired in a genteel tradition ("the cult of the fashionable, the worship of the conventional, the cultivation of the trite and artificial, the indulgence of sentimentality, and the predominance of superficiality")[2] and their compositions as so many clichés and imitations of German models. He failed to make the distinction that this book has made between the "genteel" and the "gentle." Nor did Chase convincingly explain why the composers were genteel and their compositions trite. (He, of course, should have said that his was a personal value judgment of a music that seemed stale *to him*, and he should not have prescribed his judgment for all people and all time.) A tremendous amount of subjective, even arbitrary, opinion lurks in his evaluation. Yet, many people have read the book. It is a classroom text in courses in American music, thus shaping the beliefs of many future musicians and music lovers. Its criticisms are quoted again and again by music historians and other writers, few of whom make any serious attempt to become acquainted with the composers and their music.

Then, in 1964, Wilfrid Mellers, a British writer on music, first brought out his *Music in a New Found Land*, which was reissued in a revised edition in 1987. In the later edition, he was still able to write:

> Most nineteenth-century American music is "Bracebridge Hall music."... It manifested a passive veneration from the Teutonic ... and was usually well written, cheerful and agreeable: a pretence that the wilderness did not exist, that the heart was not a "lonely hunter." We have seen that Lowell Mason tamed the fuguing hymnody of the primitives into more sophisticated, Europeanized forms, closer in harmony, cosier in texture. John Paine, George Chadwick and Arthur Foote inflated the cosiness to oratorio-like or symphonic proportions. (Paine considered Wagenr subversive, and recommended "the

present *and future* adherence to the historical forms as developed by Bach, Handel, Mozart and Beethoven.")[3]

In addition to obtrusively elaborate writing, Mellers either pontificates or is incomprehensible. What is the connection with Washington Irving's collection of tales, published in 1822? It is not spelled out. As this book points out, the six composers were hardly passive venerators of anyone; nor was their music mostly cheerful, cozy, and agreeable. What music was Mellers talking about? (Yes, the young Paine did avoid the music of Wagner, but as he matured his regard for Wagner's music increased. By the time he wrote *Azara*, he had repudiated his early opinion and had adopted several Wagnerisms.) Then again the remark about the wilderness and hearts as lonely hunters is part of Mellers's manufactured agenda and had no relevance to theirs. Yet, like Chase, Mellers has influenced the views of other writers. To give an instance, John Rockwell, in *All American Music*, praises Mellers's book and disparages "establishment histories" that treat "with solemn seriousness the generations of worthy but faceless imitators of European models who defined our art music up until the end of the last century."[4] When he wrote this, Rockwell was holding a brief for several contemporaneous composers intent on exploring experimental ideas and techniques.

In 1971 Joseph Mussulman's *Music in the Cultured Generation* came out. He follows Chase in confusing the genteel with the gentle. Mussulman relies almost completely on articles printed in the *Atlantic*, *Harper's*, *Century*, and *Scribner's* from 1870 to 1900, looking at few other sources. He quotes Paine's early evaluation of Wagner and stops there. Never is the music of the six composers examined and discussed. One cannot help wondering if he knew any of it. Grudgingly he admits that they did occasionally produce "works of recognizable intrinsic merit." On the other hand, he believes that none had true genius.[5]

Moreover, the several dissertations on these composers tend to dismiss the music. For example, E. Lindsey Merrill's dissertation, "Mrs. H.H.A. Beach: Her Life and Music," presents a mere sixteen pages of straight biography, with little attempt to learn why she thought and acted as she did. Nor do individual works receive much, let alone sympathetic, attention. Most of the study is given over to counting, for example, how many times different kinds of nonharmonic tones occur—and the same for the patterns of melody, rhythm, harmony, and modulation—as if tones and their combinations exist in a vacuum. Although Merrill thinks Beach's music sincere, he dismisses it as sentimental and reactionary. For example, he finds her widely accepted "Ecstasy" the most sentimental of her songs, and thus "nothing more needs to be said about it except that the text was original." Neither are the fine Browning songs discussed; a comment is made that they seem well written but sound "somewhat faded today."[6] That is all.

All of these charges and dismissals are echoes of attacks on nineteenth-century modes of thought, feeling, and artistic expression that crescendoed in the 1920s. Frederick Hoffman, in his examination of the 1920s, states that a new generation of militant writers and artists not located in or sympathetic to New England was trying to establish a differently conceived order of things. New England served as the focal point for their abuse. Nietzsche's attack upon democratic middle-class society was applied by Mencken and other writers to this American age just passed and to New England in particular. Their watchword was "repression." Hoffman says: "With little or no thought of personal responsibility . . . they decided that any force was evil that stood in the way of a full wholesome, primitive expression of natural impulses. Repression stood for all the social formulas that prevented the natural expression of life impulses." They declared that artistic works from this period, including music, had "conventional virtues" that embodied "dullness, conformity, and blind convictions." The artists (among whom, of course, were the six composers) and their society were judged to be Philistines nervously searching for a respectable culture and constantly concealing their inner emptiness.[7]

Explaining these assaults on nineteenth-century Americans and commentaries such as those offered by Chase, Mellers, and Mussulman, J. Meredith Neil, in *Toward a National Taste*, confirms and adds to Hoffman's critique. Neil notes that these critics' hostility also stems from a "ritualistic denial of our past," which "can best be understood as one aspect of Americans' insistence that they had a fundamental obligation to bring forth the New Adam."[8]

The adverse depiction of the six composers is to some degree odd. The records of the time support some of the statements made, to be sure. The composers' musical education was German. Their musical styles did descend from central European practices. They did have a high regard for traditional practices. They did believe in a stable community. Yet, because of the configurations that twentieth-century writers gave these matters of record, they were transmuted into a fiction about what these musicians thought and why they behaved creatively as they did.

The critics launched their inquiries with several preconceptions, most of them already voiced by European, particularly Parisian, intellectuals and aesthetes, whose affection for anything American was less than minuscule. Their perusal of American civilization and its artistic works was possibly prompted, at least in part, by a need to confirm the rightness of their initial postulates. Some militant critics selected the authentication they required in the writings and scores of the time. As a result, the six composers materialized as incredible exaggerations, figures once alive but made over into characters correctly described on the surface but otherwise false. The more respected writers like Chase and Mellers articulated no falsehoods. Yet, even they hardly ever delivered a picture faithful to the original.

Only in the late 1980s have more than one or two writers begun to view the society and composers of nineteenth-century New England in a new light. These revisionists had witnessed several decades of "primitive expression," "natural impulse," and nonconformity in behavior and creativity, and they had experienced the results. A spreading perception that much of the second half of the twentieth century has seen increased coarseness and discourtesy, and decency at a low ebb and cheap shoddy passing as art, has caused an increased appreciation for living in a stable, civilized manner and creating sound to some commonly accepted standard that reflects that stability and civility. Furthermore, these revisionists know that what uncomplimentary historians have said about this late-nineteenth-century music was due only in small part to direct experience with the works themselves. They suspect that it was molded more consequentially by unstated suppositions on the character of this music literature and by means once thought most proper for examining it.

When we take an objective look at the composers, we must agree that scarcely anything exceptional took place in their private lives. They belonged solidly to the middle class. Their waking hours were devoted to familial responsibilities, composing music, and laboring in the music world. They seem liberated from professional rivalry and always willing to assist fledgling composers. They did not normally fraternize with celebrated or modish men and women, nor seek to glorify themselves. They preferred quietness. Everything they achieved showed them holding fast to clear-cut values and convictions, which allowed them to speak with musical sureness. Religion was a source of strength, not a body of belief devoid of meaning. Thus should we understand Merrill's assertion about Amy Beach's being deeply religious and leading a life "not filled with glamor or scandal," but one that "was ordered, relaxed, and busy."[9]

These six composers inherited the postulates of the New England transcendentalism that had begun in the 1830s, believing that an all-permeating essence beyond the limits of ordinary experience had the power to activate poetic thought and feeling. One gathers that not science or reason but a trust in insight and firsthand experience helped them comprehend what they regarded as musical truths. In this view they agreed with Emerson when he spoke of nature and transcendentalism. In a young and culturally unenriched nation, and particularly in a land where the Puritan legacy was excessive, the need for a different course was obvious. Artistic inspiration could not come from the doctrine of depravity and narrow atonement, or alternately the rationalism and utilitarianism that had governed much of New England's existence. If a refreshing stimulus to creativity had not arrived with people like Emerson, Thoreau, Ripley, Alcott, and Fuller, American art music would have remained much longer in an infantile stage. Paine and Chadwick felt the transcendentalist influence in the same way that the authors Hawthorne, Melville, and Whitman did. Their boldness lay in thinking they could make an artistically viable music gush forth from such a wellhead.

The composers were conservative; they accepted change only as a step-by-step evolution from the familiar music system. They also felt the necessity for preserving their connection with the music that had gone before. However, there was change in their music, easily traceable from youth, through maturity, and into old age, from an adherence to the principles of their mentors to a fully developed style that contemporary audiences felt was their own. Assuredly, they were abreast of new musical developments, incorporating the congenial, rejecting the incompatible. As evidence of musical ripening, there is the contrast between Paine's early Mass and late *Azara*; Chadwick's early *Rip Van Winkle* Overture and late *Symphonic Sketches*; and Parker's early *King Trojan* and late *Mona*. Beach's music evolved from a moderately romantic, to a highly chromatic romantic, to a more austere style. Although MacDowell and Foote show less musical change, they grew more polished, attained greater independence, and increased their expressive power in their later compositions. Compare MacDowell's First Modern Suite for piano with the *Sea Pieces*, written twenty years later; or Foote's *In the Mountains* Overture with *A Night Piece*, written thirty-six years later.

Because nothing of the radical was in their makeup, they had enough wisdom not to emulate the newest vogues. Instead, they presented America with substantial music worthy of more attention than has been given it. The basis for the strength in their finest works varies from composer to composer. Nevertheless, all six composers reveal dedication to the highest craftsmanship, honesty and openness about what they try to express, an acute awareness of sound as something culturally significant for them and their community to share, and a psychological pressure to penetrate far into personal consciousness. They used the musical conventions of their time, aware of a tacit accord between composer and audience. This pact admitted particular liberties in, and dictated particular constraints upon, the handling of technique, formal arrangements, and subjects. By following cultural protocols, these composers facilitated the listener's appropriate comprehension of their music. At the same time, they were free to add their own individual interpretations of the conventions. When, for instance, Frederick Kopp, in his scrutiny of Foote's music, observes that Foote constantly utilized sonata structures, he also adds that this utilization was never sterotyped and showed great diversity and imagination from piece to piece.[10]

To these musicians, the "baroque," the "classical," and the "romantic" were not distinctly separate from each other and from their own era. They found the cohesion among the three approaches more vital than the dissimilarity, since composers and music publics in all three periods shared the same musical language and attitude about the significance of musical sounds. Musical tradition to them represented a sensitive awareness of the past, not something to revolt against. Indeed, the concept of revolting against tradition is rather unique in music history. The twentieth century and its avant-garde composers who accept the concept represent an anomaly. It is therefore not surprising to find Chadwick, Foote, and Beach linked to folk music and to modal scales; Paine, Chadwick, and Parker aware of early New England psalmody; all the composers save MacDowell at some point looking back to the Baroque; MacDowell preoccupied with medieval myths and legendary heroes; and Parker preoccupied with ancient British history and medieval poetry. All the composers pour romantic content into usually baroque and classical structures.

Furthermore, the six musicians were original, if we take the term to include a certain independence from their community, a pioneering of new modes of cultural expression, and a faculty for creative inventiveness and autonomous reflection on musical matters. They showed their individuality in embarking on an activity for which no solid American antecedent existed and, indeed, one that in many circles was frowned upon. They did not have the luxury afforded the twentieth-century composer, of an established American heritage involving music that they could interact with, modify, or reject. What they did was new to their world: In the midst of American society suddenly appeared professional composers, native-born Americans educated to the utmost degree in their craft, creating masterfully written music deserving of admiration by the few music lovers in America and the many more in Europe. We must keep in mind that to the general American public, who thought an art composer ludicrous, an art composer born in America was the height of absurdity. But these six composers embarked on careers unfavored by most Americans and produced artistic works different from what was normally heard and accepted. They dared to create in formats reserved to the European masters, doing so year after year. They boldly insisted on and taught music as a worthy academic subject. Their students and their students' students form an unbroken chain up to the present day. Unflinchingly, they held up a mirror of artistic excellence for their society, which was no small thing. And their music does demonstrate modifications in melody, phrase pattern, rhythm, and structure that make it more individually American rather than just counterfeit European. One takes note of Adolfo Salazar's statement, made in 1946: "What 1848 was for Europe, the year 1864 was for the United States: the moment of crisis and maturity, of the blossoming of national consciousness. The earlier part of the century is filled with minor figures marked by unmistakably American characteristics. To this period belong the native, untutored melodic genius of Stephen C. Foster (1826–64) and the Creole exoticism of Louis Moreau Gottschalk (1829–69). The second half of the century finds the times and the men in their maturity. J. K. Paine, Chadwick, and Parker signify a substantial forward step. MacDowell is the culmination, firmly rounded as to style and refined in taste. Many of these musicians were natives of, or made their home in, the New England of the Pilgrim Fathers. The Boston group served appropriately as a beacon light during the second half of the century."[11]

Nationalism held a secondary place in their thought. They felt that, because the music of African Americans and American Indians was not indigenous to the communities the composers themselves grew up in, it was better to treat it circumspectly, introducing it cautiously into art compositions. Perhaps they feared they might compromise the humanistic standards they painstakingly tried to uphold. Although Chadwick, MacDowell, Foote, and Beach allude to African, Indian, and even popoular music in some compositions, usually when they referred to an extant music, it was British-American, and Gaelic (Irish, Scottish, Welsh, Cornish) in particular. This was a more natural action for them. An astute Arthur Foote commented that he and others like him could not will or consciously cultivate nationalism. The result would have been a forced, artificial manner of writing, unnatural to the composer and unloved by his public.

Whatever shape nationalism took, it had to evolve spontaneously and be unconsciously present when the composer wrote music. According to Foote, America could never claim a national school until it produced "one great composer."[12] In Chapter 6 of this book, MacDowell was quoted as saying much the same thing.

The six composers had a firm concept of beautiful sound, and it usually led them in a different direction from nationalism. Beauty to them was the end result of the creative process. The composer constructed his work of art out of physical substance: the tones selected from a spectrum of available sounds and the instruments and voices selected to produce these tones. An expertise, acquired only after years of study, was needed to form this substance into art of aesthetic distinction. The composer tried to make a perfect product, while "besieged by dreams of beauty in his work." He proceeded "from skill . . . to good taste and from taste to charm and beauty."[13]

When performed, their music aimed to please not just specialists but the entire audience, engaging attention, occupying minds, and arousing supportive responses. Because composer and audience were substantially agreed about music's role, no debilitating compromise was involved. Although Paine spoke for his society, his was not a mindless acquiescence, but rather an attempt through music to awaken an exaltation both powerful and noble and at times with tragic sweep. His talent lay in expanding a few musical ideas into compelling effects, so as to constitute a whole more forceful than its parts. A composition like the Second Symphony scrupulously synthesizes classical with romantic methods to produce a sound abundant in variety, eloquent in rhetoric, and warm in feeling, while preserving the necessary aesthetic distance between composer and composition, thus eliminating any danger of sentimentality.

Chadwick shares many of Paine's virtues. However, his later style shows a more striking transformation from the earlier than is the case with Paine. Chadwick acquires a freer and oftentimes what may be described as an American sound in his Second Symphony and *Symphonic Sketches*. Here he samples modal and gapped scales and British-American folk and American popular-music rhythms and tunes. He ventures intrepidly into the comic, the satiric, and the poignant, and he reveals a penchant for the dramatic. The capacity for surprise is continuously present in his music. He explores the possibilities of orchestral color with an exuberance eschewed by Paine. His is a special vitality that cannot sit still but must plunge ahead, seeking broader perspectives unacknowledged by his German mentors and dimly seen by his New England community.

MacDowell's strength is mostly in his piano music. In the sonatas, he presents portraits of ancient deeds and chivalry, of love and calamity. He guided his creative labors by the light of immutable ideals that surmounted the contemporaneous world he found so harsh. He reveals a romantic delight in the rural outdoors, brought on in part by his frequent urban isolation from forest, meadowland, mountain, and ocean. The yearning for a plane of existence beyond the bleakness of the commercial and industrial city and its getting and spending finds expression in woodland scenes, seascapes, and intimations of the imagined New England of yesteryear. His was a poetic temperament with an ability to render lyrical impressions of the outdoors, giving them highly personal and nearly singular characterizations. His music is recognizably novel in its melody and harmony and capable of fleet imaging and sonorous culminations.

Parker, in his best, and usually vocal, compositions, has given us music of elevated character and spirit and with a gratifying appeal to the ear, music that shows unusual mastery in the control of polyphonic progressions. These qualities help cancel out the reserve, scholasticism, and austerity that have prompted critics to accuse him of dryness. *Hora Novissima*, in particular, manifests his gifts. He sings eloquently of a heavenly kingdom, even as he is tormented by the elemental and ruthless potency of human iniquities and earthly delusions. Living in a United States undergoing radical societal change, he imagines the just person as dissociated from the world that is coming into being, as one isolated and apprehensive (a condition familiar to twentieth-century Americans). Like an Old Testament prophet, he weighs a flawed society in the scale of immutable precepts and of truths that transcend existence and make life livable. The theme is a universal one, its music still persuasive a hundred years later.

Foote does not thunder at us. Bombast is foreign to his nature. Few works exist for full symphony orchestra, although *Francesca da Rimini* and the *Four Character Pieces* are among the finest things he composed. String orchestras and chamber ensembles receive most of his attention. The Serenade for Strings in E and the Piano Quintet contain music we must admire. He prefers smoothly coursing sounds, unfettered from stridency. Yet, he does have something to say and communicates it succinctly and with authentic flair, as in *A Night Piece*. More lyric than dramatic, melody is his forte. Hence, his excellent songs. His ensemble music may sound like introspective musing. Subtleties in tonal placement, melodic flow, harmonic construction, contrapuntal motion, and displaced accentuation abound.

Amy Beach, the youngest of the six musicians, may go to extremes in her music, from the tender fluency of a song to the expansive, assertive styling of an instrumental piece. She is a hit-or-miss composer. When a work proves unattractive, the fault lies in excessive emotionality and loquaciousness. Yet, when she exercises greater self-discipline, discernment, and care, a work can prove very attractive. A piece like the "Gaelic" Symphony throbs with rhythmic vigor and overwhelms us with its extended fervid peaks of emotion. She had confidence in her talent and the merit of her music. She wanted acceptance as a composer, not just as a *woman* composer, with the condescension that implied. To a great extent, she did gain distinction through the worth of her music. To give one instance, after the publication of her Violin Sonata, first performed by Franz Kneisel, it was admired and taken up for performance by musicians in Europe. Significantly, when Eugène Ysaÿe, the famous Belgian violinist, discovered and performed it, he believed a man had composed it.[14]

I do not expect that the music of these composers will suit everybody's tastes. The one important thing asked is that those who have rejected the music on hearsay, or whose actual listening has been guided by the remarks of hostile pundits, give it a fair hearing. Further, I suggest that the assassins of our cultural past take note of the havoc they have wrought. In besmirching the reputations of Paine, Chadwick, MacDowell, Parker, Foote, and Beach, and maligning their compositions, they condemn Americans yet once again to see their country as a musical wasteland dotted with the ruins of yesterday's composers. American composers of whatever persuasion and from whatever era deserve better.

NOTES

1. An informative discussion of these matters may be found in Simone Weil, *The Need for Roots*, trans. Arthur Wills (1953; reprinted, New York: Harper and Row, 1971), 224.

2. When he revised the book, his negative view of the New England group continued; see Gilbert Chase, *America's Music*, rev. 2nd ed. (New York: McGraw-Hill, 1966), 165.

3. Wilfrid Mellers, *Music in a New Found Land*, rev. ed. (New York: Oxford University Press, 1987), 25.

4. John Rockwell, *All American Music* (New York: Knopf, 1983), 3–4.

5. Joseph A. Mussulman, *Music in the Cultured Generation* (Evanston: Northwestern University Press, 1972), 68.

6. E. Lindsey Merrill, "Mrs. H.H.A. Beach: Her Life and Music" (Ph.D. diss., University of Rochester, 1963), 51.

7. Frederick J. Hoffman, *The 20's*, rev. ed. (New York: Free Press, 1965), 144, 357–58, 360–61.

8. J. Meredith Neil, *Toward a National Taste* (Honolulu: University Press of Hawaii, 1975), xi.

9. Merrill, "Mrs. H.H.A. Beach," 12.

10. Frederick Edward Kopp, "Arthur Foote: American Composer and Theorist" (Ph.D. diss., University of Rochester, 1957), 148.

11. Adolfo Salazar, *Music in Our Time*, trans. Isabel Pope (New York: Norton, 1946), 311–12.

12. Kopp, "Arthur Foote," 364.

13. See Samuel Alexander, *Beauty and Other Forms of Value* (New York: Crowell, 1968), 15.

14. Merrill, "Mrs. H.H.A. Beach," 8–9.

SELECTED BIBLIOGRAPHY

Aldrich, Richard. *Concert Life in New York, 1902–1923*. New York: Putnam's Sons, 1941.

———. *Musical Discoveries*. New York: Oxford University Press, 1928.

———. "Paine, John Knowles." In *Dictionary of American Biography* 14.

The American Renaissance, 1876–1917. New York: Brooklyn Museum, 1979.

Ammer, Christine. *Unsung: A History of Women in American Music*. Westport, Conn.: Greenwood Press, 1980.

Apthorp, William Foster. *By the Way*. 2 vols. Boston: Copeland and Day, 1898.

———. *Musicians and Music Lovers*. New York: Scribner's Sons, 1894.

Block, Adrienne Fried. In H. Wiley Hitchcock and Stanley Sadie, eds., *The New Grove Dictionary of American Music* (London: Macmillan, 1986), s.v. "Beach, Amy Marcy (Cheney)."

Brown, Abbie Farwell. *The Boyhood of Edward MacDowell*. New York: Stokes, 1924.

Cadman, Charles Wakefield. "The 'Idealization' of Indian Music." *Musical Quarterly* 1 (1915): 387–96.

Carter, Morris. *Isabella Stewart Gardner and Fenway Court*. Boston: Houghton Mifflin, 1925.

Chadwick, George Wakefield. *Horatio Parker*. New Haven: Yale University Press, 1921.

Cipolla, Wilma Reid. In H. Wiley Hitchcock and Stanley Sadie, eds., *The New Grove Dictionary of American Music* (London: Macmillan, 1986), s.v. "Foote, Arthur (William)."

Cobbett, Walter Willson, ed. *Cobbett's Cyclopedic Survey of Chamber Music*. 2nd ed. 2 vols. London: Oxford University Press, 1963.

Currier, T. P. "Edward MacDowell As I Knew Him." *Musical Quarterly* 1 (1915): 17–51.

Dunham, Henry Morton. *The Life of a Musician*. New York: Mrs. Henry M. Dunham, 1931.

Dvořák, Antonín. "Music in America." *Harper's New Monthly Magazine* 90 (1895): 429–34.

Dwight, John Sullivan. "Music in Boston." In *The Memorial History of Boston* 4, edited by Justin Winsor. Boston: Ticknor, 1881.

Eames, Emma. *Some Memories and Reflections*. New York: Appleton, 1927.

Ebel, Otto. *Women Composers*. New York: Chandler, 1902.

Edwards, George Thronton. *Music and Musicians of Maine*. Portland: Southworth, 1928.

Ellinwood, Leonard. *The History of American Church Music*. New York: Morehouse-Gorham, 1953.

Elson, Arthur. *Woman's Work in Music*. Boston: Page, 1904.

Elson, Louis C. *The History of American Music*. Revised to 1925 by Arthur Elson. New York: Macmillan, 1925.

———, ed. *Modern Music and Musicians* 3. New York: University Society, 1918.

———. *The National Music of America*. Boston: Page, 1900.

———. *The Realm of Music*. Boston: New England Conservatory of Music, 1897.

Engel, Carl. "George W. Chadwick." *Musical Quarterly* 10 (1924): 438–57.

———. "Views and Reviews." *Musical Quarterly* 18 (1932): 178–83.

Erskine, John. "MacDowell at Columbia: Some Recollections." *Musical Quarterly* 28 (1942): 395–405.

———. *The Memory of Certain Persons*. Philadelphia: Lippincott, 1947.

Ewen, David. *American Composers*. New York: Putnam's Sons, 1982.

Farwell, Arthur, and W. Dermot Darby, eds. *Music in America, The Art of Music* 4. New York: National Society of Music, 1915.

Fay, Amy. *More Letters of Amy Fay: The American Years, 1879–1916*. Selected and edited by S. Margaret William McCarthy. Detroit: Information Coordinators, 1986.

———. *Music-Study in Germany*. New York: Macmillan, 1896.

Ffrench, Florence. *Music and Musicians in Chicago*. Chicago: Ffrench, 1899.

Finck, Henry T. *My Adventures in the Golden Age of Music*. New York: Funk and Wagnalls, 1926.

———. *Songs and Song Writers*. New York: Scribner's Sons, 1900.

Foote, Arthur. *An Autobiography*. With an introduction and notes by Wilma Reid Cipolla. 1946. Reprint. New York: Da Capo, 1979.

———. "A Bostonian Remembers." *Musical Quarterly* 23 (1937): 37–44.

———. *Theory of Music*. London: Squire, 1908.

Gilman, Lawrence. *Edward MacDowell*. New York: Lane, 1909.

———. *Phases of Modern Music*. New York: Harper and Brothers, 1904.

———. *Stories of Symphonic Music*. New York: Harper and Brothers, 1908.

Gottschalk, Louis Moreau. *Notes of a Pianist*. Edited by Jeanne Behrend. New York: Knopf, 1964.

Hale, Philip. *Philip Hale's Boston Symphony Programme Notes*. Edited by John N. Burk. Garden City, N.Y.: Doubleday, Doran, 1935.

Hipsher, Edward Ellsworth. *American Opera and Its Composers*. Philadelphia: Presser, 1927.

Homer, Sidney. *My Wife and I*. New York: Macmillan, 1939.

Howard, John Tasker. *Our American Music*. 4th ed. New York: Crowell, 1965.

Howe, M. A. DeWolfe. *The Boston Symphony Orchestra*. Boston: Houghton Mifflin, 1914.

———. "John Knowles Paine." *Musical Quarterly* 25 (1939): 257–67.

———, ed. *Later Years of the Saturday Club, 1870–1927*. Boston: Houghton Mifflin, 1927.
Hubbard, W. L., ed. *History of American Music, The American History of Encyclopedia of Music* 8. Toledo: Squire, 1908.
Hughes, Rupert. *Contemporary American Composers*. Boston: Page, 1900.
Johns, Clayton. *Reminiscences of a Musician*. Cambridge: Washburn and Thomas, 1929.
Johnson, H. Earle. *Hallelujah, Amen!* Boston: Humphries, 1965.
Jones, F. O. *A Handbook of American Music and Musicians*. Canaseraga, N.Y.: Jones, 1886.
Kearns, William Kay. "Horatio Parker." Ph.D. diss., University of Illinois, 1965.
———. "Horatio Parker and the English Choral Societies, 1899–1902." *American Music* 4 (1986): 20–33.
———. In H. Wiley Hitchcock and Stanley Sadie, eds., *The New Grove Dictionary of American Music* (London: Macmillan, 1986), s.v. "Parker, Horatio."
Kopp, Frederick Edward. "Arthur Foote: American Composer and Theorsit." Ph.D. diss., University of Rochester, 1957.
Krehbiel, H. E. *Review of the New York Musical Season, 1886–1887*. New York: Novello, Ewer, 1887.
Krueger, Karl. *The Musical Heritage of the United States: The Unknown Portion*. New York: Society for the Preservation of the American Musical Heritage, 1973.
Langley, Allan Lincoln. "Chadwick and the New England Conservatory of Music." *Musical Quarterly* 21 (1935): 39–52.
Ledbetter, Steven, and Victor Fell Yellin. In H. Wiley Hitchcock and Stanley Sadie, eds., *The New Grove Dictionary of American Music* (London: MacMillan, 1986), s.v. "Chadwick, George Whitefield."
Lowens, Margery Morgan. In H. Wiley Hitchcock and Stanley Sadie, *The New Grove Dictionary of American Music* (London: Macmillan, 1986), s.v. "MacDowell, Edward."
McCusker, Honor. *Fifty Years of Music in Boston*. Boston: Trustees of the Public Library, 1938.
MacDowell, Edward A. *Critical and Historical Essays*. Edited by W. J. Baltzell. 1912. Reprint. New York: Da Capo, 1969.
MacDowell, Marian. "MacDowell's 'Peterborough Idea.' " *Musical Quarterly* 28 (1932): 33–38.
———. *Random Notes on Edward MacDowell and His Music*. Boston: Schmidt, 1950.
Mason, Daniel Gregory. *The Dilemma of American Music*. New York: Macmillan, 1928.
———. *Memories of a Musical Life*. New York: Century, 1901.
———. *Music in My Time and Other Reminiscences*. New York: Macmillan, 1938.
———. *Tune in, America*. New York: Knopf, 1969.
Mathews, W.S.B. "A Few Boston Notes." *Music* (January 1902): 101–7.
———, ed. *A Hundred Years of Music in America*. Chicago: Howe, 1889.
Merrill, E. Lindsey. "Mrs. H.H.A. Beach: Her Life and Music." Ph.D. diss., University of Rochester, 1963.
Mussulman, Joseph A. *Music in the Cultured Generation*. Evanston: Northwestern University Press, 1971.
Nathan, Hans. "United States of America." In *A History of Song*, edited by Denis Stevens. New York: Norton, 1970.
Parker, Horatio. *Music and Public Entertainment*. Boston: Hall and Locke, 1911.

———. "Our Taste in Music." *Yale Review* 7 (1918): 777–88.
Porte, John F. *Edward MacDowell*. New York: Dutton, 1922.
Roberts, Kenneth C., Jr. In H. Wiley Hitchcock and Stanley Sadie, *The New Grove Dictionary of American Music* (London: Macmillan, 1986), s.v. "Paine, John Knowles."
Robinson, Edward. "Horatio Parker." *American Mercury* 22 (1931): 497–501.
Rogers, Clara Kathleen. *Memories of a Musical Career*. Boston: Little, Brown, 1919.
———. *The Story of Two Lives*. Boston: Plimpton Press, 1932.
Salazar, Adolfo. *Music in Our Time*. Translated by Isabel Pope. New York: Norton, 1946.
Salter, Sumner. "Early Encouragements to American Composers." *Musical Quarterly* 18 (1932): 76–105.
Schmidt, John C. *The Life and Works of John Knowles Paine*. Ann Arbor: UMI Research Press, 1980.
Semler, Isabel Parker, in collaboration with Pierson Underwood. *Horatio Parker*. New York: Putnam's Sons, 1942.
Slonimsky, Nicholas. "Composers of New England." *Modern Music*, Vol. 8 (February–March 1930): 24–27.
Smith, David Stanley. "A Study of Horatio Parker." *Musical Quarterly* 16 (1930): 153–69.
Sonneck, Oscar G. *Suum Cuique: Essays in Music*. 1916. Reprint. Freeport, N.Y.: Books for Libraries, 1969.
Spalding, Walter Raymond. *Music at Harvard*. 1935. Reprint. New York: Da Capo, 1977.
Thomas, Theodore. *A Musical Autobiography*. Edited by George P. Upton. 1905. Reprint. New York: Da Capo, 1964.
Tick, Judith. "Passed Away Is the Piano Girl: Changes in American Musical Life, 1870–1900." In *Women Making Music*, edited by Jane Bowers and Judith Tick. Urbana: University of Illinois Press, 1986.
Tuthill, Burnet C. "Mrs. H.H.A. Beach." *Musical Quarterly* 26 (1940): 297–310.
Upton, George P. *Art-Song in America*. Boston: Ditson, 1930.
———. *Musical Memories*. Chicago: McClurg, 1908.
———. *Woman in Music*. 6th ed. Chicago: McClurg, 1899.
Yellin, Victor. "Chadwick, American Musical Realist." *Musical Quarterly* 61 (1975): 77–97.
———. "The Life and Operatic Works of George Whitefield Chadwick." Ph.D. diss., Harvard University, 1957.

MUSICAL EXAMPLES

Example 4.1. "Kyrie," from Mass in D

Example 4.2. "Et incarnatus," from Mass in D

Example 4.3. "Crucifixus," from Mass in D

Example 4.4. "Lament," from *St. Peter*

Example 4.5. "O God, my God, forsake me not!" from *St. Peter*

Example 4.6. "Remember from whence thou art fallen," from *St. Peter*

Example 4.7. Main theme of first movement, from Symphony No. 1

Example 4.8. Subordinate theme of first movement, from Symphony No. 1

Example 4.9. Main theme of the third movement, from Symphony No. 1

Example 4.10. Germinal motive of Introduction to Symphony No. 2

Example 4.11. F-minor theme of slow movement, from Symphony No. 2

Example 4.12. Main theme of prelude to *Oedipus Tyrannus*

Example 4.13. Allegro moderato of prelude to *Oedipus Tyrannus*

Example 4.14. Aria of Gontran, from Act I of *Azara*

Example 4.15. Aria of Azara, from Act II of *Azara*

Example 4.16. First Moorish Dance, from Act III of *Azara*

Example 5.1. "The Frogs," from *Five Pieces for Pianoforte*

Example 5.2. From "Sweetheart, thy lips are touched with flame"

Example 5.3. First excerpt, Mvt. I, from String Quartet No. 4

Example 5.4. Second excerpt, Mvt. I, from String Quartet No. 4

Example 5.5. Mvt. II, from String Quartet No. 4

Example 5.6. Mvt. III, from String Quartet No. 4

Example 5.7. Mvt. IV, from String Quartet No. 4

Example 5.8. Plantation Ballad, from *Tabasco*

Example 5.9. "O God, what bodings stir my troubled heart," from *Judith*

Example 5.10. "The king sends for his sword," from *Judith*

Example 5.11. Movement I: Horn motive, from Symphony No. 2

Example 5.12. Movement II: Oboe theme, from Symphony No. 2

Example 5.13. "Jubilee," from *Symphonic Sketches*

Example 5.14. "Hobgoblin," from *Symphonic Sketches*

Example 5.15. Tam's theme, from *Tam O'Shanter*

Example 5.16. Dance tune, from *Tam O'Shanter*

Example 6.1. Song: "The Sea"

Example 6.2. "Forest Spirits," from First Suite for Orchestra

Example 6.3. "Dirge," from the *Indian Suite*

Example 6.4. "An Old Love Story," from *Fireside Tales*

Example 6.5. "A Haunted House," from *Fireside Tales*

Example 6.6. Movement I, from the *Keltic Sonata*

Example 6.7. Movement III, from the *Keltic Sonata*

Example 7.1. Introduction, from *Hora Novissima*

Example 7.2. Nial's Dance, Act I, Scene 1, from *Mona*

Example 7.3. "A Roumanian Song"

Example 7.4. "Praeludium," from Suite in E

Example 7.5. ***A Night Piece***

(As the Basso is optional, the String Quartet, for which this composition was originally written, is sufficient.)

Example 7.6. "Ah, Love, but a day!"

INDEX

About the Author

NICHOLAS E. TAWA is Professor of Music at the University of Massachusetts at Boston. He is also the author of *A Most Wondrous Babble: American Art Composers, Their Music, and the American Scene, 1950–1985* (Greenwood Press, 1987).